GANGS

Selected Titles in ABC-CLIO's
CONTEMPORARY
WORLD ISSUES
Series

For a complete list of titles in this series, please visit
www.abc-clio.com.

Books in the Contemporary World Issues series address vital issues in today's society, such as genetic engineering, pollution, and biodiversity. Written by professional writers, scholars, and nonacademic experts, these books are authoritative, clearly written, up-to-date, and objective. They provide a good starting point for research by high school and college students, scholars, and general readers as well as by legislators, businesspeople, activists, and others.

Each book, carefully organized and easy to use, contains an overview of the subject, a detailed chronology, biographical sketches, facts and data and/or documents and other primary-source material, a directory of organizations and agencies, annotated lists of print and nonprint resources, and an index.

Readers of books in the Contemporary World Issues series will find the information they need to have a better understanding of the social, political, environmental, and economic issues facing the world today.

GANGS

A Reference Handbook

Second Edition

Karen L. Kinnear

**CONTEMPORARY
WORLD ISSUES**

A B C  C L I O

Santa Barbara, California
Denver, Colorado
Oxford, England

Copyright 2009 by ABC-CLIO, LLC

Library of Congress Cataloging-in-Publication Data
Kinnear, Karen L.
  Gangs : a reference handbook / Karen L. Kinnear. — 2nd ed.
    p. cm. — (Contemporary world issues)
  Includes bibliographical references and index.
  ISBN 978-1-59884-125-1 (alk. paper)
  1. Gangs—United States—Handbooks, manuals, etc.   I. Title.
  HV6439.U7K55 2009
  364.106′60973—dc22
                                    2008019138

13 12 11 10 9   1 2 3 4 5 6 7 8 9 10

E-ISBN: 978-1-59884-126-8

ABC-CLIO, LLC
130 Cremona Drive, P.O. Box 1911
Santa Barbara, California 93116-1911

This book is also available on the World Wide Web as an eBook.
Visit www.abc-clio.com for details.

This book is printed on acid-free paper. ∞

Manufactured in the United States of America

To Mike and Matt, who work tirelessly
to make their neighborhoods safe,
and to Adria, who inspires and motivates us
to find purpose in life

Contents

Preface

The purpose of this book is to provide a balanced survey of the available literature and resources on gangs. Topics addressed include the history of gangs, the types of youth who join gangs and why they join, where gangs are found, what distinguishes a gang from any other group of youngsters, how law enforcement and other intervention programs are dealing with gangs, what states and cities are doing to cope with gangs, and what other countries are doing to curb gang behavior. The book also provides statistical information, data on intervention programs, and summaries of print and nonprint resources for further information.

The nature and characteristics of gangs have changed over the years, from teenage boys getting together to have some fun and maybe create a little bit of trouble, to large, well-organized, and sophisticated groups of young men, and often women, who get together for protection and to engage in some type of criminal activity. While many gangs today are informal, loosely structured, and unorganized, others are sophisticated groups, with clear hierarchies, Web sites and blogs, and member gangs in many cities and countries around the world. Law enforcement agencies may have difficulty keeping up with changing gang structures and characteristics. It is important for all professionals involved in working with gangs to understand their changing nature and to adapt their programs and intervention strategies accordingly. This book examines and reviews current knowledge and resources in order to provide an understanding of the issues involved in this important and timely topic.

This book, like other books in the Contemporary World Issues series, provides a comprehensive review of the resources available and a guide to further research on the topic of youth gangs. Chapter 1 provides an overview of our current knowledge concerning gangs—their formation, organization, and characteristics and the various approaches law enforcement and communities are taking to prevent or eliminate them. Chapter 2 explores some of the major problems, issues, and controversies concerning gangs, including descriptions of individual gangs and their characteristics, prevention and intervention strategies, and the sophisticated use of various electronic devices to communicate information to other gang members. Chapter 3 describes the problems other countries are experiencing with gangs and international efforts to prevent the spread of gangs across national borders. Chapter 4 presents a chronology of the significant events, cases, and statutes relevant to gangs, their purposes, and their development. Chapter 5 provides short biographical sketches of individuals who have played a key role in working with gangs as well as biographies of several current and former gang members. Chapter 6 presents general facts and statistics on the prevalence and demographics of American youth gangs; descriptions of gang databases, gang alliances, and well-known gangs; descriptions of several of the major gangs in the country; state and federal statute definitions of *street gang, gang member,* and *gang activity;* and a listing of federal laws and selected U.S. Supreme Court and lower court decisions that pertain to a variety of issues that have come before the courts concerning gangs and gang activity. Chapter 7 describes organizations that work in a variety of ways with gangs and gang members as well as local community agencies that focus on stopping or preventing gang activity. Chapter 8 contains descriptions of recently published books, manuals, journal articles, and training guides on issues relating to gangs and gang behavior.

1

Background and History

Most young people join some type of social group. These groups can help youths develop social skills, fulfill many of their emotional needs, offer an environment in which they are valued, provide them with goals, and give direction and structure to their lives. Some youths will join groups that society considers prosocial, or of benefit to society, such as Boy or Girl Scouts, Little League, or fraternities and sororities. Others will join groups that are considered antisocial, such as gangs. What makes a youth decide to join a group? How can society steer children into prosocial groups? How can the influence of gangs be diminished? Researchers and other professionals in the field are trying to find answers to these and other questions. This chapter provides an overview of our current knowledge concerning gangs—their formation, organization, and characteristics and various approaches law enforcement and communities are taking to prevent or eliminate them.

What Is a Gang?

One of the first problems encountered by those who study gangs and gang behavior is how to define a gang. Is it just a group of people who hang around with each other? Can adults in a group be defined as a gang? Do the people in the group have to engage in some type of criminal behavior? From youths roaming the streets in Los Angeles following the riots in 1992 to youths rioting in Tonga in 2006 following demonstrations supporting a democratic government to youths in Kenya in 2008 taking to the streets following the presidential election, news organizations refer to these groups as "gangs of youths" or "youth gangs." Defining gangs is often a highly political issue that reflects the interests and agendas of the various individuals and agencies involved with gangs, including law enforcement personnel, politicians, advocates, social workers, the media, and researchers.

Researcher Frederic Thrasher offered this early definition in 1927: "A gang is an interstitial group, originally formed spontaneously, and then integrated through conflict. It is characterized by the following types of behavior: meeting face to face, milling, movement through space as a unit, conflict, and planning. The result of this collective behavior is the development of tradition, unreflective internal structure, esprit de corps, solidarity, morale, group awareness, and attachment to a local territory" (57). Thrasher believed that gangs were interstitial in that they were created in the cracks or along the boundaries of society. Gang members were not in the mainstream and did not have the advantages that others did; they were often composed of individuals who were of the lower class, left out, and ignored by the rest of society.

Thrasher's definition of gangs influenced other definitions developed by researchers who followed him. Malcolm Klein (1971) added the element of delinquency to his definition: "any denotable adolescent group of youngsters who (a) are generally perceived as a distinct aggregation by others in their neighborhood; (b) recognize themselves as a denotable group (almost invariably with a group name); and (c) have been involved in a sufficient number of delinquent incidents to call forth a consistent negative response from neighborhood residents and/or enforcement agencies" (13).

Desmond Cartwright also built on Thrasher's definition. He believed that a gang was "an interstitial and integrated group of persons who meet face to face more or less regularly and whose existence and activities as a group are considered an actual or potential threat to the prevailing social order" (Cartwright, Thomson, and Schwartz 1975, 4).

In the 1980s, the element of criminal activity was added to many definitions. Walter Miller (1980), after talking with criminal justice system professionals and others working with youths, defined a gang as "a self-formed association of peers, bound together by mutual interests, with identifiable leadership, well defined lines of authority, and other organizational features, who act in concert to achieve a specific purpose or purposes which generally include conduct of illegal activity and control over a particular territory, facility, or type of enterprise" (121).

Sandra Gardner (1983) added the variables of territory and delinquency in her definition: "An organization of young people usually between their early teens and early twenties, which has a group name, claims a territory or neighborhood as its own, meets with its members on a regular basis, and has recognizable leadership. The key element that distinguishes a gang from other organizations of young people is delinquency: its members regularly participate in activities that violate the law" (5).

In 1987, the California Office of Criminal Justice Planning defined a gang as "a group of associating individuals which (a) has an identifiable leadership and organizational structure; (b) either claims control over particular territory in the community, or exercises control over an illegal enterprise; and (c) engages collectively or as individuals in acts of violence or serious criminal behavior" (3–4).

George Knox (1993) believes a group can be considered a gang when "it exists for or benefits substantially from the continuing criminal activity of its members. Some element of crime must exist as a definitive feature of the organization for it to be classified as a gang. That need not be income-producing crime, because it could also be crimes of violence" (5).

Dan Korem (1994), who studied suburban gangs, defined a gang as "a group of youths who are banded together in a specific context and whose activities include, but are not limited to, criminal acts. Adults may or may not be a part of this group, but when there is adult involvement, they will only represent a small minority of the gang membership" (35). According to Finn-Aage Esbensen (2000), a gang has more than two members, its members generally range in age from 11 to 25, they have a common identity, they have endured over time, and they are involved in some type of criminal activity.

Individual jurisdictions vary on their definition of a gang, depending on their location and the characteristics of local gangs. The National Youth Gang Center defines a youth gang as a "self-formed association of peers having the following characteristics: three or more members, generally ages 12 to 24; a name and some sense of identity, generally indicated by such symbols as style of clothing, graffiti, and hand signs; some degree of permanence and organization; and an elevated level of involvement in delinquent or criminal activity" (Institute for Intergovernmental Research, n.d.).

As these definitions show, several major elements can be found in most current definitions of gangs: a group of people, some type of organization, identifiable leadership, identifiable territory, use of symbols, a specific purpose, continual association and existence, and participation in some type of illegal activity.

Most gangs today have other behaviors in common: they use graffiti to mark their territory and to communicate with other gangs; they dress alike, often adopting a particular color as a gang color (for example, red for the Bloods, blue for the Crips); they often tattoo themselves with gang names or symbols; they abide by a specific code of conduct; they have their own specific language; and they have their own set of hand signs that help them recognize other gang members.

Gang Organization

Gangs are organized in a variety of ways, depending on their primary purpose, their level of structure, and the degree of control that the gang leaders have. Carl Taylor (1990) categorized gangs, based on the reasons for their existence, as scavenger gangs, territorial or turf gangs, and instrumental or corporate gangs. Scavenger gangs are loosely organized with a leadership that may change often, and this type of gang provides its members with a purpose for their lives. Many members are low achievers or school dropouts and are likely to exhibit violent behavior. Their crimes are usually not serious and are spontaneous. Territorial gangs may claim blocks, neighborhoods, specific buildings, or even schools as their home turf. These gangs are highly organized and have elaborate initiation rites as well as rules and regulations for controlling members' behavior. Members usually wear gang colors. Instrumental or corporate gangs usually have a clearly defined leader and a finely defined hierarchy of leadership, often a military-type structure. Youths generally become members if the gang views their contribution as necessary to the success and survival of the gang itself. Crimes are committed for a specific purpose, usually profit of some sort, and not just for fun. Gangs may start off as scavenger gangs and, over time, become instrumental or corporate gangs.

Lewis Yablonsky (1970) also distinguished three types of gangs, with somewhat different definitions; he referred to them as social, delinquent, and violent gangs. Social gangs are fairly permanent and cohesive, have a permanent location, and usually do not engage in delinquent or criminal activity. Delinquent gangs are organized for some type of illegal activity, usually for profit. They tend to be small, cohesive, exclusive, and well organized, and they participate in violent as well as social activity in the process of gaining illegal profits. Violent gangs are formed for the purpose of engaging in violent activity; these gangs are loosely organized and highly unstable, membership is uncertain, and core members often are emotionally unstable.

Other researchers also have organized gangs into a variety of categories. Most gang typologies contain four general types: social gangs, retreatist gangs, conflict gangs, and criminal gangs. Social gangs, which are the most common type, are also known as territorial or street-corner gangs. They are primarily involved in social activities, which may or may not include illegal activities; have some structure; and are identified with a specific territory. Alcohol and drug use is common among retreatist gang members and often is a major focus for this type of gang—one whose members pull back or retreat from society. Conflict gangs develop in poor neighborhoods, focus on social status for the members, and often are involved in serious criminal and violent activities. Criminal gangs, somewhat rare among juvenile gangs according to some experts, have strong leadership and a strong profit motive, are highly disciplined, and do not like to draw attention to themselves (Covey, Menard, and Franzese 1992).

Gangs are also made up of a variety of member types. "Wannabes" are usually younger people who want to become gang members or are seen as potential recruits by current members. Core members and leaders are the most consistently identified group of members; core members are more likely to be involved in the major activities of the gang. Veterans or "O.G." (for "old gangsters" or "original gangsters") are usually older youths or adults who are not actively involved in gang activity; many have the respect and admiration of younger gang members and work with gang leaders to help them achieve their goals.

Why Join a Gang?

Young people join gangs for many reasons. Some join for the same reasons that they might join Scouts or Little League or later join fraternities or sororities: they want to hang out with their friends who are part of a certain group, or they are looking for ways to distinguish themselves from their parents, to develop their own identities. Other young people join for economic reasons; if the gang is selling drugs or stolen goods, many youngsters see gang membership as an easy way to make some money.

Many people believe that young people join gangs and then get in trouble by going along with the dictates of the group. Fellow gang members may display values that are conducive to crime; provide opportunities for violent and sociopathic behavior; show how to gain material wealth that would otherwise be unavailable to many youths, especially those in the inner city; and provide an environment in which young men are supposed to prove their manhood by following these examples. Other people believe that youths who join gangs are already troublemakers and are seeking an outlet for their criminal tendencies. Travis Hirschi (1969) found that gangs harbored members who had little respect for others' opinions; therefore, it is likely that those juveniles who joined gangs already knew what they wanted to do—they did not need the encouragement of others in the gang to help them decide. Earlier researchers also found that some juveniles were already delinquent before they joined juvenile gangs (Glueck and Glueck 1950).

Researchers today report similar findings. Some youths join gangs to be part of a group and are drawn or coerced into delinquent or criminal behavior. Other youths have a delinquent or criminal background before joining a gang and continue their behavior patterns while in the gang (Egley, Howell, and Major 2006; Delaney 2006).

Many theories attempt to explain why juveniles join gangs. Several of these theories are sociological in nature, focusing on structural and dynamic variables as causes of gang formation and behavior. Some of these variables include social environment, family, and economic conditions and opportunity. Most of the theories fall into one of six categories: bonding and control theory, opportunity and strain theory, labeling theory, subcultural or cultural conflict theory, social disorganization theory, and radical or sociopolitical theory.

Bonding and Control Theory

The basic social institutions in American society, including home, school, church, and workplace, can teach children socially acceptable behavior. These institutions reward individuals who follow the rules and punish those who do not, thus attempting to control behavior (Shoemaker 2000). Family processes and interaction play a particularly important role in developing social bonds that may prevent young people from committing delinquent or criminal acts. Some researchers have found that families of delinquents tend to spend little time together and provide less support and affection than families of well-behaved youths. Parents often are unemployed and have problems with alcohol, and they may provide little or no supervision for their children (Patterson 1982; Snyder and Patterson 1987). Children of such parents may not pay attention in, or even attend, school, and they may not attend church either. These children miss out on multiple opportunities to learn socially appropriate behavior.

Opportunity and Strain Theory

The media often depict the American Dream—to achieve wealth, social position, and personal goals—as attainable for everyone. Many young people have the same dream for themselves—that they will be able to do better than their parents and achieve great things in their lives. However, not all young people have an equal opportunity to achieve this dream. As a result, they grow up frustrated and may develop a sense of hopelessness, believing that they will not receive the same things from society as other people do. The resulting depression or anger can lead to delinquent behavior.

A number of researchers believe that such social strain explains juvenile and gang delinquency (Cloward and Ohlin 1960; Cohen 1971; Williams and McShane 1999). Deborah Prothrow-Stith (1991) contends that young people who think they will be able to gain their fair share of what society has to offer are likely to join clubs, Boy or Girl Scouts, or fraternities, while young people who do not believe that society will provide for them may join gangs. She believes that juveniles join gangs, including violent gangs, only when they believe that their future opportunities for success are limited.

Other researchers suggest that strain theory does not adequately explain why juveniles join gangs. For instance, it does not explain why middle-class youths become delinquent or join gangs. The strain of living with limited opportunities does not lead most inner-city youths to join gangs, only certain youths.

While this theory provides one explanation, it also demonstrates the need to examine several factors that may interact to lead youths into delinquent or gang behavior.

Robert Merton's anomie theory attempts to explain how youths cope with the strain of having high hopes for their future and the reality of their situation or the probability of becoming successful. These youths may conform to the goal of success and attempt to succeed using legitimate means. They can become innovative in their attempts to succeed, using legal or illegal means to achieve their goals. They focus on the means of achieving success, without being successful, and are absorbed in small details. They may retreat from society. Finally, they may rebel against society and create their own goals (Williams and McShane 1999).

Labeling Theory

According to sociologist George Herbert Mead (1934), an individual's self-concept is derived from how others define the individual. This concept provides the basis for labeling theory, which some have called self-fulfilling prophecy. Several theorists have applied this theory to juvenile delinquency. According to Arnold Goldstein (1991), the initial act of delinquent behavior (primary deviance) is not important in labeling theory; it is the subsequent delinquent acts perpetrated in reaction to society's response to the initial act (secondary deviance) that are relevant. An individual's good behavior may not be reinforced if other people believe he is a troublemaker; as opportunities for engaging in delinquent behavior present themselves, the individual may conclude that if most people think he is bad, he might as well be bad (Williams and McShane 1999). According to Siegel, Welsh, and Senna (2003), these "actions help solidify both the grip of deviant peers and the impact of the labels" (125).

Subcultural or Cultural Conflict Theory

Some researchers believe that delinquent behavior results from an individual conforming to the current norms of the subculture in which he grows up, if these norms vary from those of the larger society (Shaw and McKay 1942; Miller 1958; Thornton and Voight 1992). Several studies have shown that males who admit that some of their friends are delinquent also admit that they have committed delinquent acts (Johnson 1979). Other studies have shown that students who live in neighborhoods with high rates of delinquency are more likely to commit delinquent acts than students living in areas of low delinquency (Rutter and Giller 1983). Youngsters who grow up in areas that have high crime and delinquency rates may come to believe that crime and delinquency are normal aspects of everyday life and therefore do not think that they are doing anything wrong when they misbehave or commit a crime.

Social Disorganization Theory

Thrasher (1927) was one of the first to propose social disorganization theory as a way of explaining why youths find gangs so compelling: youths join gangs because they do not feel connected to the existing social institutions. Thrasher proposed that these youths joined gangs because, to them, the gang was their own society, one that provided all of the gang members' needs. According to this theory, the formation of gangs is not abnormal, but rather a normal response to an abnormal situation (Spergel 1995). Sampson (1993) posits that a primary indicator of social disorganization within communities is how well these communities "supervise and control *teenage peer-groups*—especially gangs" (267, emphasis in original). High rates of delinquency in an area indicate that social problems, including unemployment and single-parent families, are present and may lead to gang formation (Delaney 2006).

Radical or Sociopolitical Theory

In the late 1970s, several researchers developed a sociopolitical perspective on crime and delinquency, known as radical theory, or the "new criminology." Believing that laws in the United States are developed by and for the ruling elite, radical theorists hold that these laws are used to hold down the poor, minorities, and the powerless (Abadinsky 1979; Meier 1976; Bohm 2001). Radical theory is based on several propositions: (1) American life is structured around an advanced capitalist society, (2) government is organized to serve the needs of the capitalist ruling class, (3) criminal law and crime control protect the interests of the ruling class, (4) society is prepared to oppress the lower economic classes through any means necessary, and (5) only a society based on socialism will solve the crime problem (Quinney and Wildeman 1991).

Other Theories

Some researchers believe that many of today's gangs have evolved into major business enterprises. For example, Felix Padilla (1992) contends that "the gang represents a viable and persistent business enterprise within the U.S. economy, with its own culture, logic, and systematic means of transmitting and reinforcing its fundamental business virtues" (3). Gangs have become big business; many youths may join them as a means of earning money, more money than they would earn at the local fast-food restaurant or in another low-paying job. The gang may provide the same opportunities that a local business or large corporation might provide to a youth from a middle-class neighborhood.

Looking for ways in which community life affects criminality, researchers have examined such factors as anonymity, mobility, territoriality, population density, and systems of behavior reinforcement and punishment. Peers can alter how an individual views criminal or delinquent behavior. James Wilson and Richard Herrnstein (1985) claim that "the density of human settlement can affect the frequency with which one encounters opportunities for crime (by presenting a chance to steal a purse or a car when one is to the right of his 'crossover point'—that is, when the rewards of crime appear stronger than the delayed rewards of not committing the crime); and the extent of natural surveillance of the streets, provided it is carried out by persons willing to act on the basis of what they see, may affect the probability of being caught and punished" (311).

Combination of Theories

Many researchers have found it necessary to combine various theories in order to explain delinquent behavior. For example, social learning theory holds that situational, cognitive, and physiological variables interact to influence behavior (Bandura 1973). Social development theory considers the following variables important: the opportunities available to the child for bonding with the parent, life skills, and the reinforcements that are provided for good behavior (Hawkins and Weis 1985). M. Philip Feldman (1977) ties together social learning theory, individual predisposition, and social labeling theory. Differential association–differential reinforcement theory, as proposed by Robert Burgess and Ronald Akers (1966), is a combination of the differential-association perspective proposed by Edwin Sutherland (1947) and social learning theory from Albert Bandura. In *Deviant Behavior,* Akers (1985) explains differential association–differential reinforcement theory: one's behavior is shaped by imitating other people's behavior and by observing the consequences (or lack of consequences) of other people's behavior.

Most researchers focus on male juvenile delinquency and gang participation. In *Men, Women, and Aggression,* Anne Campbell observes:

> Women are curiously ignored in all three theories [structural, social control, cultural]. Structural arguments focus almost wholly on classism and racism, but it is women, not men, who bear the brunt of the poverty that results. Any theory arguing that gangs are the result of economic inequality must surely predict that women would be at least equal partners in the roster of gang members. As for social control theory, women are also exposed to the erosion of family and community control, but they are much less likely to join gangs. . . . The cultural analysis is both detailed and persuasive, but it explains only Chicano gangs. . . . During the course of the last 200 years, the predominant ethnic makeup of gangs has altered time and again. What they all have in common is the gang as a predominantly male response to poverty and lack of opportunity. The culture that has to be examined is that of poverty-level and working-class masculinity. (Campbell 1993, 129–130)

In addition to examining masculinity issues when studying gang participation and gang behavior, researchers also must be careful not to generalize about the influence of gangs on the criminality of their members, because gangs differ greatly from city to city and from ethnic group to ethnic group.

Social Factors

As can be seen from the many theories concerning the existence and growth of gangs, many factors interact to lead youths to join gangs. As Irving Spergel and his colleagues (1994) say, "Rapid urban population change, community disintegration, increasing poverty (relative and absolute), and social isolation contribute to institutional failures and the consequent development of youth gangs" (3).

Growing up in American society today can be a challenge, particularly in an inner-city neighborhood. When young people have little structure in their lives, when they have no purpose or can see no reason to excel in school, they may be more likely to join gangs. The gang gives their lives structure, makes them feel important and useful, protects them from a violent environment, and provides some sense of safety in numbers. Gang members are loyal to each other and to the gang, their group gets special attention in the community, and their association may provide financial rewards if the gang is selling drugs or involved in other criminal activities. Excitement is a part of gang life; members can get an adrenaline rush from some of their activities, and they may feel empowered by the backing and respect of the other gang members, which gives them the courage to do whatever the gang asks of them.

Racial/Ethnic Gangs

Gangs frequently are composed of members from the same race or ethnic group, although a growing number of gangs are referred to as "hybrid" gangs (see below). Generally, whites join white gangs, Hispanics join Hispanic gangs, and African Americans join African American gangs. Researchers have found that these racial/ethnic gangs have several characteristics that are specific to their gangs.

Hispanic Gangs

Hispanic gangs, also known as Latino gangs, generally have four levels of membership: peripheral, general, active, and hard core. Peripheral members identify with the gang but do not actively participate in the gang, especially in the criminal activities. General members readily identify themselves with the gang but are still working on gaining respect. Once a general member gains respect, he is expected to complete various "jobs" assigned to him; for example, carjackings and attacks on rival gangs. At this point, he is considered an active member. Finally, the hard-core members are active participants in the gang's criminal activity; in fact, these members are the ones who are in leadership positions and usually determine the gang's criminal activities.

The two major Latino gangs are the Norteños and Sureños. Many of the Latino gangs in California (and other states) claim to be either Norteños (Northerners) or Sureños (Southerners), originally determined by their location—north or south of a line that runs east-west between Delano and Salinas, California. Norteños-affiliated gangs are found primarily throughout the western United States, while the Sureños are more widespread throughout the country.

Hispanic gang members often set themselves apart from other gangs by using a slang language that is a combination of English and Spanish. Many gang members are proud to call themselves crazy, hence the common use of the word *loco* in much of their language to denote they are unafraid or macho.

African American Gangs

According to several researchers, African American gang members stay in their gangs longer than gang members from other racial/ethnic groups. This can be explained in part by the lack of economic opportunities available to these youths. According to Irving Spergel (1995), legitimate opportunities for African American youth to participate in viable economic activities are more "thoroughly blocked" than in any other community: "More limited systems of illegitimate opportunity have evolved, based pervasively on street-gang structures, than is the case for any other racial or ethnic group. . . . Because of persistent poverty associated with racism, black male youths also become overidentified as gang members" (62).

Asian Gangs

Asian youths may join gangs for many of the same reasons youths from other cultures join them. Asian youths whose parents are fairly new to the United States may feel alienated, overwhelmed, and out of place. The language barrier and other obstacles to adapting to American culture may encourage these youths to band together for protection and support.

Asian gangs are usually organized for economic reasons, and members rarely commit crimes against other cultural or racial groups. Spergel (1993), in a review of the literature, finds that these gangs, especially Japanese, Taiwanese, and Hong Kong gangs, are the best organized, the most secretive, and the best disciplined of all gangs.

Malcolm Klein (1995) found that Asian gangs were quite selective in choosing members. Non-Asians were not welcomed into the gang. While some Asian gangs are organized according to their location and fight others for turf, most public attention has been focused on their home invasion activities. They will often target Asian families, threatening their victims with death or great bodily damage if they talk to the police. Many victims refrain from going to the police because of these threats and because of their view of the police in their country of origin as corrupt or ineffective, or because reporting the crime will bring shame to the family. Most cities have few police officers, reporters, or researchers who are Asian or understand Asian culture, and few outsiders are able to gain the confidence of Asian gang members and victims in order to better understand them.

White Gangs

White gangs have the longest history among all racial/ethnic gangs; they were especially prominent in the late 1800s and early 1900s as many Europeans immigrated to the United States. White supremacist groups are popular gangs in many areas of the United States. They believe in the doctrines of Adolf Hitler and may be tied in with the Ku Klux Klan and the neo-Nazi movement. Many gang members refer to themselves as "skinheads." They tend to wear their hair short or shave their heads, wear black biker boots, and listen to punk rock music. However, some skinheads may keep their hair longer to keep from being identified as skinheads. They dislike African Americans, Asians, Hispanics, Jews, gays, lesbians, Catholics, and any other group that they do not consider part of the white Aryan race.

Many people believe that the skinheads are becoming more popular with white youth today, because many of these youths believe that the future holds little promise for them (Holthouse 2006). They do not believe that they will be better off than their parents, and they may become disaffected with society, often looking for someone else to blame for their problems. Most research indicates that the skinhead groups are loosely organized and primarily composed of high school dropouts and working-class youth. Their trademark is violence, which distinguishes them from most street gangs. Skinheads join together to commit violence against anyone they do not like or approve of, while street gangs form for a wider variety of reasons (Delaney 2006). In fact, some researchers believe that skinheads should not be considered typical street gangs but rather "constitute what can best be described as a terrorist youth subculture" (Hamm 1993, 65).

Native American Gangs

Most research concerning Native American gangs has focused on gangs in Native American communities, collectively referred to as "Indian Country" in most studies. *Indian Country* is defined in U.S. law (18 U.S.C. § 1151) as including (1) land within Indian reservations, (2) dependent Indian communities, and (3) Indian allotments. This definition encompasses 561 federally recognized tribes living in 577 communities. Gang activity on Native American reservations is difficult to measure and to compare, in large part because reservations vary greatly in size and can include both rural and urban areas.

Most research has indicated that gang activity on reservations primarily consists of unstructured and informal associations among youth (Major and Egley 2002). Native youths who have moved off the reservation with their families and then return to the reservation may bring their gang associations with them and attempt to recruit new members. Members of the Hualapai reservation in Arizona report few instances of gang behavior. However, gang membership on the Pine Ridge reservation in South Dakota is estimated at 3,500 members or more (total population on the reservation is approximately 15,000) (Grant 2004). Nearby, on the Lakota Rosebud reservation, school personnel believe that at least 77 gangs are active. Some educators see a direct causal relationship between the loss of cultural identity among the Native American children and their families and the problems of substance abuse and gangs on the reservation (Kilman 2006).

Hybrid Gangs

In the early 1900s, hybrid gangs were gangs that consisted of members from two or more races or ethnic groups. Today, hybrid gangs may have members from more than one ethnic group or race; have members who participate in more than one gang; use symbols or colors from more than one gang; or cooperate with rival gangs in certain, often criminal, activities (Starbuck, Howell, and Lindquist 2001). Communities throughout the United States are seeing an increase in the number of hybrid gangs, especially communities that had little or no gang activity prior to the 1980s or 1990s. Communities in the Midwest are more likely to have hybrid gangs than many other areas of the country, in part because gangs are fairly new to many of these areas and the gangs are trying to find their own identities. They take bits and pieces of characteristics from current gangs on the West Coast and in Chicago and create their own identities (Starbuck, Howell, and Lindquist 2001).

These hybrid gangs may pose a serious problem to local law enforcement agencies, because they do not mimic traditional gang characteristics or behavior. Citizens, as well as local law enforcement agencies, may be lulled into a false sense of security, believing that their community does not have any gang activity, while the reality is that hybrid gangs may exist but may not fit the typical view of a gang. Also, using ineffective intervention tactics based on a gang's name or other characteristic may be problematic. For example, believing that a gang is involved in drug trafficking because the name it goes by happens to be the name of a gang generally involved in drugs may lead law enforcement and others into totally inappropriate intervention activities.

Rural versus Urban Gangs

Prior to the 1980s and 1990s, most gangs were found in urban, primarily inner-city, areas. Rapid growth of immigrant groups, especially in rural areas, has contributed to the spread of gangs in these communities, as well as in more affluent urban areas (Howell and Egley 2005). Youths from immigrant families may experience problems in speaking and understanding English, may be ostracized by local youths as outsiders, and may not have strong community support systems to help them assimilate.

Some youths in rural areas may band together for friendship and protection and have the potential to develop into gangs. Rural communities may not have many activities to keep youths busy after school or during the summer, or offer few job opportunities for them, which may further alienate them and lead them into gangs. On the other hand, one study found that students in urban schools were significantly more likely to have friends who are members of a gang and were more likely to have been threatened by gangs than students in schools in rural areas (Evans et al. 1999). Youths belonging to gangs also move into other urban and rural areas with their families, bringing with them the ability to organize gangs in their new communities.

Media reports and gang studies tend to focus on gangs and violence in the inner city, leading readers to believe that gangs are primarily an urban phenomenon and primarily affect lower socioeconomic areas. However, Dan Korem (1994) has studied gangs in affluent suburban neighborhoods and contends that a certain "flow of events" leads to gang formation in these areas. This flow includes the breakdown of families in part of the community; the emergence of styles of dress, music preference, hair styles, and graffiti that are characteristic of youth subculture; increase in drug abuse; and unexpected acts of violence.

Gang Alliances

In the early 1900s, most gangs were created at the local neighborhood level and took their names from that neighborhood. Most of these gangs were autonomous. However, beginning in the 1960s, gangs began to adopt a variation of a common gang name, in essence, becoming a branch of another gang. For example, in Chicago, local gangs included the War Lords, California Lords, and Fifth Avenue Lords, all claiming to be related to and a part of the Vice Lord Nation (Miller 2001).

The 1980s saw the expansion of gang alliances. Each alliance had its own set of symbols and other means of identifying it and separating it from other gangs and gang alliances. Examples of these alliances include the People Nation (composed of Bloods [West Coast], Latin Kings, Vice Lords, El Rukn, Bishops, and Gaylords) and the Folk Nation (composed of Crips, Black Gangster Disciples, Black Disciples, Latin Disciples, and La Raza). Incentives for forming these alliances include the power associated with being part of a larger and more important organization and the coverage by the news media of these alliances, which creates publicity for them. Researchers and law enforcement personnel are divided over whether these alliances are in name only, formed primarily to create the impression of large, powerful gang networks, or whether the individual gangs actually coordinate their activities and projects with each other.

Females as Gang Members and All-Female Gangs

Early studies of gangs often did not consider females as gang members (Thrasher 1927; Miller 1975). They were seen, if at all, as girlfriends of gang members with only a superficial interest in gang activities. As more gang research has been conducted, the role of the female has expanded to include a secondary role in gang activities. Females often are seen as providing help and support to male gang members by carrying weapons, offering alibis, and gathering information on rival gang members. Studies generally estimate that between 6 and 30 percent of all gang members are female (see Chapter 6 for more detail). Female participation in gangs may be increasing, including participation in all-female gangs, and female roles may be changing.

Some researchers believe that females join gangs for many of the same reasons that males do (Campbell 1984). Others believe that females join for vastly different reasons, often because of psychological factors and problems with society's expectations for young women. Young women who have been sexually abused may also be more likely to join gangs (Moore and Hagedorn 2001). Males are more likely to need the support and encouragement of other males as they mature, while most girls do not need this type of group support. Males also usually have more freedom in their activities.

A study conducted by Beth Bjerregaard and Carolyn Smith (1993), using data from the Rochester Youth Development Study, found many similarities between female and male participation in gangs. For both males and females, a strong relationship exists between membership in a gang and instances of delinquency, drug use, and sexual activity, and the relationship between gang membership and sexual activity at an early age was stronger for females than for males. Females were also more likely than males to see their opportunities for success limited, especially educationally, and to believe that joining a gang was their best opportunity to become successful.

Some female gangs are allied with a particular male gang, while others are totally autonomous. African American and Hispanic females are the most likely to participate in gang activities, although white and Asian females are forming and joining gangs in increasing numbers. Anne Campbell (1987) studied female gangs and found that the female gang member is not simply a sexual object, hanging around the male gang members solely to provide sex. She found that the "social talk of delinquent girls generally shows that they not only reject sexual activity outside the context of a steady relationship, but even reject friendships with 'loose' girls whose reputation might contaminate them by association" (451–452). Campbell goes on to say that "[n]ew girls in the group who, unaware of the prevailing norms, slept around with a variety of men were called to account for their behavior at meetings and instructed that serial monogamy was required" (461).

More studies are currently being conducted on female gang membership in large part because law enforcement agencies are beginning to better document female participation in gangs (Egley, Howell, and Major 2006). Researchers are finding that most females join male gangs or are affiliated with male gangs in some way. Some all-female gangs do exist. Female gang member involvement in gang-related criminal activities is also growing. However, female gang members are still more likely to be killed than to kill someone else (Hagedorn 1999).

Gang Migration

Researchers are beginning to study gang migration—the movement of gang members from one area to another and the subsequent development of gangs in those new locations. In communities that are seeing the appearance of gangs in recent years, authorities believe that migratory gang members are moving into the area and recruiting local youth to establish a new branch of a gang. Known as the importation model, this strategy involves attempts by gang members to encourage the growth of their gang into new cities and is often used to establish new money-making criminal enterprises (Decker and Van Winkle 1996). Knox and his colleagues (1996) refer to this as gang franchising, while Quinn, Tobolowsky, and Downs (1994) refer to it as gang colonization.

Migrant gang members do not always establish new gangs that are extensions of an already existing gang. Some newly developed gangs do not have any structural affiliation to an existing gang. In addition, migrant gang members do not always have to find local participants in a new area to keep the gang going; this occurs when enough gang members move to a new location (Maxson 1998).

Gangs and Violence

Most experts agree that gang activity increased significantly during the 1980s and 1990s and continues to spread throughout the United States today. Law enforcement, community organizations, and the news media offer many gang members the recognition that they crave. Stories about gang activities and gang violence are a concrete example to gang members that their gangs and their actions are important. In fact, some researchers believe that the news media influence the general public's view of gangs and create the impression that gangs are more widespread and violent than they actually are. Prothrow-Stith (1991) explains that some inner-city youths believe the only way they can get any attention or recognition is to join a gang and participate in some type of criminal activity.

Researchers believe that a variety of factors have led to increasingly violent behavior on the part of gang members. The major factors are guns, territory, and drugs.

Guns

Gangs began routinely using guns during the 1980s, according to Miller (1992). Howell (2004) says that the "growing use of firearms in gang assaults is a major contributor to the growth of gang murders" (212). With their increasing availability, guns have become the weapon of choice for gang members. Many researchers believe that gang members are more likely to carry and to use guns than are other juveniles—one gang member shoots a member of another gang, that gang retaliates, then the first gang retaliates, and so on.

Gang members are able to obtain guns through legal means, through gun shops or online, as well as illegally, by stealing them during break-ins. Gang members believe carrying a gun gives them increased power and masculinity. According to Delaney (2006), gang members today "assume rivals are packing and therefore feel it necessary to pack a gun as well" (239).

Territory

With more emphasis on material possessions, territory can be considered a possession. As the distribution and sale of drugs become more popular and profitable for gangs, the amount of territory that a gang controls becomes more important. Territory plays a critical part in the life of many gangs. James Vigil (1988), reporting on the importance of territory, quotes one young gang member: "The only thing we can do is build our own little nation. We know that we have complete control in our community. It's like we're making our stand. . . . We take pride in our little nation and if any intruders enter, we get panicked because we feel our community is being threatened. The only way is with violence" (131).

However, while fighting for and controlling their territory was the primary focus of many gangs, today that focus may be changing. According to the National Youth Gang Center (2000), modern youth gangs are less focused on maintaining a certain territory than were gangs in earlier years, who vigorously defended their territory (strongly tied to their local neighborhood).

Drugs

Many of our images of gangs, based primarily on media reports, include the use of alcohol and drugs. We tend to believe that gangs sell drugs to make extra money or even that many gangs are structured as mini-corporations and are heavily involved in the drug trade. Research supports the belief that many gang members use alcohol and illegal drugs, but, while some gangs are heavily involved in the distribution of drugs, most sell and distribute drugs on a more casual, less organized, basis. In any case, the use, sale, and distribution of drugs by gangs have been increasing over the years.

In 1964, Isador Chein and his colleagues surveyed New York City Youth Board staff who worked with street-gang members in New York City and found that gangs contacted by these staff members reported little drug use or selling of drugs by gang members. However, also in 1964, Spergel found that gang members who were on the verge of leaving the gang and were involved in violent gang activity were more likely than other gang members to use drugs and sell them on a limited basis. In her studies of Chicano gang members in East Los Angeles, Joan Moore (1991) found that heroin became popular among the older gang members during the late 1940s; many members left the gang to become involved in the heroin trade. Several reports have found that gang members were likely to be using marijuana, even during the 1950s and 1960s, although they report little involvement in heavy sales activities of this substance.

Studying Mexican American gangs in Southern California, James Vigil found that gang members used drugs and were involved only minimally in the sale of drugs. He reported that gang members generally started using drugs at the age of 12.7 years and that use of more than one drug was common, but that most gang members were not heavily involved in drug sales. Explaining the popularity of drug use among gang members, Vigil said that "drinking and drugs act as a 'social lubricant' to facilitate the broadening, deepening, and solidifying of group affiliations and cohesiveness. . . . Drug and alcohol usage often facilitates gang youths' release from their felt obligations to social mores and thus increases their willingness to participate in other criminal acts, especially if such behavior seems to help them prove their loyalty and commitment to the group" (Vigil 1988, 126).

Though more gang members than nongang members use drugs and many also sell drugs, they do not generally appear to be part of larger criminal drug organizations. According to Ira Reiner (1992), former Los Angeles County district attorney, drugs and gangs should be treated as two separate issues, even though some of the same individuals who sell drugs are gang members. Reiner reports that in Los Angeles more than 70 percent of all gang members use drugs, which is four times the percentage of nongang members, and seven times more gang members sell drugs than nongang members. Younger gang members tend to focus their time and energy on intergang rivalries and see drugs only as a source of income, while older gang members lean more toward selling drugs than performing other activities usually important to gang members.

Some researchers believe that gang structure is not conducive to organized drug dealing. According to Spergel (1995), "the youth gang's fluid, unstable, emotionally charged character is not suited to a rational drug organization" (47). Leonard Dunston also sees gang structure and drug organization as separate:

In New York City, drugs are controlled by organized crime groups. Young, weak, undermanned and poorly organized street gangs cannot compete with the older more powerful and violent groups. The fragmented street gangs do not have the network organizations employing youths in various aspects of their drug business. They are employed as steerers, lookouts, dealers, enforcers or protectors from robbers and other drug organizations. The primary difference between a drug organization and a youth gang is that in a drug organization all members are employees while youth gang membership only requires affiliation. We do not see our youth gangs become drug organizations. (Dunston 1990, 7)

Other researchers similarly believe that gangs are too unorganized, unfocused, and unable to effectively operate a serious drug organization. Klein, Maxson, and Cunningham (1988) indicate the gang-drug connection has been overstated and should not be considered a single social problem.

During the 1980s, some gang members recognized the economic opportunity presented by the appearance of crack cocaine; however, nongang youths also capitalized on this opportunity (Fagan 2004). In addition, according to Howell and Decker (1999), the economic opportunities encouraged some youths to prolong their gang membership, because this was the best opportunity they had to make money.

However, even though a gang member sells drugs, it does not necessarily follow that he also uses drugs. In fact, some gangs involved in the distribution of drugs do not allow members to become users. For example, Ko-Lin Chin (1990) found that, while many of the early Chinese gangs in New York City distributed heroin, most of these gangs refused to use heroin themselves. While studying gangs in Detroit, Thomas Mieczkowski (1986) found that the street-level juvenile drug runners, primarily running heroin, rejected the use of heroin for themselves. However, many of these youths used other drugs, primarily marijuana and cocaine, for recreational purposes.

The relationship between drug sales and homicides by gangs is not very strong or persuasive. Klein, Maxson, and Cunningham (1988) found no relationship between drug sales and gang homicides in a study of Los Angeles gangs, drugs, and homicides. Lawrence Bobrowski (1988), an analyst for Chicago's

Gang Crime Unit, examined the relationship between gang-related drug dealing and violence using statistics from the Chicago Police Department. While he found a relationship between gangs and drug use, he did not find a relationship between arrests for drug dealing or possession by gang members and gang violence. In a 1994 report, the Institute for Law and Justice also reported that it found no strong relationship between drugs and gangs. It claimed that "if gangs were to disappear overnight, drugs would remain a serious problem, and if drugs were to disappear overnight, gangs would still be a serious problem. These two problems intersect and complicate each other, but there are still large areas in which they are independent of each other" (8–9).

Approaches to Dealing with Gangs

Three basic approaches exist in dealing with gangs: prevention, intervention, and suppression. The most successful programs generally employ a combination of these activities to discourage gang participation and activities in local communities. Many of the actions employed by these approaches overlap.

Prevention

Prevention programs were the first type of strategy employed in attempts to rid communities of gangs. These programs generally attempt to keep young people from joining gangs, as well as to prevent the formation of gangs. Most of these programs focus on community organization activities intended to improve economic and living conditions and provide early childhood programs, school-based programs, and after-school activities.

Community organization programs involve local groups in providing or improving resources for young people so they are not tempted to join gangs. These activities can include recreational activities, community improvement, and advocacy activities. Leaders of programs that focus on improving economic and living conditions believe that children will be less likely to join gangs if their living conditions are improved, more health and social services are offered to families, and their communities are safe places to live. Early childhood programs focus on providing very young children with the resources they will need to avoid gang involvement through preschool programs, parent training, and services to pregnant mothers, including nutritional, health, safety, and educational services. School-based programs generally involve activities to keep students safe while in school, enrichment activities that keep students interested in school, networking with local community programs, and some type of gang intervention program. After-school activities can offer young people alternatives to gang membership by keeping them active and interested in safer, more productive endeavors.

The importance of these types of programs was confirmed in a study conducted by Hill and his colleagues (1999) that examined childhood risk factors that lead to gang membership. They found that family characteristics that are more likely to place a child at risk for gang participation include family instability, severe economic deprivation, low attachment to the mother, family management problems, family conflict, parents displaying proviolence attitudes, and siblings displaying antisocial behaviors. They also found that children who lived in communities with readily available drugs had a higher probability of joining gangs.

Intervention

Intervention programs focus on encouraging youths to quit their gang memberships and encouraging gangs to reduce or eliminate their criminal activities through the provision of alternative opportunities and rehabilitation options. Intervention programs typically include community outreach, crisis intervention, job training, and social intervention.

Communities can take many steps to help create successful intervention and prevention programs. The extent of the gang problem within the community must be assessed, local representatives of concerned agencies should provide information for the assessment effort, and factors contributing to gang activities should be discussed. An effective organizational system must be implemented to coordinate activities among all participating agencies. Policies and strategies have to be developed with input from all concerned agencies. Gang members need to be held responsible for their behavior, but the community also has to provide opportunities to help them change their behavior. Staff members must be well trained in all aspects of gang behavior and current research findings in the field.

Suppression

Suppression programs use legal means, including police response, prosecution, and incarceration, to discourage or eliminate gangs, primarily by removing individual gang members from the streets.

Police departments use a variety of techniques to gather information about gangs and individual gang members. These techniques include staking out territory where gangs are known to congregate; patrolling and enforcing the law aggressively in gang territories; surveilling individual gang members and gang hangouts; following up on investigations into gang activities; developing an extensive information system on gang members and their activities; and infiltrating locales in which gangs may be found, such as schools, activity centers, and malls. According to Spergel (1995), "Gang information systems are expected to improve crime analysis, surveillance, communication, investigation, and other techniques to monitor gang activity, especially gang-related drug trafficking. Law enforcement officials argue that improved data systems and coordination of information across different justice system agencies will lead to more efficiency, more gang members being removed from the streets, more rapid prosecution, and more imprisonment with 'less hassle' for longer periods" (195).

The various responses to gangs were one of the areas explored in a federally funded national youth gang survey conducted by Spergel and Curry (1993). Suppression activities were reported as those most frequently adopted to control gangs; these types of activities were also reported to be the least effective in controlling gang behavior.

Legal Approaches

Many police departments currently have special units to deal with the problem of gangs. These units range in size from 1 to 500 staff members and are either centrally located or have offices spread throughout the city. The size of the gang unit often depends on the seriousness and extent of the city's gang problems as well as the extent of other problems that may take precedence, the financial strength of the police department, and the importance the public and city officials place on reducing gang problems. For example, in the late 1980s, eight officers were assigned to a variety of tasks within the Preventive Patrol Unit of the Philadelphia Police Department. The unit worked with gang youth, runaways, sexually abused children, and at-risk youth. During the same time, both the Los Angeles Police Department and the Los Angeles County Sheriff's Department developed special gang units of approximately 200 officers each. By 1992, the Chicago Police Department's gang unit employed more than 500 specially trained police officers (Spergel 1995).

Federal authorities from such agencies as the Bureau of Alcohol, Tobacco, Firearms and Explosives (ATF); the Federal Bureau of Investigation (FBI); the Drug Enforcement Administration (DEA); and the Immigration and Naturalization Service (INS) sometimes get involved in efforts to intervene in gang activities. At the local, state, and federal levels, the FBI sponsors 131 task forces in 41 states; Washington, D.C.; Puerto Rico; and the U.S. Virgin Islands to fight gang- and drug-related violence (http://www.fbi.gov/hq/cid/ngic/natgangtfs.htm).

Within the past 20 years, many law enforcement agencies have focused on gangs as criminal organizations and have set up or advocated elaborate information and tracking systems, primarily at the local level, though state governments are now beginning to see the value of these types of systems. Robert Philibosian (1989) asserts that the growth of gangs and their involvement with drugs underscore the need for a statewide information system in California: "The expansion of gangs and their importation of drugs throughout the state make it even more critical to design and develop a statewide gang information network and clearing house. The statewide system should provide local law enforcement officials with gang analysis files. The system would greatly improve communication, cooperation, and coordination among all criminal justice entities through the state" (55).

Many people believe that law enforcement officials already spend too much time gathering information and intruding into the lives of suspected gang members and their families and that the police harass blacks in the inner cities. In Los Angeles, police are alleged to pick up gang members and drop them off in a rival gang's territory. Several studies do suggest that the police are sometimes out of line. As a result of the beating of Rodney King, a black man, by white Los Angeles police officers, an incident that was videotaped by a bystander and broadcast on national television in 1991, the Independent Commission on the Los Angeles Police Department, commonly known as the Christopher Commission, found many documented instances of police brutality and harassment of racial minorities. Mexican Americans, both gang members and nongang members, experience harassment at the hands of the police in the barrios of Los Angeles, although it is possible that the bad feeling that exists between the police and gangs may lead to some false reports of harassment (Mirande 1981; Vigil 1988).

Prosecutors often take what they call a vertical approach to dealing with gang youth. Once assigned to a case, they stay with the case from the beginning to the end. As a result of this strategy, the conviction rate has gone up. Prosecutors have become more experienced, more specialized, and often more community oriented in dealing with gang crime.

Prosecutors are responsible for protecting witnesses in all criminal cases; they often must resort to extraordinary measures to protect witnesses in gang-related cases. The 1992 NIJ survey found that 89 percent of prosecutors in large jurisdictions and 74 percent in smaller jurisdictions reported that obtaining the cooperation of witnesses was a significant problem. Prosecutors said witnesses were afraid to cooperate because of possible retaliation, a neighborhood culture that frowned on informers, or personal connection with the gang member(s) in question. Some prosecutors' offices ask the police to videotape witness statements in case witnesses change their minds later, "forget" what they saw, or are murdered. Many witnesses are also afraid of and do not trust the police; because of personal experiences, these witnesses often protect each other and their neighbors.

Few judges have developed special approaches to dealing with gang youth. Those who have not tend to emphasize a get-tough approach, often based on community desires, trying many youths as adults. Some judges have developed a community-oriented approach, taking into account social aspects of each case. Many communities look for a get-tough approach; they do not want to see violent gang youth treated leniently.

Most probation offices do not have special programs or officers to deal with gang members, but some cities have developed special units for working with gang members placed on parole. Some jurisdictions in California, including Los Angeles, San Jose, San Diego, and Orange County, have instituted special units that provide intense supervision and often work closely with local community social service agencies. Some programs also work with other agencies to provide group counseling, remedial education, employment training, and job placement services.

Prison officials attempt to suppress all gang activity within the prison system. They may move gang leaders from one facility to another in an attempt to prevent them from associating with one another. Some youth correctional systems coordinate activities with local law enforcement and community agencies as well as provide employment training and work programs.

Legislation and Gangs

Thirty-one states have enacted Racketeer Influenced and Corrupt Organizations (RICO) Act statutes to help their officials combat gang crime. The writers of these statutes portray gangs as a serious, organized threat to society (Spergel 1995). However, according to the 1992 NIJ study, only 17 percent of prosecutors in large counties and less than 10 percent in smaller counties have ever used RICO statutes to prosecute gang members (Johnson, Webster, and Connors 1995).

State conspiracy laws have been used to combat gang crime along with state drug kingpin statutes. The NIJ study found that state conspiracy laws were used against gang members by 37 percent of prosecutors in large jurisdictions and by 26 percent of prosecutors in small jurisdictions, while 36 percent of all prosecutors used state drug kingpin laws against gang members (Johnson, Webster, and Connors 1995). Many cities have tried arranging gang treaties and truces to lessen gang crime. In some cases, these truces have worked for a while, but in most cases something eventually triggers an end to the truce.

Street Terrorism Enforcement and Prevention (STEP) acts have been passed in 16 states (Arizona, Arkansas, California, Florida, Georgia, Illinois, Indiana, Iowa, Louisiana, Minnesota, Mississippi, Montana, Nevada, North Dakota, Rhode Island, and South Dakota) to combat gang activities. STEP acts are based on RICO statutes and deal with gangs in a comprehensive way, with one law, and they address constitutional issues related to the prosecution of street-gang activities. The California law has been challenged on various constitutional grounds regarding freedom of association, vagueness, and overreaching but has managed to survive all challenges to date.

Other states and local jurisdictions have passed legislation to deal with their specific gang-related problems. These statutes focus on such gang activities as drive-by shootings, member recruitment, weapon possession, loitering, and pointing weapons from a vehicle. The statutes also address law enforcement issues such as vehicle forfeiture, witness protection programs, accessibility of juvenile records, the age limit for juvenile offenses, and automatic treatment of juveniles as adults in trials for gang-related crime.

Why Youths Leave Gangs

Some individuals are able to walk away from gang activity on their own, without the help of outside intervention. Various reasons account for this ability. As a youth gets older, he may lose interest in the gang, in large part because he is maturing and sees the gang as a dead end (literally or figuratively) for himself. Or a youth may find other activities or interests that become more important than the gang. Others decide that they do not like or support violent activities. A youth may join a gang for specific reasons; once in the gang, however, he discovers that gang life does not meet his expectations, so he quits. Some gang members may discover that they are being used or exploited by the leadership and decide that they want to be needed, not used. In some cases, the home environment may improve, reducing the need for a youth to join a gang to feel part of a family. Some youths may realize that the benefits of being in a gang are not worth the increased likelihood of being incarcerated for gang activity.

Positive Functions of Gangs

For the most part, young people are hurt by gang membership; they may get shot at or killed, they may commit criminal acts, they may terrorize a neighborhood, and they may end up in jail or prison. However, Klein (1995) found that positive aspects of gangs and gang life may be realized as well. For example, many young people who join gangs gain a measure of self-confidence and self-respect, and, in some cases, these young people will eventually see that gangs cannot give them what they want in life and will leave their gangs as better people. In some cases, the skills that gang members learn, such as cooperation, organization, and teamwork, can be used to improve their neighborhoods and their futures, if applied in the right way. Finally, gangs may have a stabilizing effect on the communities in which they are found, providing activities for the children and a focus to the neighborhood as the community aims to keep the next generation out of gangs.

Outlook for the Future

Clearly, gangs are becoming more widespread and more violent; they reflect the society in which they operate. More families today are composed of single mothers or single fathers trying to raise children and work or of two-parent families in which both parents work and do not have the time to spend with their children. Many experts believe that this lack of time spent with children by parents, combined with living in a society often focused on the accumulation of material goods and individual rights but not individual responsibility, has led to increases in juvenile delinquency and juvenile crime. The growing trend of violence on television, in movies, and in video games may also have a strong influence on our children. In a materialistic culture such as that found in the United States, it is easy to understand why youths from low-income communities as well as those from more affluent areas find it easier and more attractive to join a gang and sell drugs or other high-cost items than to work at the local fast-food restaurant or some other place for minimum wage.

Until American society understands that the behavior of the children reflects the attitudes and standards of the society in which they are brought up, levels of violence and the growth of gangs will most likely continue. Gangs provide their members with a sense of belonging, a sense of family and identity that so many children today do not find at home or at school. Programs must be put into place that help children develop these values outside of gang membership. Families must be supported in the search to find positive alternatives to gang participation. In addition, government agencies, private organizations, and community members must work together to find positive alternatives to the negative aspects of gang life.

References

Abadinsky, H. 1979. *Social Service in Criminal Justice.* Englewood Cliffs, NJ: Prentice-Hall.

Akers, R. L. 1985. *Deviant Behavior.* Belmont, CA: Wadsworth.

Bandura, A. 1973. *Aggression: A Social Learning Analysis.* Englewood Cliffs, NJ: Prentice-Hall.

Bjerregaard, Beth, and Carolyn Smith. 1993. "Gender Differences in Gang Participation, Delinquency, and Substance Use." *Journal of Quantitative Criminology* 9 (4): 329–355.

Bobrowski, Lawrence. 1988. *Collecting, Organizing, and Reporting Street Gang Crime.* Chicago: Chicago Police Department, Special Functions Group.

Bohm, Robert M. 2001. *Primer on Crime and Delinquency Theory,* 2nd ed. Belmont, CA: Wadsworth.

Burgess, R. L., and R. L. Akers. 1966. "A Differential Association-Reinforcement Theory of Criminal Behavior." *Social Problems* 14:128–147.

California Office of Criminal Justice Planning. 1987. *Report of the State Task Force on Youth Gang Violence.* Sacramento, CA: California Office of Criminal Justice Planning.

Campbell, Anne. 1984. *The Girls in the Gang: A Report from New York City.* Oxford: Basil Blackwell.

Campbell, Anne. 1987. "Self-Definition by Rejection: The Case of Gang Girls." *Social Problems* 34:451–466.

Campbell, Anne. 1993. *Men, Women, and Aggression.* New York: Basic.

Cartwright, Desmond S., Barbara Thomson, and Hershey Schwartz, eds. 1975. *Gang Delinquency.* Monterey, CA: Brooks/Cole.

Chein, Isador, Donald L. Gerard, Robert S. Lee, Eva Rosenfeld, and Daniel M. Wilner. 1964. *The Road to H: Narcotics, Delinquency, and Social Policy.* New York: Basic.

Chin, Ko-Lin. 1990. *Chinese Subculture and Criminality: Non-traditional Crime Groups in America.* New York: Greenwood Press.

Cloward, Richard A., and Lloyd E. Ohlin. 1960. *Delinquency and Opportunity: A Theory of Delinquent Gangs.* Glencoe, IL: Free Press.

Cohen, Albert K. 1971. *Delinquent Boys: The Culture of the Gang.* Glencoe, IL: Free Press.

Covey, Herbert C., Scott Menard, and Robert J. Franzese. 1992. *Juvenile Gangs.* Springfield, IL: Charles C. Thomas.

Decker, S., and B. Van Winkle. 1996. *Life in the Gang.* New York: Cambridge University Press.

Delaney, Tim. 2006. *American Street Gangs.* Upper Saddle River, NJ: Prentice-Hall.

Dunston, Leonard G. 1990. *Reaffirming Prevention. Report of the Task Force on Juvenile Gangs.* Albany, NY: New York State Division for Youth.

Egley, A., J. C. Howell, and A. K. Major. 2006. "National Youth Gang Survey: 1999–2001." Washington, DC: U.S. Department of Justice, Office of Juvenile Justice and Delinquency Prevention.

Esbensen, Finn-Aage. 2000. *Preventing Adolescent Gang Involvement.* Washington, DC: Office of Juvenile Justice and Delinquency Prevention.

Evans, William P., Carla Fitzgerald, Dan Weigel, and Sarah Chvilivek. 1999. "Are Rural Gang Members Similar to Their Urban Peers? Implications for Rural Communities." *Youth & Society* 30:267–282.

Fagan, Jeffrey. 2004. "Gangs, Drugs, and Neighborhood Change." In *Understanding Contemporary Gangs in America*, edited by Rebecca D. Petersen. Upper Saddle River, NJ: Prentice-Hall.

Feldman, M. Philip. 1977. *Criminal Behavior: A Psychological Analysis.* London: Wiley.

Gardner, Sandra. 1983. *Street Gangs.* New York: Franklin Watts.

Glueck, Sheldon, and Eleanor T. Glueck. 1950. *Unraveling Juvenile Delinquency.* Cambridge, MA: Harvard University Press.

Goldstein, Arnold P. 1991. *Delinquent Gangs: A Psychological Perspective.* Champaign, IL: Research Press.

Grant, Chris. 2004. "Native Gangs." [Online article; retrieved 4/15/08.] http://www.knowgangs.com/gang_resources/native/native_001.htm.

Hagedorn, John M. 1999. "Girl Gangs: Are Girls Getting More Violent?" *Streetwise* 8 (2): 9–22.

Hamm, Mark S. 1993. *American Skinheads: The Criminology and Control of Hate Crime.* Westport, CT: Praeger.

Hawkins, J. D., and J. G. Weis. 1985. "The Social Development Model: An Integrated Approach to Delinquency Prevention." *Journal of Primary Prevention* 6:73–97.

Hill, K. G., J. C. Howell, J. D. Hawkins, and S. R. Battin-Pearson. 1999. "Childhood Risk Factors for Adolescent Gang Membership: Results from the Seattle Social Development Project." *Journal of Research in Crime and Delinquency* 36 (3): 300–322.

Hirschi, Travis. 1969. *Causes of Delinquency.* Berkeley, CA: University of California Press.

Holthouse, David. 2006. "Motley Crew." *Intelligence Report* 123:36–44.

Howell, James C. 2004. "Promising Programs for Youth Gang Violence Prevention and Intervention." In *Understanding Contemporary Gangs in America*, edited by Rebecca D. Petersen. Upper Saddle River, NJ: Prentice-Hall.

Howell, James C., and Scott H. Decker. 1999. "The Youth Gangs, Drugs, and Violence Connection." In *OJJDP Juvenile Justice Bulletin*. Washington, DC: U.S. Department of Justice.

Howell, James C., and Arlen Egley, Jr. 2005. "Gangs in Small Towns and Rural Counties." In *NYGC Bulletin*. Washington, DC: Office of Juvenile Justice and Delinquency Prevention.

Institute for Intergovernmental Research. N.d. "Frequently Asked Questions Regarding Gangs." [Online information; retrieved 4/15/05.] http://www.iir.com/NYGC/faq.htm.

Institute for Law and Justice. 1994. *Gang Prosecution in the United States*. Washington, DC: National Institute of Justice, Office of Justice Programs, U.S. Department of Justice.

Johnson, Claire, Barbara Webster, and Edward Connors. 1995. "Prosecuting Gangs: A National Assessment." In *Research in Brief*. Washington, DC: National Institute of Justice.

Johnson, R. E. 1979. *Juvenile Delinquency and Its Origins*. Cambridge, UK: Cambridge University Press.

Kilman, Carrie. 2006. "Learning Lakota." *Teaching Tolerance* 2:28–35.

Klein, Malcolm W. 1971. *Street Gangs and Street Workers*. Englewood Cliffs, NJ: Prentice-Hall.

Klein, Malcolm W. 1995. *The American Street Gang: Its Nature, Prevalence, and Control*. New York: Oxford University Press.

Klein, Malcolm W., Cheryl L. Maxson, and Lea C. Cunningham. 1988. "Gang Involvement in Cocaine 'Rock' Trafficking." Project Summary/Final Report. Los Angeles: Center for Research on Crime and Social Control, Social Science Research Institute, University of Southern California.

Knox, George W. 1993. *An Introduction to Gangs*. Buchanan, MI: Vande Vere.

Knox, G. W., J. G. Houston, E. D. Tromanhauser, T. F. McCurrie, and J. Laskey. 1996. "Addressing and Testing the Gang Migration Issue." In *Gangs: A Criminal Justice Approach*, edited by J. M. Miller and J. P. Rush. Cincinnati: Anderson.

Korem, Dan. 1994. *Suburban Gangs: The Affluent Rebels*. Richardson, TX: International Focus Press.

Major, Aline K., and Arlen Egley, Jr. 2002. *2000 Survey of Youth Gangs in Indian Country. NYGC Fact Sheet #1*. Washington, DC: National Youth Gang Center.

Maxson, Cheryl L. 1998. "Gang Members on the Move." In *OJJDP Juvenile Justice Bulletin*. Washington, DC: Office of Juvenile Justice and Delinquency Prevention.

Mead, George Herbert. 1934. *Mind, Self and Society*. Chicago: University of Chicago Press.

Meier, R. 1976. "The New Criminology: Continuity in Criminological Theory." *Journal of Criminal Law and Criminology* 67:461–469.

Mieczkowski, Thomas. 1986. "Geeking Down and Throwing Down: Heroin Street Life in Detroit." *Criminology* 24:645–666.

Miller, Walter B. 1958. "Lower Class Culture as a Generating Milieu of Gang Delinquency." *Journal of Social Issues* 14 (3): 5–19.

Miller, Walter B. 1975. *Violence by Youth Gangs and Youth Gangs as a Crime Problem in Major Cities*. Washington, DC: U.S. Department of Justice.

Miller, Walter B. 1980. "Gangs, Groups, and Serious Youth Crime." In *Critical Issues in Juvenile Delinquency*, edited by D. Shichor and D. Kelly. Lexington, MA: Lexington Books.

Miller, Walter B. 1992. *Crime by Youth Gangs and Groups in the United States*. Washington, DC: U.S. Department of Justice, Office of Justice Programs, Office of Juvenile Justice and Delinquency Prevention.

Miller, Walter B. 2001. *The Growth of Youth Gang Problems in the United States: 1970–1998*. Washington, DC: Office of Juvenile Justice and Delinquency Prevention.

Mirande, Alfredo. 1981. "The Chicano and the Law." *Pacific Sociological Review* 24 (1): 65–86.

Moore, Joan W. 1991. *Going Down to the Barrio*. Philadelphia: Temple University Press.

Moore, Joan W., and John Hagedorn. 2001. "Female Gangs: A Focus on Research." In *OJJDP Juvenile Justice Bulletin*. Washington, DC: U.S. Department of Justice.

National Youth Gang Center. 2000. *1998 National Youth Gang Survey*. Washington, DC: U.S. Department of Justice, Office of Justice Programs, Office of Juvenile Justice and Delinquency Prevention.

Padilla, Felix M. 1992. *The Gang as an American Enterprise*. New Brunswick, NJ: Rutgers University Press.

Patterson, G. R. 1982. *Coercive Family Process*. Eugene, OR: Castalia.

Philibosian, Robert H. 1989. "Gang Violence and Control." Testimony Presented to the Subcommittee on Juvenile Justice of the Senate Committee on the Judiciary. 98th Congress, 1st session hearings, Sacramento, CA, February 7, 9.

Prothrow-Stith, Deborah. 1991. *Deadly Consequences: How Violence Is Destroying Our Teenage Population and a Plan to Begin Solving the Problem*. New York: HarperCollins.

Quinn, J. F., P. M. Tobolowsky, and W. T. Downs. 1994. "The Gang Problem in Large and Small Cities: An Analysis of Police Perceptions in Nine States." *The Gang Journal* 2 (2): 13–22.

Quinney, Richard A., and J. Wildeman. 1991. *The Problem of Crime: A Peace and Social Justice Perspective,* 3rd ed. Mountain View, CA: Mayfield.

Reiner, Ira. 1992. *Gangs, Crime, and Violence in Los Angeles.* Los Angeles: Office of the District Attorney of the County of Los Angeles.

Rutter, Michael, and Henri Giller. 1983. *Juvenile Delinquency: Trends and Perspectives.* New York: Guilford.

Sampson, Robert J. 1993. "The Community Context of Violent Crime," in *Sociology and the Public Agenda,* edited by W. J. Wilson. Newbury Park, CA: Sage.

Shaw, Clifford R., and Henry D. McKay. 1942. *Juvenile Delinquency in Urban Areas.* Chicago: University of Chicago Press.

Shoemaker, Donald. 2000. *Theories of Delinquency.* New York: Oxford University Press.

Siegel, Larry J., Brandon C. Welsh, and Joseph J. Senna. 2003. *Juvenile Delinquency,* 8th ed. Belmont, CA: Wadsworth.

Snyder, J. J., and G. R. Patterson. 1987. "Family Interaction and Delinquent Behavior." In *Handbook of Juvenile Delinquency,* edited by H. C. Quay. New York: John Wiley.

Spergel, Irving A. 1964. *Slumtown, Racketville, Haulburg.* Chicago: University of Chicago Press.

Spergel, Irving A. 1993. *Gang Suppression and Intervention: An Assessment.* Chicago: School of Social Service Administration, University of Chicago.

Spergel, Irving A. 1995. *The Youth Gang Problem: A Community Approach.* New York: Oxford University Press.

Spergel, Irving A., and G. David Curry. 1993. "The National Youth Gang Survey: A Research and Development Process." In *The Gang Intervention Handbook,* edited by A. P. Goldstein and C. R. Huff, 359–400. Champaign, IL: Research Press.

Spergel, Irving A., David Curry, Ron Chance, Candace Kane, Ruth Ross, Alba Alexander, Edwina Simmons, and Sandra Oh. 1994. *Gang Suppression and Intervention: Problem and Response.* Chicago: School of Social Service Administration, University of Chicago.

Starbuck, David, James C. Howell, and Donna J. Lindquist. 2001. "Hybrid and Other Modern Gangs." In *Juvenile Justice Bulletin.* Washington, DC: Office of Juvenile Justice and Delinquency Prevention.

Sutherland, Edwin H. 1947. *Principles of Criminology.* Philadelphia: Lippincott.

Taylor, Carl S. 1990. *Dangerous Society.* East Lansing, MI: Michigan State University Press.

Thornton, William E., and Lydia Voight. 1992. *Delinquency and Justice,* 3rd ed. New York: McGraw-Hill.

Thrasher, Frederic. 1927. *The Gang.* Chicago: University of Chicago Press.

Vigil, James Diego. 1988. *Barrio Gangs: Street Life and Identity in Southern California.* Austin: University of Texas Press.

Williams, Frank P., and Marilyn D. McShane. 1999. *Criminological Theory,* 3rd ed. Toronto: Prentice-Hall.

Wilson, James Q., and Richard J. Herrnstein. 1985. *Crime and Human Nature.* New York: Simon and Schuster.

Yablonsky, Lewis. 1970. *The Violent Gang,* rev. ed. Baltimore: Penguin.

2

Problems, Controversies, and Solutions

This chapter explores some of the major problems, issues, and controversies concerning gangs. Some of these problems relate to the accurate determination of gangs, gang members, and their characteristics. The questions of whether participation in gangs can be prevented and what schools can do and have done to prevent or control gang activities within the school environment are discussed. Authorities have developed a variety of strategies to cope with gangs, including gang databases, civil gang injunctions, curfews, the application of Racketeer Influenced and Corrupt Organizations (RICO) Act statutes to gangs, sentencing enhancements, and Global Positioning System (GPS) monitoring. Finally, gangs are becoming increasingly sophisticated in their use of electronic devices to communicate information to each other, and the Internet has provided them with additional opportunities for criminal activities.

A number of controversies surround gangs and the prevention or suppression of their activities as well as their attempts to thwart prosecution. The extent to which gangs are involved in drugs is still being debated by many researchers and those in the field of law enforcement. The use of racial profiling by police officers and others is a critical issue in the field of gang research and gang prevention. Some officials in the U.S. government believe that certain gangs are involved in terrorist activities against the United States. The media are criticized by some who believe that news stories of grisly gang attacks encourage the participation of youths in gangs. The media are also believed by some to perpetuate the stereotypes of African Americans and Hispanics as being responsible for a large majority of gang and criminal activity.

Gangs also are believed to have developed a growing presence in the armed forces, resulting in gang members potentially transferring their knowledge of weapons and warfare to their neighborhoods when they return from military service. Some still debate whether white racist organizations, such as the skinheads, are true gangs. The plight of youths who are being deported back to their countries of origin from the United States is of great concern to many professionals; their return to some countries is seen as a certain death sentence by many child advocates. Finally, intimidation of witnesses by gang members is a serious problem, which often results in the release of violent gang members as witnesses change or retract their previous testimony in response to threats by the gang member.

Gang Characteristics

Lack of agreement among law enforcement and other professionals concerning how to define a gang, who is likely to join a gang, and whether females are true gang members or are just adjuncts to male gang members; current stereotypes of gang members; and determining the best, most effective means of dealing with gangs are just some of the difficulties facing professionals in the field today. This section discusses many of the problems faced by law enforcement and other professionals in attempting to measure gang presence and influence, prevent children from joining gangs, and prevent or suppress gang activity.

Definition of a Gang and Identifying Gang Members

One of the problems encountered by law enforcement and other professionals is the lack of a consistent definition of a gang. As discussed in Chapter 1, the definition of a gang varies from one jurisdiction to another and among experts in the field, although generally a gang is defined as three or more individuals with a common purpose who are engaged in criminal activity. No generally accepted methodology for defining or identifying gang members and gangs exists. Definitions of gangs in state statutes vary from state to state (see Chapter 6 for individual state statutes). Surveys that are conducted to determine the depth and

breadth of gang activity often leave it up to the individual respondents to define the term *gang.*

The problem of defining gangs is described by Delaney
(2006) as follows:

> In fact, there is no single definition, although every defi-
> nition includes some mention of the word, *group.* For ex-
> ample, is a group of young people hanging out together
> a gang? What if this group is hanging outside a conve-
> nience store talking loud and acting proud? What if this
> group creates a name for itself, starts identifying mem-
> bers with specific clothing, and uses secret hand signals
> and handshakes and intimidating nicknames such as
> "killer" and "assassin"? But the group just described
> could actually be a sports team! Add to this description
> the commission of a number of deviant acts and frater-
> nities and sororities would also fit this profile. (6)

The difficulty posed by not having one single definition of a
gang creates a major problem when attempting to study the size
and extent of gangs and gang behavior. Without a consistent,
widely accepted definition, statistics concerning the number of
gangs and gang members are only estimates. In addition, when
law enforcement agencies and researchers rely on an individual
to answer the question, "Are you a gang member?" the results
may not be realistic or consistent from group to group. This problem limits the reliability and usefulness of data collection for research purposes as well as for criminal reporting. The lack of a
consistent definition limits the usefulness of data collection as
well as the "ability to quantify and understand the extent of the
gang problem and complicates any national public policy response" (Franco 2006, 6).

Stereotypes—Are Most Gang Members African American, Hispanic, or Asian?

Most of the literature on street gangs focuses on African American, Hispanic, and Asian gang members and may lead one to believe that most gang members are nonwhite. In fact, racial
stereotyping is common in many communities. Gang databases
are primarily composed of Hispanic, African American, and

Asian (fewer) males. Beres and Griffith (2004) examined statistics contained in the Gang Reporting Evaluation and Tracking (GREAT) database, which was a predecessor to California's Cal/Gang database. Operated by the Los Angeles district attorney's office, the GREAT database "listed over 37,000 Black gang members and over 58,000 Hispanic gang members. Asian and Pacific Islanders had slightly more than 4,000 listings. However, White gang members apparently were so scarce in Los Angeles that they did not even warrant their own category, but were sorted with individuals of 'miscellaneous' ethnicity into a 'Misc/White' class with only 358 entries" (Beres and Griffith 2004, 6).

A report from the Justice Policy Institute suggests that more than 90 percent of gang members are nonwhite, according to law enforcement officials, although youth surveys report that 40 percent of adolescent gang members are white (Greene and Pranis 2007). White gangs generally display many of the same characteristics, have similar delinquency and crime rates, and have similar rates of gang involvement as Hispanic and African American gangs, but have not received the same attention from law enforcement and the media as nonwhite gangs. Greene and Pranis (2007) say that this "disparity raises troubling questions about how gang members are identified by police" (4).

One example of this disparity, suggest Beres and Griffith (2004), is in the reporting of the Columbine High School massacre in Colorado in 1999. Dylan Klebold and Eric Harris, both white, instigated an all-out assault on Columbine High School during an otherwise normal school day. When it was over, they had murdered 12 students and one teacher and then killed themselves. They were reportedly members of a group known as the Trenchcoat Mafia, although the rest of the group disavowed them and their actions. The media never referred to this group as a gang, although they would likely have been characterized as one if the definitions of a gang used by many police departments were applied to them.

Another example is the Spur Posse, a group of 15- to 18-year-old white males in Lakewood, California. In 1993, nine members of the group were arrested for the rape and sexual assault of several girls, including one who was only 10 years old. The boys had developed a system of earning points for having sexual relations with young girls and were competing with each other to see who could earn the most points. Prosecutors ended up dropping all but one of the charges against the boys, claiming that most of the sexual encounters turned out to be consensual, even though some of the girls were underage. The girls were described by some as "sluts," and the boys were seen by many as "just being boys." The group would have met most of the criteria used by police as constituting a gang, including the wearing of San Antonio Spurs caps and displaying intimidating behavior but were not referred to as a gang by many in the media. Some members of the Spur Posse claimed they were not part of a gang because they did not have guns and did not shoot people. They believed that a gang consisted of a group of guys hanging out and smoking pot (Beres and Griffith 2004).

Even descriptions of girls on probation differ depending on their race. Miller (1994) examined the impact of ethnicity and race on processing cases of juvenile girls in 1992 and 1993. She reviewed probation officers' reports and discovered major differences in the way the behavior of the girls was described, what she referred to as "racialized gender expectations." In particular, descriptions of the perceived causes of the delinquent behavior of African American girls referred to "inappropriate 'lifestyle' choices." On the other hand, descriptions of the causes of white girls' delinquent behavior were more likely to include low self-esteem, the fact that they were easily influenced by others, and the idea that their behavior was caused by being abandoned by parents or other family members (Miller 1994). In other words, the behavior of the white girls was blamed on forces external to the girls, while the behavior of African American girls was their choice, implying that the white girls had no choice—they were not at fault—whereas the African American girls made a conscious (obviously bad) choice.

Asian American young women have also been assumed to be gang members because of their dress. For example, outside a café in downtown Garden Grove, California, Minh Tram, 15, and her two friends, all Vietnamese Americans, were waiting to use a pay phone. An unmarked police car drove past them, and an Asian officer was in the front passenger seat watching them. The car circled around, then the police officer in the car stopped the girls, saying they looked like gang members. The girls said they were just waiting to use the nearby pay phone to page Tram's brother to pick them up, although the two police officers suggested that they were waiting to page someone for drugs. They were lined up against a wall, and the police took their pictures and told them that they looked like street gang members. Although they were not arrested, their information was added to the state's gang database. The American Civil Liberties Union (ACLU) filed a class-action lawsuit against the police department on the girls' behalf, and in 1995 the case was settled, with the young women receiving $85,000. The police agreed to obtain written voluntary consent from individuals before taking their pictures and agreed that they would photograph individuals only if they had a reasonable suspicion that they were involved in criminal activity.

This discrepancy in approaches to white versus nonwhite youths has major policy implications. The U.S. Department of Justice, in a 2001 survey regarding the racial disparities in death penalty cases, explained that federal agents did not intend to discriminate against African Americans, but the agents were intent on fighting violent drug gangs, and the members of these gangs were African Americans (U.S. Department of Justice 2001). This way of thinking emphasizes the need to examine statistics regarding gang membership carefully. If law enforcement officials believe that most gang members are members of minorities, then they will focus on watching and arresting minorities more often than whites, which only reinforces the belief that most gang members are members of racial minorities.

According to Coker (2003), "the link in white consciousness between African Americans and criminality remains strong" (866). Taslitz (2003) suggests that some educational programs continue to reinforce this connection. Until this link is broken, we will continue to rely on statistics that may not provide a true picture of the extent of white participation in gangs. Many white groups of youths are not currently considered gangs by law enforcement and the general public (see section below on racial profiling), in large part because we are led to believe by what we read in the newspaper and see on television that gang members are primarily African American or Hispanic.

Females in Gangs—Are Females Being Exploited, or Are They True Gang Members?

During the early 1900s, females rarely participated in gangs. Over time, their participation has increased and their role has evolved. Beginning in the 1970s, researchers started noticing female gang members and studying their behavior and role in the gang. They were seen primarily as sexual objects—they were girlfriends of gang members or at least provided sex to them, and they played the role of temptress, luring unsuspecting members of rival gangs into certain areas where those gang members were attacked. Females also were employed at times to carry drugs or weapons, because law enforcement generally would go easier on them than on their male counterparts if they were caught by the police.

Today, more gangs are composed of both males and females. One study reported that in 2000, 42 percent of all jurisdictions reporting gang problems in the New York Gang Survey indicated that a majority of their gangs had female members (Egley, Howell, and Major 2006).

Females tend to join gangs for reasons similar to those of male gang members: to stake out and protect a specific territory, for the sense of belonging to some type of group, and to achieve a feeling of power from being in such a group. Some females have also indicated that they joined a gang because they felt freed from typical societal stereotypes toward women. Some research has suggested that females join gangs for protection from neighborhood crime, as a result of conflicts with their families, because it provides an exciting money-making opportunity, and because it offers an exciting alternative to an otherwise boring life (Walker-Barnes and Mason 2001). However, many female gang members also report that they are exposed to sexual exploitation, abuse, and violence.

Female gang members tend to join gangs during early adolescence and leave earlier than their male counterparts (Egley, Howell, and Major 2006; Thornberry et al. 2003). Research has also indicated that the presence of females in a gang influences the delinquency rate of that gang. Specifically, gangs that were composed of all females or were mostly female had the lowest delinquency rates, while gangs in which the males outnumbered the females had the highest delinquency rates (Peterson, Miller, and Esbensen 2001). Other research has shown that violence perpetrated by female gang members is highest between the time they join the gang and their first pregnancy, and decreases from pregnancy on (Fleisher and Krienert 2004).

However, female gang members can be violent. For example, in 1992, in Chicago, two boys were lured into a park by three female members of the Maniac Latin Disciples gang, thinking they were going to have some fun partying with the girls. Instead, all of them entered the bathroom, where one of the boys was shot execution style in the back of the head by one of the girls, who then passed the gun to her girlfriend. The girlfriend shot the other boy in the back of the head. The girls claimed to have killed the boys in "retaliation for murdering one of their friends" [*State v. Mulero*, 680 N.E. 2d 1329 (Ill. 1997)].

Overall, female participation in gangs varies from gang to gang and among ethnic groups. For example, in Hispanic gangs, females are less likely to participate as full-fledged gang members than in other gangs. This is in large part because of the Hispanic concept of machismo, in which the males have a strong sense of their masculinity that focuses on strength, courage, and superiority over women. The males believe that females need to be protected. Another reason that male gangs, especially Hispanic gangs, do not encourage females to join them is that females may have more difficulty withholding certain information about the gang from the police. For example, Mike Prill from the Greeley, Colorado, police gang unit explains that a female gang member may be more likely than a male gang member to "rat" on a male gang member; perhaps he is a former boyfriend who has dumped her for someone else, and she wants revenge. Female gang members are also more likely to cave in to police pressure and provide other information on the gang. Male gang members are much less likely to provide information concerning other gang members to law enforcement officials.

Some researchers believe that law enforcement personnel and others within the criminal justice system dismiss or ignore the behavior of female gang members, even though female gang members behave as badly as their male counterparts; they have initiated or participated in drive-by shootings and murders and will do anything to protect their home turf (Sikes 1997).

Prevention of Gangs and Their Activities

Communities have tried a variety of means to prevent gangs from forming in their neighborhoods and to prevent young people from joining gangs. Many researchers believe a prevention strategy is the only effective way to eliminate or greatly reduce gangs and gang activity. Once a youth joins a gang, he or she has more difficulty getting out of it.

Can Gangs Be Eliminated or Prevented?

Many communities are reactive in their treatment of gangs; that is, they look for ways to eliminate gangs once they become aware of their presence rather than working to prevent gangs from establishing a presence in their community. This is a natural response, one that is primarily based on economics—communities are more likely to spend money to resolve issues rather than working to prevent something that may not occur in the first place.

Most experts agree that gangs are highly unlikely, if not impossible, to be eliminated. They are too entrenched in too many cities, especially Los Angeles and Chicago. Some smaller towns and limited areas within larger towns and cities may be able to eliminate them from certain areas, but research has shown that gangs that are forced out of one area or town simply move their activities to another area. Many researchers believe that as long as economic disparity exists in society, gangs will also exist. According to Fagan (2004), the "future of gangs is tied to the future of urban crises in social control, social structure, labor markets, and cultural processes in a rapidly changing political and economic context" (255). In order to eliminate gangs, society must eliminate the economic disparity among individuals as well as provide well-paying jobs, economic security, and the belief that it is possible to be successful in today's society. Only then may at-risk individuals turn away from gangs and other criminal activities (Delaney 2006).

Role of Schools in Preventing Gangs

Schools are seen by many as providing the best and most effective means of preventing gang participation. Because most youths attend public schools, many experts believe that schools are in the best position to recognize at-risk youths and to work with them or divert them to other prevention programs in order to persuade them to stay away from gangs.

Many schools have adopted regulations and dress codes to describe clothing that is not permitted in school, including the wearing of gang colors. Some schools have gone so far as to outlaw gang membership. Courts have generally ruled for the schools when civil suits have challenged the constitutionality of school rules prohibiting certain gang attire or other evidence of gang membership. This is primarily because the states' interest in protecting the safety of children outweighs the children's constitutional rights of freedom of expression or association. However, the schools must prove that their prohibitions are reasonable and that otherwise, gang activities would be present on the school campus.

One popular means of limiting gang influence that many schools have adopted is having a well-defined dress code that prohibits students from wearing gang-related clothing. However, schools have had some difficulty in controlling such dress codes because of the ease with which gangs can select new clothing or accessory options when their current selection is banned. Some gang-related clothing is easily recognized. For example, wearing red or blue may signify membership in the Bloods (red) or Crips (blue). Students wearing bandannas or baseball caps may also be members of gangs and are advertising their membership; for example, in some areas, wearing a Duke University baseball cap signifies membership in the Folk Nation gang.

Schools have run into several difficulties in trying to cover all possibilities. The wide variety of clothing that can be worn, the multiple combinations of clothing and accessories, and the ease with which gangs can change the combinations depending on what is banned at the moment all make crafting dress codes that ban all gang-related clothing difficult.

One way to avoid this dilemma is to create a broad definition of gang-related clothing; however, this approach has caused some problems for school districts. Students have challenged this policy in court and, in some cases, have won on freedom of speech grounds. In one case, *Chalifoux v. New Caney Independent School District* [976 F. Supp. 659 (S.D. Tex. 1997)], the school dress code prohibited wearing of gang-related apparel and listed oversized clothing, baseball caps, hair nets, bandannas, sweatbands, and "any attire which identifies students as a group (gang-related)." The school's handbook also indicated that an updated list of items that were considered to be gang related would be kept in the principal's office. In this case, two students, David Chalifoux and Jerry Robertson, were told that they would not be allowed to continue wearing their rosaries, because the principal had seen three other students known to be gang members wearing rosaries. The principal believed that rosaries were gang-related apparel, even though Chalifoux and Robertson had been wearing the rosaries for several weeks, were not gang members, and had not been approached by any gang members. The boys filed suit against the school district for violation of their First Amendment rights to free speech and free exercise of religion. The court agreed with the boys, ruling that the phrase "gang-related apparel" was ambiguous as to the specific clothing and accessories prohibited and was unconstitutionally vague.

Some schools have also outlawed, or attempted to outlaw, gang membership. This attempt is effective only to the extent that the definition of gang membership is clear and specific. For example, the Board of Education for Bremen High School in Midlothian, Illinois, banned gang membership and gang activity at the school. This ban included the wearing of gang symbols, jewelry, and emblems. The school suspended Darryl Olesen for wearing an earring (wearing of earrings by male students was part of the ban on gang activities), and Olesen sued the school board, arguing that the ban violated his First Amendment right of free speech and expression as well as his Fourteenth Amendment right to equal protection. The court found in favor of the school board, noting that the "school's policy of banning the wearing of earrings by male students was directly related to the safety and well-being of its students" [*Olesen v. Board of Education*, 676 F.Supp. 821 (N.D.Ill 1987)].

Intervention Strategies

Law enforcement agencies, state and federal governments, and local communities attempt to control or eliminate gangs in a variety of ways. Each of these methods has proponents and detractors, advantages and disadvantages. Some methods, such as antiloitering laws, were ruled unconstitutional but have been modified to pass legal scrutiny. Prosecution of gang members frequently takes place in state courts, where gang members are charged with a variety of offenses, including drug trafficking, homicide, robbery, and assault. Occasionally, the prosecution of gang members is more appropriate in federal court, using federal statutes, including the RICO Act, weapons, and drug statutes. This section discusses the issues surrounding many of the techniques attempted by local communities, states, and the federal government to prevent, control, or eliminate gangs.

Gang Databases

Gang databases in some form are used by many police departments to encourage information sharing and assist in the prosecution of gang members. They may be detailed, computerized
collections of data or a simple listings of gang members known
to the police. Problems with gang databases stem from the fact
that no consistent and reliable means exist to determine who belongs in the database. Individuals can be entered into most databases on the word of one police officer, as was the case of Minh
Tram and her friends, discussed earlier. The database is used to
provide information to local, state, and federal law enforcement
agencies to help solve gang-related crimes, locate individual suspects, determine the extent of a gang's influence in a specific
area, and aid in the prosecution of criminal defendants (Wright
2005).

There are two primary ways for an individual to have his or
her name entered into a database. First, following the commission
of a crime (homicide) and the issuance of a crime report, the gang
unit receives a copy of the report, and if it is gang related, the individual is entered into the database. If the case is not a homicide,
the suspects named in the crime report are checked against the
database and the crime is tagged as gang related if any of the suspects are listed as gang members. The other way for an individual to end up in the database is through field interviews
conducted by police officers. Police frequently come into contact
with known gang members and other youths who may be gang
members. These youths are interviewed, and if they admit to
being in a gang or if the police officer suspects that they are in
a gang, their information will be entered into the database. This
is the more common way for individuals to be entered into the
database.

An individual is usually not informed that he has been
placed in the database and therefore has little or no recourse to
get his name removed from the database, even if he is not a gang
member. In addition, many agencies have not established specific
protocols to review entries or remove the names of those who are
no longer active, or never were active, in gangs. While some police departments have a policy that suggests purging names after
a specified amount of time, often five years, the reality is that
purging often is not done in a timely way. In some cases, if police
make any type of contact with an individual, even a simple

chance encounter on the street, that contact will be entered into the database and start the five-year purge cycle all over again.

Many of the problems with databases relate back to the issue of defining a gang member. An individual who is caught loitering on a street corner can be identified in a database as a gang member, even if he is not truly a gang member. Also, the definition of "gang related" varies from jurisdiction to jurisdiction. In most jurisdictions, an individual can be entered into a database following a gang-related crime. For example, statutes in Los Angeles define a crime as gang related if either the victim or the perpetrator is a gang member; if a gang member is caught selling drugs, the crime is considered gang related, even if he is acting on his own (Beres and Griffith 2004). Another classification of crime sometimes used by law enforcement is "gang motivated," which refers to those crimes committed for the benefit of or in association with a gang.

The consequences to an individual listed in a database can be serious and include an increased chance of conviction, the imposition of longer sentences if found guilty in a criminal case, loss of employment, and other social and legal consequences. Once gang membership has been established, the individual is exposed to sentence enhancements if found guilty and the possibility of future prosecution as a gang member. During a trial, testimony from law enforcement personnel that an individual is identified as a gang member in the state's database is usually sufficient to establish him as a gang member.

Information in the database may also be shared with potential employers and with schools (Katz 2003). This practice can have serious consequences for an individual who is in the database but, in reality, is not a gang member. Because the police are not required to notify an individual that he or she has been entered into the database, the repercussions could be serious, as well as unknown, to the individual.

The GREAT system is a nationwide database, linking many state and local GREAT databases with each other. It includes a master index of gang member records that state and local law enforcement agencies can search. In addition, six regional databases are funded by the U.S. Department of Justice and run by the Regional Information Sharing Systems (RISS) program, which contain gang information available to all members of the RISS. The six program locations are Phoenix, Arizona; Sacramento, California; Needham, Massachusetts; Springfield, Missouri; Trenton,

New Jersey; and Newtown, Pennsylvania. RISS programs conduct a variety of analyses for their members, including criminal, financial, and investigative activity.

Many local communities have developed their own databases, with specific criteria that must be met for inclusion. For example, the police department in Tucson, Arizona, developed a comprehensive database in 1994 that tracks all known gang members. In order to be entered into the database, the gang member must meet at least one of the seven criteria for classification as a criminal street gang, according to the Arizona Revised Statutes (see Chapter 6). According to the police and local community, the database has been effective in capturing gang members.

Portland, Oregon, police have established a list of 15 criteria, any one of which can establish an individual as a gang member. These criteria were developed following a civil lawsuit that was filed against the police alleging that their criteria at that time were too vague. The current criteria are based on providing clear and convincing evidence that a person is a gang member; they include committing or planning to commit a crime on behalf of the gang or for the gang's benefit, displaying knowledge of the gang's history and rituals, having gang tattoos, or self-identifying as a gang member.

Civil Gang Injunctions

Civil gang injunctions are used by some communities to prohibit certain individuals from participating in specific activities. With respect to gangs, these generally focus on otherwise legal behavior and include banning gang members from congregating in certain areas, such as public parks; from wearing certain types of clothing or colors of clothing; or from carrying materials that could be used in creating graffiti. Some advocates of injunctions encourage their use in conjunction with other community policing activities, in an attempt to encourage the community to become involved in suppressing gang activities.

Civil injunctions often begin with community involvement, specifically its frustration with growing gang activity in the neighborhood. Attempts to impose civil injunctions begin in civil court, when prosecutors file a complaint petitioning the court for relief from a public nuisance. The prosecutors must prove to the court that certain gangs or gang members are responsible for creating this public nuisance. Two sources are used for presenting proof: individuals from the community who can provide sworn statements testifying to the criminal behavior and police and informants who are aware of gang activities.

Several problems exist in obtaining information that can be used in requesting an injunction. One problem is that once the prosecutors file the complaint in court, each individual who is a known gang member must be served with the complaint. Service of the complaint lets the gang members know what the police know about them. Some researchers believe that this, in itself, may help reduce gang activity because the gang will now know that it is being watched and investigated by law enforcement. As a result, its members may back off from some of their criminal activities. On the other hand, this knowledge may just force the gang to move, scale back but not eliminate its criminal activities, or in some other way hide its activities from the authorities.

Gathering statements from the police and informants is often easier than getting them from community members, who are frequently afraid to provide information to law enforcement. Members of the community may receive threats from gang members, suggesting retaliation against them if they talk to the authorities. They also may believe that the authorities will not actually do anything to help curb crime in their neighborhoods or may not believe that the authorities will have the power to stop the gang's activities.

Once the complaint is filed with the court, a hearing date is set, at which time some defendants may be removed from the complaint if it cannot be proven that they are actual participants in the public nuisance activities. The judge also has the option to modify the injunction in some way, although injunctions are usually issued unmodified. Once the order for the injunction has been served on the defendants, it goes into effect.

As with other attempts to suppress or prevent gang activities, civil injunctions have been challenged in the courts. For example, in *Gallo v. Acuna* [929 P.2d 596 (1997)], a civil gang injunction that prohibited 38 members of a San Jose, California, gang from entering a four-square-block area was challenged in California (see Chapter 6 for a summary of this case). In 1997, the California Supreme Court upheld the constitutionality of this antigang injunction.

In addition to the constitutional concerns regarding these injunctions, other concerns include (1) the fact that most civil injunctions are used against Hispanic and African American youth, which raises equal protection concerns; (2) how local communities define gangs, how they identify gang members, and how they collect information concerning alleged gang members; and (3) the question of whether gang members are receiving procedural safeguards to which they are entitled under the due process clause of the Fourteenth Amendment (Werdegar 1999).

In California, concern has been voiced over the naming of a particular gang as the defendant in some of these cases, as opposed to naming individual gang members. While California law appears to allow gangs to be considered unincorporated associations, which may allow the gang to be sued as an entity, the general lack of structure, named officers, and other characteristics of more typical organizations makes knowing who should receive service of the complaint difficult. Some cases [for example, *People ex rel. Totten v. Colonia Chiques* (Cal. Super. Ct., June 1, 2005)] name the gang as the defendant, along with a certain number of John Does. This allows police to serve individual gang members without prior knowledge of their names. However, it also raises questions of due process protection.

In an attempt to evaluate the effectiveness of these injunctions, Grogger (2002) studied data from Los Angeles County, which imposed 22 injunctions between 1993 and 2002. He found that the injunctions did appear to reduce crime in the county—by approximately 5 to 10 percent—during their first year of implementation. Another study also found some reduction of gang activity with the use of injunctions, including a reduction in gang visibility, intimidation, and community fears of criminal activity perpetrated by gang members (Maxson, Hennigan, and Sloane 2005).

The ACLU Foundation of Southern California examined the use and effectiveness of civil gang injunctions, focusing on the 1993 Blythe Street injunction in Panorama City (Los Angeles), which is one of the broadest injunctions. The ACLU found that the injunction did not immediately reduce violent crime and drug trafficking, one of its major goals, and its attempt to reduce crime only resulted in a shift of crime to a neighboring area. The ACLU concluded that civil gang injunctions led communities to believe, falsely, that they were safer as a result, and should no longer be adopted (ACLU Foundation of Southern California 1997).

Over time, gang injunctions may work in positive ways to lower gang crimes in various communities, but the help of community members is needed to effect lasting change. Community members need to become involved in their local organizations and monitor what is happening in the community. The injunctions may work for a while, but most gangs, if they have not moved out of the neighborhood, will find other ways to create trouble in the community.

Research must be conducted to determine whether gangs just move their activities to another location in the city following imposition of an injunction, therefore negating the overall effects by simply relocating their activities. In addition, the continuing questions concerning the denial of fundamental rights, including the right to appointed counsel, the right to a jury trial, and the concern over the vagueness of these injunctions, will need to be balanced against the need for communities to feel safe from gangs in order to continue advocating for these injunctions.

Antiloitering Legislation

Antiloitering laws allow law enforcement to disperse or arrest individuals believed to be gang members who are associating with each other in public areas, such as parks and street corners. These laws have a long history and have been enacted in many cities, but have been overturned on constitutional grounds. One of the most well-known antiloitering laws applied to gangs was passed in Chicago in 1992. Known as the Gang Congregation Ordinance, it stated that "Whenever a police officer observes a person whom he reasonably believes to be a criminal street gang member loitering in any public place with one or more other persons, he shall order all such persons to disperse and remove themselves from the area. Any person who does not promptly obey such an order is in violation of this section" [Chi. Ill. Mun. Code § 8-4-015 (1992)]. During the three years that it was in effect, 45,000 individuals were arrested under this ordinance. The law was challenged as unconstitutional in 1993 by Jesus Morales and other suspected gang members in that it violated their First, Fourth, and Fourteenth Amendment rights. The case went all the way to the U.S. Supreme Court, which found the law to be unconstitutional (as did each court below it). Other antiloitering laws in other cities have been successfully challenged as well.

One problem with these laws is their vagueness. These statutes often forbid individuals from doing something that requires them to guess at the legal implications of that action, which violates their due process rights to receive adequate and clear notice of the law. In a 1983 case, the U.S. Supreme Court defined the vagueness doctrine as requiring "that a penal statute define the criminal offense with sufficient definiteness that ordinary people can understand what conduct is prohibited and in a manner that does not encourage arbitrary and discriminatory enforcement" [*Kolender v. Lawson*, 461 U.S. 352 (1983), 357].

These actions may also violate the Fourteenth Amendment's equal protection clause, which prohibits states from denying any of their citizens equal protection of the law. The laws of the state must treat an individual within its jurisdiction in the same manner as it does others who are in similar circumstances. For example, the antiloitering ordinances would prohibit gang members from loitering but would allow other individuals who were not gang members to loiter; therefore, these ordinances are considered unconstitutional based on the Fourteenth Amendment.

Also, police officers are given a great deal of latitude in enforcing the law, which may lead to "arbitrary and discriminatory" enforcement of these laws (Santo 2000). Police enforcing these laws are often accused of discriminatory behavior, because they may single out African Americans or Hispanics for arrest. In its ruling in the Morales case mentioned earlier, the Illinois Supreme Court indicated that the ordinance was "drafted in an intentionally vague manner so that persons who are undesirable in the eyes of police and prosecutors can be convicted even though they are not chargeable with any other particular offense" [*City of Chicago v. Morales*, 687 N.E.2d 53 (Ill. 1997), 64].

Another problem with antiloitering laws is that they are overly broad and may violate freedom of speech, freedom of association, and freedom of assembly. Individuals have the right to associate with others of their own choosing and, as the Supreme Court ruled in *Chicago v. Morales*, "the freedom to loiter for innocent purposes is part of the 'liberty' protected by the due process clause of the Fourteenth Amendment" (53).

Some antiloitering statutes have been challenged and have passed constitutional muster, and therefore remain on the books as valid laws. Most of these statutes are written in narrow terms and are specific in their language. For example, an antiloitering statute in Birmingham, Alabama, was written to cover two specific activities: (1) blocking free passage on a sidewalk by loitering and (2) continuing to loiter after being told to disperse by a police officer. In 1965, Fred Shuttlesworth, an African American minister, was arrested and convicted for violating both ordinances; his appeal went all the way to the U.S. Supreme Court. The Court overturned his conviction but let the ordinances stand and remain in effect. Its decision was based on the fact that the prosecutor was unable to provide evidence that Shuttlesworth had violated the statute, ruling that it was a "violation of due process to convict and punish him without evidence of his guilt" [*Shuttlesworth v. City of Birmingham*, 382 U.S. 87 (1965)].

Curfews

Curfew laws are designed to keep minors from being on the streets during specific hours, often between 11 p.m. and 6 a.m. The theory behind these laws is that minors are more likely to be influenced by peer pressure and become involved in some type of criminal behavior when they are out during the night than when they are out during the day. In a study of curfew ordinances in the 200 largest cities in the United States, Ruefle and Reynolds (1995) found that 93 cities had curfews in effect as of January 1, 1990, and between January 1990 and the spring of 1995, another 53 cities enacted curfew ordinances. As of 1995, 146 cities, or 73 percent of the largest cities in the United States, had curfew laws on the books.

The effectiveness of these laws has been examined by several researchers. Pratcher (1994) found that significant reductions of gang-related crime occurred during curfew periods in Long Beach, California. Another study found that in Phoenix, 21 percent of all curfew violators were members of street gangs and, following the implementation of a strict curfew policy, a 10 percent drop in juvenile arrests was seen (Fritsch, Caeti, and Taylor 2003).

Juvenile curfew laws, like other means to prevent gang activity, have been challenged in the courts on constitutional grounds, including the rights to free assembly, to not be deprived of liberty without due process, to privacy, and to equal protection against unreasonable stopping and detainment. Most challenges, however, are based on the equal protection clause of the Fourteenth Amendment, in that curfew laws create a "suspect classification based on age, and that they result in selective enforcement to the detriment of minority youth" (Ruefle and Reynolds 1995, 349).

Laws that restrict fundamental constitutional rights, such as curfew laws, must pass a two-pronged test if their supporters do not want them overturned. Jurisdictions are required to demonstrate a compelling state interest and to narrowly describe the ways the law meets the needs of the jurisdiction. For example, Dallas, Texas, enacted a curfew law in 1991 that was challenged by the ACLU. The curfew was upheld by the U.S. Court of Appeals for the Fifth Circuit [*Qutb v. Strauss* 11 F.3d 488 (5th Cir. 1993)]. The Dallas curfew exempted juveniles who were with an adult; on their way to or from work; participating in activities related to interstate commerce or protected by the First Amendment; responding to an emergency; married; or attending a supervised school, religious, or recreational activity. As a result, the court found that the law met the requirement that it should be narrowly structured to avoid issues based on the First Amendment to the U.S. Constitution.

Successful curfew programs generally have several elements in common. These include (1) establishment of a central area, for example, a church or recreational center, where the juveniles can be held until released or picked up by a parent; (2) staffing of the central area by social service professionals; (3) intervention options, including referrals to counseling and social service providers; (4) specific policies or programs for repeat offenders, such as established fines or other penalties; (5) recreational activities and job programs; (6) antidrug and antigang programs; and (7) crisis intervention hotlines and crisis follow-up activities (Bilchik 1996).

RICO Statutes

The Racketeer Influenced and Corrupt Organizations Act was enacted in 1970 to fight organized crime. In the 1990s, the federal government began using it against motorcycle gangs (Delaney 2006). While most state laws generally address individual crimes, RICO statutes allow police to arrest individual gang members for being members of a group engaged in criminal activities. Prosecutors must prove only that the gang committed the crime, not that each individual is guilty; however, they do need to prove that the individual profited from the crime. Penalties also are more severe than under state statutes; for example, under the RICO statute in federal court, a murder conviction carries a sentence of life without the possibility of parole.

Some researchers believe that gangs generally are not a good fit for RICO prosecution, in large part because many gangs are not well organized and therefore do not fit the definition of a crime organization. However, RICO statutes have been used successfully against gangs in several states, including California, Georgia, Maryland, Oklahoma, and New York. For example, the prosecution of the Boot Camp gang in New York is one success story in the application of the RICO statute to gangs. In 2003, various federal and state law enforcement agencies began to investigate street gangs in Syracuse, focusing on the illegal activities of the Boot Camp gang, which was involved in narcotics trafficking, gun sales, and various violent crimes. After analyzing old arrest and conviction reports and other relevant documentation, the law enforcement agencies built a strong case, using the RICO statute, against 26 members of the gang, all of whom eventually pleaded guilty or were convicted of one or more federal offenses. Gang activity in Syracuse dropped following the Boot Camp arrests and convictions (New York State Commission of Investigations 2006).

Sentencing Enhancements

Some states have enacted legislation that increases the penalties for crimes committed by gangs in an attempt to discourage gang crime. For example, California first passed the Street Terrorism Enforcement and Prevention (STEP) Act in 1988 in an attempt to control and suppress criminal activity by gangs. The STEP Act describes what constitutes a "criminal street gang," enumerates the offenses that are considered "gang offenses," and includes increased penalties for crimes that are gang related. Law enforcement personnel target a particular gang that they believe fits the STEP Act's criteria as a criminal street gang. A notification process informs alleged gang members that they have been identified as gang members of this particular gang and that they may be prosecuted under the STEP Act. If the gang member is found guilty, the enhanced penalties will apply. An additional two to four years can be imposed for general felonies, five years are added to the sentence for serious felonies, and ten years are added for violent felonies.

Other states, including Arizona, Arkansas, Florida, Georgia, Illinois, Indiana, Iowa, Louisiana, Minnesota, Mississippi, Montana, Nevada, North Dakota, Rhode Island, and South Dakota, have enacted similar legislation in an effort to deter street gangs from engaging in criminal acts. Many advocates of these laws believe that they are effective in reducing gang activity. Others believe that these laws only demonize the gang "as purposefully criminal conspiracies, as violent organizations" and end up by labeling "youth as gang members and to incarcerate them for as long as possible" (Klein and Maxson 2006, 9). These stereotypes encourage law enforcement and other professionals to see criminal street gangs as identical, not allowing for the wide variety that exists among gangs and gang members.

GPS Monitoring

Some communities are trying a different approach to tracking gang members—the use of monitoring devices employing a GPS satellite navigation system to keep track of violent gang members. The California Department of Corrections and Rehabilitation (CDCR) entered into a partnership with the City of San Bernardino in a pilot program to use GPS devices to track the movements of local street gang members. All participating gang members have been released on parole from state prisons. The CDCR began using GPS devices to track sex offenders and, in 2005, expanded the program to track gang members on parole. The city of Los Angeles has also begun to use GPS devices to track the movements of their local street gang members as a condition of their parole.

Gang Communications

Gangs are becoming increasingly sophisticated in the ways they use cell phones, pagers, and computers to spread word of their activities, communicate with each other, and seek new members. They use cell phones to call gang members together, warn each other when law enforcement personnel are approaching certain areas, and forward photos of gang activity, among other uses.

Some communities have attempted to ban the use of cell phones, pagers, and/or beepers by gang members, based on the premise that gang members use these devices to coordinate or plan illegal activities. Police and prosecutors in Oceanside, California, were granted an injunction in 1997 that banned gang members from carrying pagers and cell phones, among other devices. On February 13, 1998, David Englebrecht was seen hanging out with a fellow gang member after he was warned earlier in the day by the police not to do so. He was arrested and charged with violating the gang injunction provision that prohibits association with other gang members and the provision banning the possession and use of pagers. He was found guilty and appealed. The California Court of Appeals upheld the provision banning associating with known gang members; however, the provision banning the possession and use of pagers was found to be unconstitutional, violating the First Amendment to the Constitution. The court ruled that cell phones and pagers were "important communication devices that were protected by free speech, and that the provision was overbroad by banning all possession and use, even for legitimate reasons" [*In re Englebrecht*, 67 Cal. App. 4th 486 (1998)]. Other jurisdictions have attempted to ban the use of pagers and cell phones for criminal activities, and as of this writing, these injunctions have not been challenged.

In addition to cell phones and pagers, gangs are using the Internet for communication and promotional purposes. In addition to using e-mail or text messaging to keep in touch with other gang members, many gangs have established their own Web sites. For example, the Crips and the Bloods have their own Web sites, offering free e-mail service to gang members, space to promote individual gangs, and private chat rooms for members.

Law enforcement personnel are beginning to monitor Web sites and blogs for information on gangs and their individual members. In some cases, materials, including photographs of gang exploits, that have been posted to Web sites have helped law enforcement officials build cases against individual gang members. For example, in a California case, a judge ruled that two teenagers who were charged with beating a boy so severely that he ended up in a coma could be tried as adults. Prosecutors convinced the judge that the teenagers were indeed gang members when they showed him photographs the teenagers had posted on MySpace.com. The photos showed them flashing the hand signs of a local gang.

Some professionals argue that gang Web sites should be shut down, while others believe that if they assist law enforcement in monitoring gang activities or in finding evidence of crimes, they should be allowed to continue. Also in question is whether gang sites are protected under the First Amendment right to freedom of speech.

Controversies

In addition to the issues surrounding prevention and suppression activities are more controversial issues concerning gangs. These include distribution of illegal drugs in the United States, terrorism activities, racial profiling, immigration and asylum, witness intimidation, the role of the media, gangs in the military, and white supremacist groups being considered gangs.

Gangs and Drug Distribution

While many researchers believe that gangs are too unorganized to run efficient drug operations (Klein and Maxson 1994; Decker and Van Winkle 1996), others suggest that gangs can be formal organizations with established leadership roles and structures that would lend themselves to drug distribution (Taylor 1990; Sanchez-Jankowski 1991). One of the first studies to examine the connection between gangs and drugs was conducted by Skolnick and his colleagues in 1988 (cited in Howell and Decker 1999). They found that the Crips and the Bloods, two of the major Los Angeles gangs, were involved in drug trafficking and in fact were expanding their operations to other cities. In a study for the U.S. Congress, the General Accounting Office (1989) determined that in the United States, the Crips and Bloods gained control of 30 percent of the crack cocaine market during the late 1980s. During this same period, the U.S. Federal Bureau of Investigation (FBI) estimated that members of the Bloods and Crips had migrated from Los Angeles to 45 other cities throughout the United States and had established crack cocaine trafficking operations in those locations (Skolnick 1989; also cited in Howell and Decker 1999).

Howell and Gleason (1999) analyzed the results of the 1996 Youth Gang Survey and found that respondents to the survey reported that gang members were involved in 43 percent of the drug sales in their jurisdiction. However, they found that the distribution of drugs in most of the jurisdictions was not controlled by gangs: More than two-thirds of the respondents reported that gangs controlled less than 50 percent of the drug distribution, while 47 percent of the respondents reported that gangs controlled less that 25 percent of all drug distribution in their communities. For small cities and rural communities with populations under 25,000, gang members were more heavily involved in drug sales, and gangs controlled a substantial amount of the distribution of drugs; almost one-third of these respondents reported that gang members accounted for two-thirds of all drug sales and that gangs controlled more than half of all drug distribution. Results from the 1997 Youth Gang Survey showed similar results.

One of the primary sources of income for gangs is believed to be the distribution of drugs. According to the National Drug Intelligence Center (2005), illegal drugs are distributed in the United States primarily by street gangs, outlaw motorcycle gangs, and prison gangs. Street gangs are primarily involved in converting powdered cocaine into crack cocaine and in producing PCP (phencyclidine), a dangerous hallucinogen.

Because of the growing amount of drug distribution by gangs, researchers are beginning to distinguish between street gangs and drug gangs. Klein (1995) suggested that this distinction needed to be made in order to better understand the growth and development of gangs. Researchers as well as law enforcement personnel often have difficulty defining drug gangs, as they do street gangs. This issue creates a problem when the distinction is not clear; statistics concerning street gangs and drug gangs are unreliable and unclear as to their meaning and interpretation.

Another distinction that must be made is that between the gang distributing drugs and individuals within the gang distributing drugs. According to Fagan (2004), "not all gang members sell drugs even in gangs where drug selling is common. Drug-selling cliques within gangs are responsible for gang drug sales. These cliques are organized around gang members who have contacts with drug wholesalers or importers" (240). Decker (2004) understands the difference as well, as he explains that "most research has demonstrated that gang members sell drugs as individuals, and that gangs exert little instrumental control over the patterns of sales and the profits made by their members" (264).

Some of the larger well-known and well-organized gangs are overlooking their past conflicts with each other and creating alliances to sell drugs. The Crips and the Bloods have reportedly been working together to sell drugs in Portland, Oregon, and the Folk and People gang alliances in Arlington Heights, Illinois, have joined forces to sell narcotics (National Alliance of Gang Investigators Associations 2005).

Profiling

Racial profiling is generally defined as the "discriminatory practice by law enforcement officials of targeting individuals for suspicion of crime based on the individual's race, ethnicity, religion or national origin. Criminal profiling, generally, as practiced by police, is the reliance on a group of characteristics they believe to be associated with crime" (ACLU 2005). Do law enforcement personnel use racial profiling in stopping and arresting alleged gang members?

One of the problems with the antiloitering statutes discussed earlier in this chapter is that police officers have been accused of racial profiling when they have asked groups of young Hispanics or African Americans to disperse. The officers were accused of singling out minorities in the mistaken belief that if the gathered youths were Hispanic or African American, they must be members of a gang.

Charges of racial profiling are not just brought by Hispanics and African Americans. For example, racial profiling was at issue in the lawsuit brought by Minh Tram and other young Asian Americans against the police department in Garden Grove, California, mentioned earlier. The police department settled the racial profiling lawsuit, which claimed that the civil rights of the young girls were violated when police officers believed they were gang members based solely on their ethnicity and the clothing they were wearing.

Native Americans also have charged officials with racial profiling. In March 2006, 10 Native American families with children in the Winner, South Dakota, school system filed a class-action suit against the school district. The children and their families claimed, among other allegations, that the schools discriminated against Native American students by disciplining them unfairly, accusing them of "engaging in gang-related activities when they walk, talk, or stand in a group of three or more, wear bandanas, or write 'Native Pride' or draw medicine wheels on their notebooks. Caucasian students who engage in similar behavior are not subject to the same accusations. In fact, during a basketball tournament hosted by Winner High School in November 2004, Caucasian students wore bandanas with the school's explicit consent" (*Antoine et al. v. Winner School District*, 2006). The parties settled the case, with the school district agreeing to set up a committee of Native American parents and school officials that reviews all disciplinary incidents for racial disparities and recommends changes to reduce these disparities (ACLU 2007).

Gangs and Terrorism

Some law enforcement professionals and government officials believe that gangs are somehow involved in terrorist activities against the United States. For example, in testimony before the U.S. Senate Committee on Intelligence in February 2005, Robert S. Mueller, director of the FBI, indicated that gangs are becoming more violent and pose a serious "threat to the safety and security of Americans" (Mueller 2005). He claimed that gang members "travel from city to city, between states and, on occasion, between countries to commit their crimes."

The Immigration and Customs Enforcement Agency, part of the Department of Homeland Security, also has focused on violent street gangs as a threat to national security. Beginning in 2005, it began its ongoing Operation Community Shield, a program that, in cooperation with other federal and state authorities, targets gang activity. Secretary of Homeland Security Michael Chertoff has referred to violent street gangs as a threat to our national security (Bansal 2006).

Some gang leaders have actually contacted foreign dictators and others that the U.S. government considers a threat to the security of the United States. For example, Jeff Fort, the leader of the El Rukn gang in Chicago, reportedly contacted Muammar Qaddafi seeking $2.5 million from him to engage in terrorist activities in the United States on behalf of Qaddafi. Approximately 3,500 hours of conversations involving Fort, who suggested that the El Rukn could conduct terrorist activities throughout the United States, were collected by the FBI. When the El Rukn bought a rocket launcher from an undercover agent, federal agents moved in and arrested Fort. Trammel Davis, an official in the El Rukn gang, testified against Fort and the gang in exchange for $10,000 for his family. In 1987, five members of the gang were convicted of conspiring to commit terrorist acts against the United States.

The Media and Gangs

Advances in technology have created the ability to communicate a greater amount of information than ever before and to do it faster. People die every day on the streets of U.S. cities, not always as a result of gang violence, but as a result of drunken driving, exposure, and other non-gang-related violence. Most often, however, the deaths and shootings that are reported are the more violent, gang-related, "newsworthy" items. Many researchers believe that while gang violence may have increased over time, news coverage of gangs and gang-related violence has also likely increased, thereby giving the impression that gang-related violence has increased more significantly than is actually the case.

Several researchers have suggested that the media, especially television, have encouraged the growth of gangs and their increasingly violent activities (Tovares 2002). By providing news coverage of drive-by shootings, murders, and other violent gang activities, the news media may be seen as encouraging gangs to continue these types of activities and persuading the public that gangs are present in their communities. In addition, news coverage provides gangs with free advertising to an audience of potential new members and informs rival gangs of their activities.

Media coverage provides the only source of information that most people receive concerning gangs. The types of information reported by the media concerning individual gangs, the kinds of gangs they select to report on, and the actions that are reported are frequently chosen by news organizations and their directors, who make the decisions based on the newsworthiness of the incidents rather than how accurately the incidents reflect reality (Barbour 2006).

The news media may also encourage stereotypes of local gangs, especially African American and Hispanic gangs. For example, Tovares (2002) studied the ways in which Mexican American youth gangs have been portrayed on local television news in Austin, Texas. He suggests that the public is led by local television coverage, using media-driven clichés, to believe that a tide of violence is rising, widespread drug use and addiction exists among Mexican American gangs, and minority youth are alienated from the larger society. Tovares argues that these beliefs are gross exaggerations of reality and have led to reinforcing stereotypes concerning Mexican American youth. Continuing distortions and selective reporting by the press and television only encourage these stereotypes of young Mexican American males as prone to violence and a danger to society.

Gangs and the Military

Some researchers and other professionals in the field believe that
increasing numbers of gang members are joining the military.
The FBI suggests several reasons why gang members enlist in
the military: they may be trying to escape an uncomfortable situation at home, to escape from gang participation, to receive
weapons and combat training, or to learn other techniques that
will benefit themselves and their gang once they have completed
their service.

A 2007 report by the FBI indicates that gang activity is increasing in the military, and this activity poses both a law enforcement and a national security threat. Members of most of the
major street gangs in the United States have been found on local
as well as international U.S. military bases (National Gang Intelligence Center 2007). These gangs participate in many of the activities in which civilian gangs participate, including drive-by
shootings, assaults, robberies, weapons violations, drug distribution, vandalism, money laundering, extortion, and domestic
disturbances.

Military investigators have briefed local law enforcement
agencies in many major U.S. cities, including New York, on the
increased potential for gang members from the armed services to
return to their homes and share their weapons and warfare tactics knowledge with civilian gang members (CBS News 2007). In
some cases, criminals convicted of certain crimes may be offered
the opportunity to join the military in lieu of serving a prison
sentence. In fact, the FBI has documented several cases in which
gang members have been recruited while on parole or probation,
or even while facing criminal charges. Army recruiters have reportedly concealed gang membership of recruits in order to bol-
ster their enlistment numbers (National Gang Intelligence
Center 2007).

The children of military personnel may also be at higher
risk for joining gangs, in large part because of their transient
lifestyle. Many children feel isolated and vulnerable and find
making friends difficult. A survey conducted in 1998 indicated
that street gangs have spread to communities that have military
installations and local neighborhoods where the dependents of
military personnel reside (National Gang Intelligence Center
2007).

68 Problems, Controversies, and Solutions

Are White Racist Extremist Organizations Gangs?

Groups generally included in white racist organizations are the Ku Klux Klan, racist skinheads, the Aryan Brotherhood, the National Alliance, and the White Nationalists, along with several other smaller, less well-known groups. The Ku Klux Klan is probably the best known of all of these groups, with its long history of violence. The Klan has lost a great deal of its power in the last 10 to 20 years but still exists in some areas of the country. According to the Southern Poverty Law Center (2006), 165 individual Klan groups were found in 35 states and the District of Columbia. The Klan generally views itself as a Christian organization and not a gang.

The racist skinheads began as a working-class movement in the United Kingdom during the 1960s. Today, racist skinheads are organized in small "crews" and are found in 25 states (Southern Poverty Law Center 2006). They do not fight over neighborhoods or turf, but they do share a hatred for anyone who is different from them. They are known for their aggressive tactics; use of violence to communicate their message of hate to others; and criminal activities, including assaults, burglaries, vandalism, and theft.

The Aryan Brotherhood was founded in San Quentin prison in 1967 to provide protection for white inmates from Hispanic and African American gangs. It is considered to be a white supremacist organization and is known for its criminal activity and racial hatred. Members wear tattoos, although today many members cover up or remove their tattoos in an effort to hide their association with the group from law enforcement personnel.

The National Alliance has been one of the better known neo-Nazi organizations. It owns Resistance Records, a white power music company that is popular with skinheads. According to the Anti-Defamation League (ADL 2006), it has lost many of its members as a result of dissatisfaction with the leadership; many of them have joined the National Vanguard, which was started in 2005.

The White Nationalists are another white supremacist organization that focuses on the inferiority of nonwhites and often professes white separatist ideologies. According to the Southern Poverty Law Center (2006), 110 White Nationalist groups were found to be active in 32 states and the District of Columbia.

Researchers and law enforcement agencies debate whether these racist extremist organizations can be considered gangs. Based on the most common elements in the definition of a gang, that is, a group of three or more individuals who participate in some sort of criminal activity, the answer is that these groups could be considered gangs. Many members have swastikas tattooed on their bodies; wear distinctive clothing, such as "white power" t-shirts; and shave their heads. These characteristics would also define them as a gang. Out of all the white racist groups, the skinheads and the Aryan Brotherhood are the most likely groups to be considered a gang.

However, gang experts do not generally characterize most of these groups as gangs. They are more likely to be considered ideological, or hate, groups by most researchers. They do not generally have a neighborhood area, or turf, that they protect. Their focus is generally not considered to be criminal activity as a means for economic gain, but rather communicating messages of hate through the use of violent, and often criminal, activities.

Witness Intimidation

Intimidation of witnesses in gang cases can have serious repercussions in many instances. When witnesses to gang crime are persuaded to change their testimony, gang members may go free because prosecutors cannot prove their case. Two primary types of witness intimidation are overt intimidation and implicit intimidation. Overt intimidation occurs when an explicit action forces the witness to change, falsify, or withhold his or her testimony, such as an explicit threat to witnesses that they will be harmed if they testify. Gang members may also show up in court or outside the courtroom and stare at the witness, take his or her picture, or wear clothing that contains messages such as "stop snitching" (Anderson 2007). Implicit intimidation occurs when the individual witness knows that the threat is there, even though it is unexpressed. This may be experienced by residents in specific neighborhoods that are terrorized by gang members; they refuse to tell the police who committed the crimes, even though they know who the perpetrators are. They are afraid the gang members will come after them if they provide law enforcement officials with information concerning gang activities.

Today's gangs are "sophisticated and flagrant in use of violence and intimidation tactics," according to the National Alliance of Gang Investigators' Associations (2005, v). Respondents to their survey believed that gangs frequently used witness intimidation to avoid criminal convictions and that witness intimidation was widespread throughout the United States.

A variety of means are available to counteract these threats, but many are expensive and not always successful. One means is some type of witness protection program, which may involve as little effort as protecting the witness up to and during the trial or as much effort as temporarily relocating the witness, in which the witness is moved to a safe place until the trial is over. According to Finn and Healey (1996), gang members generally do not retaliate against a witness who has already testified because they do not want to be arrested, charged, and convicted of retaliation.

However, in some cases of witness intimidation, permanent relocation is necessary. The federal Witness Security Program is the most well-known program for permanent witness relocation. It is used primarily for federal organized crime and racketeering, serious federal felony, and similar state cases. The witnesses' lives must be threatened and the threat must be serious in order to be admitted into this program. Some states have developed similar witness protection programs, including the State of California, which reimburses local law enforcement agencies for a variety of costs related to the protection of a witness, including armed protection and escort services, temporary relocation services, and services related to the permanent relocation of witnesses (Anderson 2007).

Some legal barriers exist in attempting to prevent courtroom intimidation, such as excluding the public from the courtroom, allowing hearsay evidence from law enforcement officers, impeaching inconsistent witness testimony, and keeping witness and jury information confidential. The Constitution provides defendants with the right to a fair and public trial and witnesses with the right to testify without the threat of retaliation. Judges are generally reluctant to exclude certain individuals from the courtroom or to close the courtroom, but these actions have been used on a selective basis and often have been upheld on appeal (Finn and Healey 1996).

The issue of allowing hearsay evidence from law enforcement officers has been examined in many states. California now allows certain specially trained law enforcement officers to testify on behalf of the victims and witnesses. In most cases, the officer must have been involved with the case from its early stages. In Vermont, a statute provides that depositions may be used at trial if the person who was deposed is unavailable for trial or, if at trial, the witness gives conflicting testimony, leading prosecutors to believe that he or she has been threatened.

Witnesses in gang cases have been known to change their testimony from the time they were originally interviewed by police to when they testify during hearings or at trial. Some state and local jurisdictions have amended their rules of evidence to allow prior inconsistent testimony by witnesses to be admitted at trial. For example, California law has allowed the introduction of inconsistent witness statements since 1967. Officials there believe that early statements by witnesses are more likely to be true than later ones, which can be influenced by a number of factors, including intimidation (Finn and Healey 1996).

Prosecutors in many jurisdictions have worried about the ability of defendants to obtain the names and addresses of witnesses as well as those of the members of the jury in an attempt to intimidate them. The courts have allowed prosecutors in New York to withhold the names of witnesses until the day they testify in some gang cases. Jurors in New York City are only required to provide the area of Manhattan in which they live, not their specific address. In some cases, prosecutors have been allowed to provide the names of witnesses to the defendant's attorneys but have barred the attorneys from revealing the information to their clients. In other cases, witnesses have been allowed to testify under a pseudonym and the courtroom cleared during their testimony (Finn and Healey 1996).

Many prosecutors are continuing to look for ways to prevent witness intimidation. Attempts have been made to develop comprehensive witness protection programs that include sharing of local resources, community policing, anti-intimidation legislation, and gang suppression statutes. All agencies involved should work together to help protect witnesses and to encourage their testimony. Police departments must strengthen their ties to the community through the use of mobile precincts or storefront precincts in order to establish a positive presence. Increasing the penalties for witness intimidation and more aggressively prosecuting gang members who threaten witnesses may also deter gang members from intimidating witnesses.

Asylum

Another serious issue regarding gangs is the growing number of youths from other countries, especially Central American countries, who come to the United States seeking asylum. In their home countries, they may have been gang members who are fearful for their lives, because the gang has threatened to kill them for leaving the gang, or they have never been a member of a gang but are being threatened with death if they do not join the gang. Many of these youths are threatened by the MS-13 (also known as Mara Salvatrucha) gangs in El Salvador and other Central American countries.

According to U.S. immigration law, in order to be granted asylum, a person must demonstrate that he or she is a refugee, which is defined as "any person who is outside any country of such person's nationality . . . and who is unable or unwilling to avail himself or herself of the protection of that country because of persecution or a well-founded fear of persecution on account of race, religion, nationality, membership in a particular social group, or political opinion" [8 U.S.C. § 1101(a)(42)(A) (2005)]. Youths seeking asylum because of fear of gang retaliation often are not granted asylum because they do not qualify as a member of a "particular social group," which is typically the only category in the above definition that may apply to them. Because the definition of the term *particular social group* is unclear, immigration judges have wide latitude in deciding whether to grant asylum. Some judges may suspect that the youth is not totally innocent if he is a former gang member, believing that he was probably involved in criminal activities, and may deny asylum on that basis. Each judge's interpretation of a particular social group may differ, and a youth may or may not be granted asylum, depending on which judge hears his case (Voss 2005).

During the hearing to establish the facts in the case, youths may not be able to fully explain the reasons they have for seeking asylum. Many may not be fluent in English, while others are unable to clearly explain the reasons for their fears of returning to their country. The conditions within the country or the legal ramifications of these conditions often are not fully understood by the youth. Most are not represented by counsel; fewer than half of all aliens were represented by attorneys during their Immigration Court hearings in 2003 (Voss 2005).

If asylum is denied, the denial may be appealed to the Board of Immigration Appeals. While the youth may not need to be represented by an attorney during the primary asylum hearing, when he is just establishing the facts concerning the need for asylum, the appeal process is more complicated and knowledge of the law is a critical part of the appeal process; thus, legal representation is necessary. However, many of these youths are not able to afford an attorney or even know how to retain one and are thus unable to appeal the decision.

One of the better known cases of a gang member being deported to his country of origin is that of Edgar Chocoy Guzman, who was abandoned by his parents and living in the slums of Guatemala City. He was recruited into the Mara Salvatrucha gang when he was in grade school. He quit the gang in 2003, when he was 15 years old, and fled the country after the gang threatened to kill him if he did not remain with the gang. He came to the United States to join his mother in California. He became involved with a gang in Los Angeles and was eventually charged with weapons and drug possession. Facing deportation, he sought asylum, claiming he feared for his life if he was sent back to Guatemala. Asylum was denied in January 2004, and he was sent back to Guatemala, where he was shot to death within three weeks of his return. His aunt claimed that he was shot by gang members who heard he had returned to Guatemala (James 2005; Voss 2005).

These youths deserve more protection in these situations, according to James (2005) and other researchers, child welfare workers, and other professionals in the field of children's rights. James believes they should be treated favorably by immigration officials; they should not be held to the adult standard of responsibility for joining a gang, in part because they have the potential to be rehabilitated and to become responsible members of society. In addition, immigration officials should understand the pervasiveness of gangs throughout Central America and the inability of those governments to protect their young people.

Immigration officials also must understand that children who are gang members in these countries are not protected by the police; in some cases, the government encourages the police to actively pursue gang members and arrest them. Many gang members are tattooed with the name of their gang, which helps the police identify them. Also, the simple fact that a child is a gang member does not necessarily mean that he participates in gang violence. Young children, especially in Central American countries, are often coerced into joining a gang by current gang members who threaten them with bodily harm, even death, if they refuse to join (James 2005).

Conclusion

Many problems exist in attempting to control or eliminate gangs and gang activities, especially criminal activity, beginning with accurate identification of gangs and gang members. Prejudices and stereotypes held by law enforcement, the media, and the general public can seriously influence the perception of who is a gang member and what strategies are used to intervene in or prevent gang activity. Gangs can no longer be considered only an American phenomenon, as they have developed from internal forces within other countries or from external forces, such as migration of gang members into other countries. Law enforcement authorities throughout the world currently face many challenges in controlling gangs and their criminal activities.

References

American Civil Liberties Union (ACLU). 2005. "Racial Profiling: Definition." [Online information; retrieved 4/15/08.] http://www.aclu.org/racialjustice/racialprofiling/21741res20051123.html.

American Civil Liberties Union (ACLU). 2007. "Native American Families and Winner School District Announce Settlement in Case Alleging Discrimination." [Online article; retrieved 4/15/08.] http://www.aclu.org/crimjustice/juv/30155prs20070618.html.

American Civil Liberties Union (ACLU) Foundation of Southern California. 1997. *False Premise/False Promise: The Blythe Street Gang Injunction and Its Aftermath.* Los Angeles: ACLU Foundation of Southern California.

Anderson, John. 2007. "Gang-Related Witness Intimidation." In *National Gang Center Bulletin.* Tallahassee, FL: National Gang Center.

Anti-Defamation League (ADL). 2006. "Racist Skinhead Project: White Supremacist Groups and Skinheads." [Online information; retrieved 4/15/08.] http://www.adl.org/racist_skinheads/.

Antoine et al. v. Winner School District. 2006. Complaint. [Online information; retrieved 4/15/08.] http://www.aclu.org/pdfs/antoinevwinner 03282006.pdf.

Bansal, Monisha. 2006. "Chertoff: Street Gangs a Threat to National Security." [Online information; retrieved 5/16/08.] http://www.cnsnews. com/ViewNation.asp?Page=%5CNation%5Carchive%5C200603%5 CNAT2006/

Barbour, Scott, ed. 2006. *Gangs.* Farmington Hills, MI: Greenhaven Press.

Beres, Linda S., and Thomas D. Griffith. 2004. "Gangs, Schools and Stereotypes." *Loyola of Los Angeles Law Review* 37:935–978.

Bilchik, Shay. 1996. "Curfew: An Answer to Juvenile Delinquency and Victimization?" In *OJJDP Juvenile Justice Bulletin.* Washington, DC: U.S. Bureau of Justice.

CBS News. 2007. "Are Gang Members Using Military Training?" [Online article; retrieved 4/15/08.] http://www.cbsnews.com/stories/2007/ 07/29/eveningnews/printable3108597.shtml.

Coker, Donna. 2004. "Foreword: Addressing the Real World of Racial Injustice in the Criminal Justice System." *Journal of Criminal Law and Criminology* 93:827–879.

Decker, Scott H. 2004. "Legitimating Drug Use." In *Understanding Contemporary Gangs in America,* edited by Rebecca D. Petersen. Upper Saddle River, NJ: Prentice-Hall.

Decker, Scott H., and Barrik Van Winkle. 1996. *Life in the Gang: Family, Friends, and Violence.* New York: Cambridge University Press.

Delaney, Tim. 2006. *American Street Gangs.* Upper Saddle River, NJ: Pearson Prentice-Hall.

Egley, Arlen, Jr., James C. Howell, and Aline K. Major. 2006. *National Youth Gang Survey: 1999–2001.* Washington DC: Office of Juvenile Justice and Delinquency Prevention, U.S. Department of Justice.

Fagan, Jeffrey. 2004. "Gangs, Drugs, and Neighborhood Change." In *Understanding Contemporary Gangs in America,* edited by Rebecca D. Petersen. Upper Saddle River, NJ: Prentice-Hall.

Finn, Peter, and Kerry Murphy Healey. 1996. "Preventing Gang- and Drug-Related Witness Intimidation." In *Issues and Practices.* Washington, DC: National Institute of Justice, U.S. Department of Justice.

Fleisher, Mark S., and Jessie L. Krienert. 2004. "Life-Course Events, Social Networks, and the Emergence of Violence among Female Gang Members." *Journal of Community Psychology* 32 (5): 607–622.

Franco, Celinda. 2006. *Youth Gangs: Legislative Issues in the 109th Congress.* Washington, DC: Congressional Research Service.

Fritsch, Eric J., Tory J. Caeti, and Robert W. Taylor. 2003. "Gang Suppression through Saturation Patrol and Aggressive Curfew and Truancy Enforcement." In *Policing Gangs and Youth Violence,* edited by Scott H. Decker. Belmont, CA: Wadsworth.

General Accounting Office. 1989. *Nontraditional Organized Crime.* Washington, DC: U.S. Government Printing Office.

Greene, Judith, and Kevin Pranis. 2007. *Gang Wars: The Failure of Enforcement Tactics and the Need for Effective Public Safety Strategies.* Washington, DC: Justice Policy Institute.

Grogger, Jeffrey. 2002. "The Effects of Civil Gang Injunctions on Reported Violent Crime: Evidence from Los Angeles County." *Journal of Law and Economics* 45:69–90.

Howell, James C., and Scott H. Decker. 1999. "The Youth Gangs, Drugs, and Violence Connection." In *Juvenile Justice Bulletin.* Washington, DC: Office of Juvenile Justice and Delinquency Prevention.

Howell, James C., and D. K. Gleason. 1999. *Youth Gang Drug Trafficking.* Washington, DC: U.S. Department of Justice.

James, Melissa. 2005. "Fleeing the Maras: Child Gang Members Seeking Refugee Status in the United States." *Children's Legal Rights Journal* 25:1–22.

Katz, Charles M. 2003. "Issues in the Production and Dissemination of Gang Statistics: An Ethnographic Study of a Large Midwestern Police Gang Unit." *Crime and Delinquency* 49 (3): 485–497.

Klein, Malcolm W. 1995. *The American Street Gang.* New York: Oxford University Press.

Klein, Malcolm W., and Cheryl L. Maxson. 1994. "Gangs and Cocaine Trafficking." In *Drugs and Crime: Evaluating Public Policy Initiatives,* edited by Doris L. MacKenzie and Craig D. Uchida. Thousand Oaks, CA: Sage.

Klein, Malcolm W., and Cheryl L. Maxson. 2006. *Street Gang Patterns and Policies.* New York: Oxford University Press.

Maxson, Cheryl L., Karen Hennigan, and David C. Sloane. 2005. "It's Getting Crazy Out There: Can a Civil Gang Injunction Change a Community?" *Criminology and Public Policy* 4 (3): 577–605.

Miller, Jody. 1994. "Race, Gender and Juvenile Justice: An Examination of Disposition Decision-Making for Delinquent Girls." In *The Intersection of Race, Gender and Class in Criminology,* edited by Martin D. Schwartz and Dragan Milovanovic. New York: Garland Press.

Mueller, Robert S. 2005. Testimony before the U.S. Senate Committee on Intelligence, February 16. [Online information; retrieved 4/15/08.] http://www.fbi.gov/congress/congress05/mueller021605.htm.

National Alliance of Gang Investigators' Associations (NAGIA). 2005. *2005 National Gang Threat Assessment.* Washington, DC: Bureau of Justice Assistance.

National Drug Intelligence Center. 2005. *Drugs and Gangs: Fast Facts: Questions and Answers.* Washington, DC: National Drug Intelligence Center.

National Gang Intelligence Center. 2007. *Gang-Related Activity in the US Armed Forces Increasing.* Washington, DC: Federal Bureau of Investigation.

New York State Commission of Investigations. 2006. *Combating Gang Activity in New York: Suppression, Intervention, Prevention.* New York: New York State Commission of Investigations.

Peterson, D., J. Miller, and F. Esbensen. 2001. "The Impact of Sex Composition on Gangs and Gang Delinquency." *Criminology* 39 (2): 411–439.

Pratcher, S. D. 1994. "A Response to Juvenile Curfew Violations." *Police Chief* 61:58.

Ruefle, W., and K. M. Reynolds. 1995. "Curfew and Delinquency in Major American Cities." *Crime and Delinquency* 41:347–363.

Sanchez-Jankowski, Martin S. 1991. *Islands in the Street: Gangs and American Urban Society.* Berkeley: University of California Press.

Santo, Jocelyn L. 2000. "Down on the Corner: An Analysis of Gang-Related Antiloitering Laws." *Cardozo Law Review* 22:269–314.

Sikes, Gini. 1997. *8 Ball Chicks: A Year in the Violent World of Girl Gangs.* New York: Anchor.

Skolnick, Jerome H. 1989. *Gang Organization and Migration—Drugs, Gangs, and Law Enforcement.* Unpublished manuscript.

Skolnick, Jerome H., T. Correl, E. Navarro, and R. Rabb. 1988. *The Social Structure of Street Drug Dealing.* Unpublished report to the Office of the Attorney General of the State of California.

Southern Poverty Law Center. 2006. "Intelligence Project." [Online information; retrieved 4/15/08.] http://www.splcenter.org/intel/map/hate.jsp.

Taslitz, Andrew. 2003. "Racial Auditors and the Fourth Amendment: Data with the Power to Inspire Political Action." *Law and Contemporary Problems* 66:221–246.

Taylor, Carl S. 1990. "Gang Imperialism." In *Gangs in America,* edited by C. Ronald Huff. Newbury Park, CA: Sage.

Thornberry, Terrence P., Marvin D. Krohn, Alan J. Lizotte, Carolyn A. Smith, and Kimberly Tobin. 2003. *Gangs and Delinquency in Developmental Perspective.* New York: Cambridge University Press.

Tovares, Raul Damacio. 2002. *Manufacturing the Gang: Mexican American Youth Gangs on Local Television News.* Westport, CT: Greenwood Press.

U.S. Department of Justice. 2001. *The Federal Death Penalty System: Supplementary Data, Analysis and Revised Protocols for Capital Case Review.* [Online report; retrieved 4/15/08.] http://www.usdoj.gov/dag/pubdoc/deathpenaltystudy.htm.

Voss, Michele. 2005. "Young and Marked for Death: Expanding the Definition of 'Particular Social Group' in Asylum Law to Include Youth Victims of Gang Persecution." *Rutgers Law Journal* 37:235–275.

Walker-Barnes, Chanequa J., and Craig A. Mason. 2001. "Perceptions of Risk Factors for Female Gang Involvement among African American and Hispanic Women." *Youth and Society* 32 (3): 303–336.

Werdegar, Matthew Mickle. 1999. "Enjoining the Constitution: The Use of Public Nuisance Abatement Injunctions against Urban Street Gangs." *Stanford Law Review* 51:409–445.

Wright, Joshua D. 2005. "The Constitutional Failure of Gang Databases." *Stanford Journal of Civil Rights & Civil Liberties* 2:115–142.

3

Worldwide Perspective

Many people once believed that gangs were primarily found in the United States. After all, most of the research on gangs was conducted in the United States. However, more countries are becoming aware of gangs within their borders and beginning to study their growth and development. International efforts are underway to avoid the spread of gangs across national borders. Gangs are becoming a problem in some countries in part because gang members in the United States are being returned to their countries of origin. This chapter explores the existence and growth of gangs in other countries and is organized according to continent or region of the world, and then alphabetically by country. A representative sample of countries is included to give the reader a broad view of the existence of gangs in other countries.

Understanding the gang presence in other countries is important for several reasons. First, the sheer number of gang members around the world is staggering. The executive director of the United Nations Human Settlement Programme (UN-HABITAT), Dr. Anna Kajumulo Tibaijuka (2005), estimated that the membership of youth gangs around the world is in the millions, with "institutionalized youth gangs concentrated in cities that have high violence rates" (3). Second, because many gangs migrate across national borders, an understanding of gangs, their motivations and activities, and effective deterrence and prevention strategies is important. Third, the similarities and differences among gangs in different countries may help us understand the reasons for gang formation and lead to the development of effective intervention techniques.

Many developed countries have problems with gangs similar to those experienced in the United States. Other countries, especially developing countries, have different types of experiences with gangs. Some gangs are specific to individual countries, and some are international gangs, that is, they cross national borders. For example, the Crips and the Bloods have member gangs in other countries, such as Canada and the United Kingdom. The Mara Salvatrucha (MS-13) and the 18th Street (or Calle 18) gangs originated in the United States but have spread into Mexico and many Central American countries.

In both industrialized nations and developing countries, gangs are a result of similar circumstances. In industrialized nations, gangs often are formed by individual immigrant and ethnic groups, who join together for protection against other ethnic groups. In developing countries, gangs form for a variety of additional reasons. In some countries, especially in Latin America and Africa, struggling economies lead to conditions that may trigger gang development; many countries have growing problems of rural migration into urban areas, lack of education and employment opportunities for young people, and little infrastructure to help these families and individuals escape poverty. Several countries are experiencing a growing youth population, which leads to a tighter job market and fewer legitimate economic opportunities. Other countries, especially developing countries, have weak justice systems, which may not be able to control civil unrest and gang development. Gangs have also spread from one country to another as criminal gang members are deported or travel to other countries in search of better economic opportunities.

Gathering information on street gangs in other countries presents several problems. Many countries have not devoted the resources necessary to studying street gangs; they are plagued with other, more serious problems or do not believe that street gangs are a serious issue. The problem of a lack of a consistent, acceptable definition of youth gangs also makes comparing research conducted in different countries, or even in different regions of the same country, difficult. Standards of research vary from country to country, which also contributes to problems with attempting to compare one country with another. Finally, language barriers make it difficult for Americans to learn about gangs in other countries; research results are reported in native languages and not often translated into English.

Gangs in North America

Characteristics of gangs in North America vary from country to country. While Canada has experienced similar issues to those of the United States, Jamaica and Mexico have had different experiences with gangs.

Canada

The history of youth gangs in Canada is similar to the history of youth gangs in the United States. Both countries have similar experiences with youth gangs and are seeing a growing number of gangs and gang members. Canadian youth gangs are frequently organized along ethnic lines, as in the United States. In addition, several gangs have patterned themselves after the major gangs in the United States, including Bo Gars and Crack Down Posse, which have adapted their behavior to conform to that of the Bloods and the Crips, respectively.

The problem of defining the term *youth gang* has also created issues for the police, government officials, and policy makers; different regions across the country have different definitions based on the unique aspects of gangs within their territories. This lack of a consistent definition makes gathering and comparing statistics across the country difficult. As one researcher has stated, "There is no single theory or definition that can account for the pluralistic or heterogeneous gang/group phenomenon in contemporary Canadian society" (Mathews 1999, 4).

In 2002, a Canadian police survey on youth gangs was conducted on behalf of the solicitor general of Canada in order to determine the depth and breadth of gang activity throughout the country. No such survey had ever been conducted before this study; therefore, it will provide a baseline for future research on gangs. In the study, municipal police services, Ontario Provincial Police detachments, and Royal Canadian Mounted Police detachments were surveyed. Results indicated that 434 gangs are active, with 7,071 members in the participating communities. The authors caution that these figures may not reflect the true numbers of gangs throughout the country for a variety of reasons, including underreporting, lack of consistent definition of a youth gang, limited abilities to track the numbers of youth gangs, political reasons for not wanting to report the existence of a gang in one's local community, and limitations of law enforcement data collection practices (Astwood Strategy Corporation 2004).

According to the results of the survey, Canadian gangs are widely distributed throughout the country, with 216 gangs in Ontario, 102 in British Columbia, 42 in Alberta, and 28 in Saskatchewan. Most gang members are males under the age of 18, and they are ethnically diverse, with a higher incidence of African Canadian (25 percent), First Nations/Native (21 percent), and caucasian (18 percent) members. Female gang members were found in several parts of the country. Youth gangs are often hybrid-type gangs, which defy simple characterizations and make it more difficult for law enforcement agencies to provide a unified approach to resolving the problems these gangs create. Gang members are involved in a variety of criminal activities, including assaults, burglaries, vandalism, and drug trafficking, and there are indications that some youth gangs are connected with organized crime groups (Astwood Strategy Corporation 2004).

In its 2006 annual report on organized crime in Canada, the Criminal Intelligence Service Canada (CISC) reported that more than 300 street gangs existed, with more than 11,000 members throughout the country. Individual provinces and territories vary in the number of gangs present, according to the CISC; for example, it identified 20 street gangs in British Colombia; 30 in Alberta; 21 in Saskatchewan; 25 in Manitoba; 80 in Ontario; 50 in Quebec; 10 in Nova Scotia; 7 in New Brunswick; and none in Prince Edward Island, Newfoundland, the Yukon Territory, Northwest Territories, and Nunavat. Gang members were commonly between 20 and 30 years old and were involved in a variety of criminal activities, including drug distribution, theft, assaults, property damage, threats of retaliation, and murder (CISC 2006).

In a study of gangs in a midwestern Canadian city, Barron and Tindall (1993) described gang members as wearing black clothing and dying their hair black. They displayed weakened social bonds with the larger community and little organizational structure.

A comprehensive study of street gangs in Montreal was conducted by Le Blanc and Lanctôt (1994), who interviewed gang members and nongang members from disadvantaged backgrounds and compared them on a number of variables. Street gang members were more likely to have social and emotional problems. The youths who were not in a gang were more likely to come from a home with higher levels of parental supervision, reported lower stress levels in school, were more likely to follow traditional norms of behavior, and had fewer opportunities for deviance. Regarding gang characteristics, Le Blanc and Lanctôt found that gang members reported that their gangs had a highly defined structure, strong leaders, and a strong sense of territory.

In a study examining incarcerated males and street gangs in Vancouver, British Columbia, Gordon (1998) found that street gangs participated in a variety of criminal activities, including burglary and theft and drive-by shootings. Gang members were primarily male; an average age of 18 years old, with most members being under 25; and most often caucasian (40 percent) or Asian (34 percent), with the remainder made up of immigrants from various countries.

Very little research has been conducted on females in gangs. In one study of 37 female gang members in correctional institutions, Mackenzie and Johnson (2003) found that these gang members were generally aggressive and antisocial, had little education, had unstable employment histories, and had prior experiences with law enforcement officials. Female gang members have also been used as prostitutes, or, in some cases, gangs have forced female runaways into prostitution for the benefit of the gang (Gordon 2002). These prostitutes were sometimes used to entice rival gang members into traps or to carry weapons.

Some studies have been conducted on immigrant gangs. Tamil street-gang members in Toronto are between 15 and 26 years old, and their gangs fight with each other over territory and are involved in extortion and home invasions. Many gang members who have moved from a very traditional society to a more open one test the limits to their freedoms in unsanctioned, often criminal, ways. Many residents in these gangs' local communities are afraid of them and, like immigrants in other countries, are wary about reporting them to the police, because they do not always trust the police to take care of the problem (Covey 2003).

Youths in Native communities have also formed gangs. Members of the Indian Posse consist of indigenous young people from low-income families. The Indian Posse in Winnipeg, Manitoba, is known as a violent street gang, participating in car thefts, drug distribution, assaults, and breaking and entering (Bergman 1995). In Saskatchewan, aboriginal youth gangs include the Crips, Junior Mixed Blood, and Tribal Brotherz. Adult aboriginal street gangs include the Native Syndicate, Indian Posse, Redd

Alert, and Crazy Cree. Many youths continue or graduate into adult gangs because they grow up in low-income communities with few educational or employment opportunities (Criminal Intelligence Service Saskatchewan 2005).

In 2003, a gang task force in Edmonton, Alberta, found 12 aboriginal gangs in the city, including more than 400 members and another 2,000 associates. Similar to other Canadian gangs and to many American gangs, aboriginal gang members are identified by the colors they wear; the hand signals they use; and the clothing worn in a certain way, such as a cap worn sideways, an untied shoelace, or a bandanna. These youths join gangs primarily for the excitement, for power, and for a source of income.

Several local law enforcement agencies have established gang units to meet the challenges of dealing with street gangs. Some agencies have established school-based programs to reach children at risk of joining a gang. The Canadian government has also begun deporting individuals involved in criminal gang activities; the Canadian Immigration Act permits the deportation of an immigrant who belongs to a gang and is convicted of a crime.

Law enforcement agencies, correctional facilities, and social service organizations provide a wide range of programs to prevent at-risk children from joining gangs and to encourage current gang members to leave their gangs. Some programs focus on educational and public awareness activities, some focus on at-risk youth in an attempt to increase educational and employment opportunities for them to remain out of gangs, and some focus on rehabilitation of current gang members (Mellor et al. 2005).

Jamaica

Gang violence is only part of the larger problem of urban violence in Jamaica. Research has shown that violence has continued to grow in the country since its independence in 1962. A World Bank study reported that in 1961–1962, 183 murders were committed in the country; in 1989–1990, 981 murders were committed; in 1996, the number was 922 (Moser and Holland 1997).

Youth gangs in urban areas of Jamaica were primarily found in low-income neighborhoods, consisted of males between the ages of 12 and 15 years, and were generally well armed. Individuals in the neighborhoods were often fearful of the gangs and planned their activities around the times of day and night when the gangs were most often absent. For one group of young males in the World Bank study, the researchers saw lack of work and education as a major problem that contributed to the violence (Moser and Holland 1997). As a result, some youths were drawn into gang activity because they believed they had no options. It was also reported that not all gang members were poor and un-educated; males from middle-class, educated families were sometimes involved in gang activities.

The most serious type of violence was gang violence, ac-cording to findings from four out of the five communities in the World Bank study. The researchers saw this violence as a virtual war, influencing all aspects of neighborhood life. Many individ-uals also reported that the violence increased when the neigh-borhood had no strong leader to reduce the territorial fighting and build strong community ties.

Mexico

Gangs in Mexico differ from traditional American gangs and Central American gangs. While much of the gang activity in Cen-tral America can be traced to the deportation of Guatemalan, Sal-vadoran, and Honduran refugees from the United States back to their original countries, gangs in Mexico have not gone through the same process. Along the northern border of Mexico, gangs may be related to their American counterparts, while those along the southern Mexican border are more likely related to Central American gangs.

The Mexican government and local authorities classify gangs primarily as youth, street, or organized criminal gangs, with the implication that youth and street gangs are not typically involved in criminal activities. They may be involved in petty crimes, such as robbery, pickpocketing, theft, and minor drug distribution, but not in serious drug distribution, murder, human trafficking, or other serious criminal activities. Gang activities have not been ex-amined or measured on a consistent basis, so no overall picture of youth and street gang activity in Mexico has emerged. Most re-search and intervention activities have focused on the more seri-ous drug cartels and other criminal organizations.

Systematic tracking of gangs or gang members in Mexico does not take place. The government's Ministry for Public Secu-rity has estimated that approximately 5,000 individuals were members of the Mara Salvatrucha (or MS-13) gang in Mexico in 2005, and approximately 15,000 were members of the Calle 18, or

18th Street, gang in 24 Mexican states. Other sources believe that more than 200 gangs are affiliated with the MS-13 and 18th Street gangs in the southern Mexican border towns (USAID 2006).

Regional and local authorities also have reported gang activity in other Mexican cities. For example, local authorities in Nuevo Laredo estimate that 24 local gangs are active there. In Ciudad Juarez, authorities report that 320 local gangs are active, including 17,000 gang members. Thirty percent of youths in Ciudad Juarez between the ages of 12 and 15 years do not attend school and do not have jobs; local authorities believe these factors contribute to the high number of youths in gangs. They also report that most gangs are involved in petty crimes and vandalism, while the majority of violent crime is committed by only 30 gangs (USAID 2006).

The line between gangs and drug cartels has become somewhat blurred along the northern Mexican border. Many gangs appear to have morphed into drug cartels—in the past, drug cartels have used gang members to provide a variety of services, and many gang members have now become active members of these criminal organizations. A former gang member interviewed by a U.S. Agency for International Development assessment team member said that "There are no more gangs here. What exists now is more dangerous. . . . The gang member obeys orders from drug cartels. The gangs used to fight for territory, culture, and identity. Now the cartels recruiting them just fight for power and money" (USAID 2006, 111).

Many of the gangs across the northern border are also generational in nature. That is, young people are joining gangs that their fathers and grandfathers joined when they were young. This tradition provides a path for the children to follow once they are old enough to join. It also makes it difficult for authorities to prevent these at-risk youths from joining gangs.

Along the southern border, gangs include MS-13 and 18th Street, which many authorities believe have migrated from Central America. The Mexico National Institute of Migration reported that from January through October 2005, the number of migrants detained along Mexico's southern border included more than 15,000 Salvadorans, almost 47,000 Guatemalans, and 23,000 Nicaraguans (USAID 2006). It is likely that many of these individuals are young males looking for better economic opportunities in Mexico or are making their way to the United States.

Some are gang members, while some may become gang members. Many of the MS-13 or 18th Street gang members are involved in human and/or drug trafficking, along with other criminal activities.

Reasons that Mexican youths give for joining gangs are similar to reasons youths give in other countries. Educational and economic opportunities are lacking for many youths. Many live in overcrowded, poverty-stricken neighborhoods and see themselves as having no future. In addition, Mexican youths are tempted by the opportunities along the country's southern border to profit from the drug, human, and weapons trafficking activities, as well as the generational nature of gangs along the northern border.

Gangs in Central America

After the United States, the area that garners the most focus concerning the subject of gangs is probably Central America. Many countries in Central America are faced with increasing levels of crime, especially gang crime. Hearings before the U.S. Congress and other government reports indicate a concern that gang problems in these countries may contribute to the region's political and economic instability. Gangs are exerting an increasing amount of influence in many Central American countries. The presence of some gangs in these countries is believed to be a direct result of the deportation of gang members from the United States during the 1990s.

Many Central American countries are vulnerable to growing gang violence for four main reasons. First, the location of these countries places them between South America, from which a large portion of illegal drugs originate, and North America, which is the primary market for these illegal drugs. Second, the growth of street gangs and increasing competition among them contribute to increasing levels of violence in these countries. Third, easy access to weapons facilitates violent crime; this availability is often the result of the internal conflicts that many of the Central American countries have recently experienced. Finally, a large proportion of the population in these countries is under the age of 18; 50 percent of the population in Honduras is under the age of 18, with similar numbers in other Central American countries (Castillo 2007).

Officials in many Central American countries began crack-ing down on the increasingly violent MS-13 gang and its princi-pal rival, the 18th Street gang. A variety of "zero tolerance" laws were enacted; these provided the governments with the author-ity to imprison suspected gang members simply on the basis of an appearance of gang membership, such as wearing gang-specific tattoos. These hard-line policies have been denounced by many human rights organizations on basic human rights grounds. Another problem with these policies is that they have resulted in overcrowded prisons that have become training grounds for gang members.

The gang problem has been blamed on the U.S. deportation policy during the 1990s by several Central American government officials. In February 2005, in response to these concerns, the U.S. Department of Homeland Security implemented a project that targets gang activity by native Central Americans in the United States. Known as Operation Community Shield, the project was designed to work in cooperation with Central American govern-ments and law enforcement agencies. Between the time it was implemented and 2007, its efforts have led to the arrest of more than 800 MS-13 members; some of them will be prosecuted crim-inally, and others will be deported.

Many Central American countries are beginning to work to-gether to solve their gang problems. For example, government leaders in El Salvador, Honduras, Guatemala, Nicaragua, and the Dominican Republic signed an agreement in 2004 to establish a unified database tracking gangs and gang members, agreed to share information about gangs, and agreed to focus on tracking gang and gang member activities.

Regional and international organizations also have an inter-est in reducing gang and other youth violence in these countries. The World Bank and the Inter-American Development Bank pro-vide economic opportunities for businesses in many Central American countries; they worry about the impact that gang and other youth violence has on the climate for investment and other development activities. Several public health projects focusing on youth violence are supported by the Pan American Health Or-ganization. The United Nations, primarily through the United Nations Children's Fund (UNICEF) and the United Nations De-velopment Programme, is a participant in regional discussions on preventing youth violence. The U.S. Agency for International Development has focused its efforts on educational projects, helping to strengthen school systems and teachers in many countries, which may have a secondary effect of reducing youth gang involvement.

El Salvador

The growth of gangs in El Salvador is a direct result of the flight of Salvadorans to the United States during the civil war in the 1980s, where they were granted special refugee status. After the civil war ended in 1992, the U.S. government ended the special refugee status of many of these Salvadorans, including many gang members, and they were sent back to El Salvador. Many of the people who returned to El Salvador were very young when they left the country and had few family or friends to connect with when they returned. Gang members stayed connected with their fellow gang members, and MS-13 has flourished in El Salvador and spread throughout much of Central America.

Estimates of the number of gangs and gang members vary, depending on the source. According to El Salvador's National Civil Police, approximately 10,500 gang members were active in 2005. The National Council on Public Security counts approximately 39,000 gang members. MS-13 is the best-known gang in El Salvador. The gang was originally formed in Los Angeles sometime in the 1980s after many refugees from the civil war in El Salvador settled in Southern California. The other major gang is the 18th Street gang, and several other smaller gangs also exist (USAID 2006).

During the heated presidential campaigns in 2003, the Mano Dura (Firm Hand) program was established. It authorized law enforcement agencies to arrest young men who were suspected of being gang members involved in illegal activities. These types of law enforcement programs led to the arrests of many gang members, but they are not believed to have been effective in decreasing gang activities (Reisman 2007).

In 2004, the president of El Salvador, Tony Saca, proposed a package of antigang legislation known as Super Mano Dura (Super Firm Hand), which was passed unanimously by the Congress. The United Nations and other human rights organizations were among its detractors, because many of its provisions violated international human rights standards (Ribando 2007).

The government of El Salvador has attempted other approaches to reduce gang membership and violence. In 2005, the legislature modified gun ownership laws, making it more difficult for youths to own guns. In 2006, the new Ministry of Public Security and Justice was created at the national level; some of its antigang activities included stepping up patrols using joint military and police personnel in high-crime neighborhoods and drafting a law concerning organized crime (Ribando 2007).

Guatemala

In Guatemala, violent crime is a major problem; participants in violent crime include corrupt security officials, members of organized crime groups, and drug cartels. While some government officials believe that gangs were involved in a majority of the country's 5,629 murders in 2006, others believe that organized crime and drug cartels are primarily responsible for these murders (Ribando 2007).

The two major gangs, as in many other Central American countries, are the MS-13 and Calle 18 (18th Street) gangs. Many Guatemalans fled the country because of civil wars and unrest during the 1970s and 1980s and settled in the United States. Similar to the situation in El Salvador, many Guatemalans were deported from the United States in the early to mid-1990s and, because many were young, had no family connections or other ties to the country, and did not speak the local language, joined gangs to protect themselves.

Almost one-half of Guatemala's population is under the age of 18 years. Estimates of gang membership indicate that most gang members are under the age of 24 years; many join gangs when they are as young as 8 years old. Estimates of the number of gang members varies, but the National Civilian Police report an estimated 340 gangs, and estimates of the number of gang members range from 14,000 to 165,000. Most gang members are male, and females who do join gangs are generally placed in a subordinate role; they are frequently sexually used and abused by the male gang members.

According to Jose Guillermo Castillo, the ambassador to the United States from Guatemala, in testimony before the U.S. Congress, more than 300 gangs are active in Guatemala, the largest of which are MS-13 and Calle 18. The gang has operations from the United States all the way through Central America to Nicaragua (Castillo 2007). The government of Guatemala believes that the only approach to solving the problems of these gangs is through a transnational method. In 2006, the Central American Integration System organized a security commission to develop such a regional effort regarding security, and it is in the process of developing a plan of action. The U.S. government in 2007 offered approximately $4 million to help develop this regional antigang strategy. Officials from Central American countries believe they may ultimately need between $600 million and $800 million to implement and support this approach (Ribando 2007).

In the meantime, the Guatemalan government has adopted its own antigang strategy, known as Plan Escoba (Sweep Plan). Proponents of this plan are running into objections similar to those faced by other countries, usually based on human rights concerns. The police have conducted major sweeps in high-crime neighborhoods, picking up hundreds of male youths; they know that most will have to be released without any charges brought against them, but the police are able to gather information from many of these youths (Washington Office on Latin America 2006). In addition, former soldiers are believed to have joined with rogue groups and law enforcement agencies in these sweeps to eliminate youth gangs. Many in the human rights community have expressed concern that these groups are engaging in "social cleansing" actions, which are similar to actions taken by Guatemala's past military governments to reduce crime (Campbell 2007).

The Trust for the Americas, a nonprofit affiliate of the Organization of American States, is actively involved in prevention activities aimed at at-risk youth. Following concerns expressed by the Guatemalan government over the large numbers of small children recruited by gangs, the U.S. Department of State provided a grant to the trust to establish and operate a civic education program in Guatemala. Known as MI ZONA (My Community), the program teaches children between the ages of 6 and 10 appropriate ways to deal with difficult situations involving drugs, crime, and gangs. Children and parents attend workshops and seminars to learn prevention and refusal techniques, parents and teachers learn how to develop effective prevention curricula and support activities, and journalists are encouraged to present more balanced and accurate coverage of various youth-related issues (Eddleman 2007).

Individuals are also having an impact on youth participation in gangs. According to a recent UNICEF report, several years ago a group of youths grew tired of the gang activity and violence in their neighborhood in a sprawling shantytown about an hour's drive from Guatemala City. Fifteen members of two rival gangs were invited to come together and participate in a theater project that was aimed at getting them to know one another and discuss their problems and their hopes for the future. Participants learned that they all had a lot in common and realized that they had the ability to change the circumstances that led to their gang participation. Out of this effort grew Iqui Balam, a group run by youths that focuses on bringing rival gangs together to help improve living conditions and future possibilities for many youths. UNICEF helps support this program and provides leadership training to program members. The program has been quite successful in helping young people stay off drugs and out of gangs and see a future for themselves (UNICEF, n.d.).

Honduras

Approximately one-half of the population of Honduras is under the age of 18 years. Government officials believe the number of active gang members is approximately 20,000, primarily between the ages of 12 and 25 years old. In addition, approximately 15,000 youths aspire to join gangs, and 30,000 people are considered *paisas,* or family members, collaborators, or employers of gang members. The main gangs are Mara Salvatrucha and Calle 18; criminal activities of gang members include auto theft, kidnapping, extortion, homicide, drug distribution, trafficking, and arms distribution. Organized crime groups in Honduras are known to use gang members to carry out many of their activities. Honduran police have observed growing violence and younger participants in gangs; they estimate that between 1998 and 2003, criminal activities of gang members increased by 250 percent (Flores 2007).

Young people, primarily males, join gangs for many of the same reasons youths in other countries join: few opportunities for education, employment, or recreation; family disintegration; poverty; resentment of common established values; and encouragement from current gang members.

According to Ambassador Roberto Flores Bermudez of Honduras in testimony before the House Committee on Foreign Affairs, many government agencies are involved in initiatives to curb gang membership and violence. In 2007, more than 40 government-sponsored projects throughout the country either targeted gangs specifically or focused on alleviating or eliminating the root causes by addressing education, health, vocational training, housing, small business development, and other local government programs. Law enforcement agencies have increased penalties for gang membership and associated criminal activities (Flores 2007). However, nongovernment sources report that the government relies on private groups to operate most intervention and prevention programs. The Honduran president, Manuel Zelaya, addresses gang problems as a part of the overall crime problem in the country, and his government has funded only a small antigang office with the National Police. Combined police and military personnel patrol high-crime areas, and, while they arrested more than 1,200 gang members in September 2006, instances of crime and violence have continued at steady or growing rates (Ribando 2007).

In 2001, the Honduran legislature enacted the Honduran Law for the Prevention, Rehabilitation and Social Reinsertion for Persons Belonging to Gangs or Maras, which instituted the legal grounds for establishment of a committee to define various prevention, rehabilitation, and social reinsertion policies for gang members. In 2005, the National Institute on Youth was established to execute the guidelines developed by this committee. Program implementation, coordination, and consolidation are conducted through the National Program for the Prevention, Rehabilitation, and Social Reinsertion, which operates out of the office of the president of Honduras (Flores 2007).

Private, nongovernment agencies are also active in working to prevent or reduce gang membership and involvement. Several churches are involved in the rehabilitation and social reinsertion activities. Nongovernmental organizations (NGOs) are working to help youths involved in gangs. One well-known NGO, the COFADEH (Committee of Relatives of Disappeared Detainees in Honduras) is active in the support of human rights in Honduras; encourages initiatives that will improve the living conditions and opportunities for young people; and observes government actions concerning gang members, ensuring that their basic legal rights are observed.

Several human rights organizations opposed strong antigang legislation passed in 2003 that created stiff prison sentences for gang membership. The public supported this legislation as it saw crime rates drop, but the law was opposed by human rights groups that saw it as providing police forces and vigilante groups with power to abuse gang members and deprive them of their civil liberties. This legislation was part of the Mano Dura legislation that many Central American countries adopted to stem gang violence.

Nicaragua

The emergence of youth gangs in Nicaragua is not primarily a result of American gang culture or deportation of Nicaraguans from the United States, but rather an outgrowth of poverty and the struggle for survival. Nicaragua's population is quite young, according to statistics from the United Nations Educational, Scientific and Cultural Organization (UNESCO): 40 percent of the population is under the age of 12, and 35 percent is between the ages of 13 and 29 years (UNESCO Institute for Statistics 2005). Following the conflicts during the 1980s, many people moved from rural to urban areas in search of jobs. Often, these individuals and families were unable to locate well-paying jobs, and the population of squatter settlements quickly grew. Several neighborhoods had local gangs, or *pandillas,* by the mid-1990s.

During the 1990s, gangs and gang members participated in muggings, robbery, shoplifting, and other similar criminal activities. Confrontations with other gangs, primarily over territory, were common. Battles were originally fought with minor weapons, including sticks and stones, but gang members quickly grew accustomed to the use of guns, fragmentation grenades, and mortars. Marijuana and alcohol use was fairly common, but by 2000, many gangs became involved in the trafficking of narcotics (USAID 2006).

Even though Nicaragua's economy is not yet strong, gang activity has decreased from its height in the late 1990s. According to Rodgers (2003), Managua had approximately 8,500 gang members in 110 gangs in 1999. By 2004, the number had dropped to 2,614 gang members in 184 gangs, and in 2005, 2,200 gang members were in 108 gangs. While the government initially adopted a hard-line approach in 1999, it changed its focus to prevention in 2000. National legislation has created a variety of resources to help youths avoid gang and other violent activities by providing alternative activities and programs. The Co-Existence and Citizen Security program, established by the Ministry of the Interior and coordinated with seven other government entities and several NGOs, has established pilot programs in 11 cities throughout the country that focus on gang members, youths at risk for gang membership, and those already in the penal system (USAID 2006).

The National Police in Nicaragua have established the Prevention of Juvenile Violence program, which coordinates activities among various state institutions, the media, NGOs, and the private sector to help rehabilitate members who have left gangs and to prevent other youths from joining gangs. Services provided include educational opportunities, psychological counseling, vocational training, and job placement.

Panama

Panama has also experienced gang activity, although not to the extent that has been seen in El Salvador, Guatemala, and Honduras. However, the government has established some programs to help fight gangs and their criminal activities. For example, President Martin Torrijos has established Mano Amiga (Friendly Hand), which provides positive alternatives, including sports and theater activities, to youths between the ages of 14 and 17 years old who are at risk for becoming gang members. The program is supported by several domestic and international human rights organizations (Ribando 2007).

In March 2007, President Torrijos reacted to spreading violence by ordering a police crackdown on youth gangs. He also asked the Panama Congress to tighten laws to keep immigrants with criminal records out of the country as well as to increase penalties for gang members convicted of murder.

Gangs in South America

Research on gangs in South American countries is not very comprehensive, wide ranging, or widely available. Many sources have not been translated into English from Portuguese or Spanish. However, some research is available from several countries in South America; findings from Argentina, Brazil, Chile, and Colombia are presented below.

Argentina

DeFleur studied gangs and other forms of juvenile delinquency in the slums of Cordoba in 1970. Gathering information from court records as well as in-depth interviews with gang members serving prison sentences, DeFleur determined that youth gangs, or *barras*, generally had between five and eight members, all male, who were an average age of 16 years old and were involved in both nonviolent activities (including playing soccer, gathering on street corners and socializing, going to movies, and smoking cigarettes and drinking alcohol) and criminal activities (including shoplifting, purse snatching, breaking into cars, and other petty criminal activities, with only occasional armed robberies and assaults) (DeFleur 1970). The primary reason for gangs and gang activities, according to DeFleur, centered on economics, in that most youths who joined gangs came from lower-class neighborhoods; youths had few educational and economic opportunities, and they turned to gangs to help them survive.

In a study of gangs in Buenos Aires, Kuasñosky and Szulik (1996) found that these gangs were typically composed of between 30 and 40 members, with 15 core members, between the ages of 18 and 23 years old. The gangs formed as a result of their social exclusion as well as their poverty. The researchers described the gang members as having an apathetic and nihilistic outlook toward society and their future and displayed few connections with each other or with their communities (Kuasñosky and Szulik 1996; also cited in Rodgers 1999).

Brazil

An estimated 7 million to 8 million children live on the street in Brazil's urban areas. The potential advantages of joining a gang for protection, social connections, and survival are tempting for many youths.

According to Lamm (1993), Rio de Janeiro has approximately 600 slums, known as favelas, which contain various organized crime syndicates and street gangs. The street gangs often work for the organized crime syndicates; gang members see members of the crime syndicate as role models and want to have the money and power that these men have. The criminal activities of both groups are disliked by law-abiding residents of the favelas, but they adhere to an unwritten law of silence and do not cooperate with police or other authorities who investigate crimes in the favelas.

Dimenstein (1991) describes Brazil's street children as being recruited by street-gang members, because children are not held responsible by the justice system for the criminal acts in which they participate. Young girls may join gangs to avoid becoming prostitutes.

According to Rodgers (1999), gangs in Brazil are more diversified and violent than in any other country in Latin America. One type of gang, the *quadrilhas,* is composed of youths between the ages of 13 and 25 years and is primarily involved in drug trafficking. Its members are territorial and will protect their neighborhoods from other gangs, which often results in the murder of gang members who threaten them, as well as innocent bystanders.

Another type of gang is the *galeras cariocas;* its gang members spend more time focusing on enjoyable, noncriminal activities such as dancing, drinking, and using drugs. They are known to fight other gangs over territory; will protect their communities; and, according to Rodgers, are more likely to reflect characteristics of youth culture, unlike the drug trafficking gangs (Rodgers 1999).

Chile

Valenzuela studied Chilean youth living in three low-income areas of Santiago in 1984. He interviewed more than 600 youths between the ages of 15 and 24 years old and identified various forms of youth collective action. Youth gangs, also known locally as *pandillas,* are identified as one type of youth mobilization group. Gangs were more likely to participate in drug and alcohol consumption and violent delinquent activities than other forms of youth groups. Valenzuela found that gang members hung out listening to music and playing pinball, displayed violence toward outsiders, destroyed public property, and participated in a variety of criminal activities (Valenzuela 1984; also cited in Rodgers 1999).

Colombia

Youth crime is responsible for most of the violent crime in Colombia, although the youths involved are not always gang members. This crime includes more than 250,000 violent deaths between 1985 and 1996 (Rodgers 1999). Colombia experienced gang activity before the formation of the drug cartels in the 1970s, and today both often work together for their mutual benefit.

More than 120 youth gangs, with 3,000 members, existed in Medellin in 1990, many of them located in the poorer areas of the city (Salazar 1990). Gang members ranged in age from 12 to 20 years old; the average age was 16 years old. Young people joined the gangs primarily because they had few opportunities to improve their lives in legitimate activities. Most of these gangs were extremely violent; criminal activities included extortion, theft, burglary, robbery, drug sales, and murder.

Youth gangs began associating with drug cartels in the late 1970s; most gang members were young males from poor neighborhoods who were unemployed and were recruited to become paid killers of rival gang members. They initially committed murder in order to protect their own gangs, but over time they became more violent. During the 1980s, as the government tried to intervene in their activities, they murdered policemen, judges, and other public officials (Salazar 1990). These gang members have become increasingly involved in other criminal activities, including robbery, theft, drug use, assault, and battles with rival gang members. Some gangs get along with and protect members of their local neighborhoods, while other gangs target local community residents as part of their criminal activities (Human Rights Watch/Americas 1994).

Gangs in Europe

Concerned about the growing presence of American-style gangs in Europe, leading experts on gangs in the United States and Europe banded together in 1998 to develop a "common framework for comparative research." Known as the Eurogang project, it has three major objectives: (1) to build a strong base of knowledge of the basic conditions that may lead to the development of gangs, (2) to create a basic structure that will encourage and facilitate comparative research on gangs, and (3) to disseminate information gained to the appropriate authorities and researchers. The project maintains a Web site (http://www.umsl.edu/~ccj/eurogang/euroganghome.htm) to help disseminate knowledge gained.

Denmark

Between 15 and 20 gangs exist in Copenhagen, according to Stevns (2001). Most of these gangs have between 5 and 20 members, who are between the ages of 15 and 20 years old, and they are made up primarily of ethnic minorities. Their members have joined gangs mainly for protection, because they have limited educational and employment opportunities, and because they believe they are discriminated against by the majority society.

Some gangs are composed of local Danish youth and pattern themselves after American street gangs. In 1994, an intervention project, known as the Dog Sledge Project, was created as a cooperative effort between social service and education personnel and the police to help encourage gang members to leave the gang and become productive citizens. They focused their efforts on a Danish gang whose members were between the ages of 12 and 21 years and worked with them to leave the gang.

Germany

Gangs have been observed in Germany since the 1950s. Following World War II, groups of German youth joined together and patterned themselves after American youth, wearing blue jeans and American hairstyles and listening to American music. They roamed the streets and were involved in petty crimes and black market goods distribution (Covey 2003). Other groups of youth, known as *Halbstarke* (half-strong), listened to rock-and-roll music and roamed the streets projecting a tough gang image.

In a study comparing German and American street gangs, Huizinga and Schumman (2001) examined the characteristics of youth gangs through the use of longitudinal data in Bremen, Germany, and Denver, Colorado. They found that 13 percent of the youths studied identified themselves as members of street gangs in Bremen compared with 14 percent of the youths in Denver. Bremen youths were more likely to remain in the gang longer than their American counterparts (2.3 years for Bremen youth, 1.5 years for Denver youth). Most gang members were more violent than nongang members; however, the gang members in Denver were more involved in the sale of drugs and more focused on territory than the gang members in Bremen.

Skinhead gangs also exist in Germany. These gangs typically target Vietnamese, Turkish, Middle Eastern, and African immigrants who are seen by the skinheads as posing a serious threat to Germany's culture and economy. In response to these attacks, many immigrant youths have joined together in gangs to protect themselves from this violence (Klein 2001).

The Netherlands

Youths began joining gangs in the Netherlands during the 1990s, following the popularity of gangsta rap. Leon Bing's (1991) book on gangs and Sanyika Shakur's (1993) autobiography were translated into Dutch and became popular reading for many young males. American-style gangs grew in popularity, including variations of the Crips.

According to Van Gemert (2001), who studied several Crips gangs in the Netherlands, the average age of gang members in the Eastside Crips was approximately 15 years old, most were male, and most were from Surinam or Dutch Antilles. These youths were having trouble assimilating into the major society, had few job opportunities, and were from poor neighborhoods. They were known for committing violent thefts, usually victimizing girls.

The Eight Tray Crips were generally involved in street robberies, stealing bicycles, and committing violence against other gang members or former gang members. The average age of members of the Southside First Tray Crips was 18 years, many were ethnic minorities from the southern part of Rotterdam, they were tattooed, and they were known for their graffiti (Van Gemert 2001).

Norway

Youths in Norway have been joining gangs for many years. In Oslo, two of the best-known gangs during the 1950s were the Frognerbanden and Blackie gangs; they committed primarily petty crimes, such as robberies, and fought with their fists. During the 1960s and 1970s, most of the local youth gangs were known as Punks and Rockers. Members of all of these gangs were local, native Norwegians.

However, during the 1990s, youth gangs made up of immigrants began appearing. The most well known was the Young Guns, a group of Pakistani youth who came to Norway when they were between 10 and 12 years old. They fought with other gangs, and many were imprisoned for their criminal activity. Once they were released from prison, some gang members were able to turn their lives around and become productive citizens, while others became more deeply involved in gangs and other criminal groups (Lien 2001).

Between the late 1990s and 2000, the Young Guns recruited new members and changed their name to the A-gang. They have become international in scope, creating a network with gangs in Denmark and England; authorities believe they also work with criminal gangs in Turkey and Morocco. Some of the gang members have split off from the A-gang and refer to themselves as the B-gang (Lien 2001).

Other immigrant youth gangs have not created special names for themselves, and just go by the name of their country of origin, such as the Somali gang or the Vietnamese gang. Many of these gangs are youths from individual ethnic groups, while others have members from several different ethnic groups or nationalities.

Russia

Prior to the transformation of the Soviet Union to Russia, information on street gangs was not easily found. Officials in the Soviet Union regarded juvenile delinquency and all its manifestations as a problem unique to Western capitalistic societies. Therefore, juvenile delinquency, including participation in street gangs, was not evident in the Soviet Union.

However, following the dissolution of the Soviet Union, many Russian families were faced with economic difficulties. The lack of viable educational institutions and after-school activities in many areas, as well as the desires of many youths for Western goods, led youths into delinquent behavior, which included alcohol and drug abuse and involvement in crime.

Pilkington (1994) examined Liubertsy street gangs. Gang members were primarily male; more than half were usually under the age of 18; they participated in gang fights, thefts, robberies, and assaults, frequently on specific Westernized groups (for example, punk rockers); they were territorial; and they frequently prohibited the use of alcohol. They generally had one to three leaders, collected dues to support their activities, and sometimes were linked to organized crime. While many of the Liubertsy gang members were apolitical, Pilkington viewed them as protecting their culture from the decadent Western foreign influences.

Omel'chenko (1996) studied gangs in Ul'ianovsk and determined that three characteristics were specific to Russian youth gangs: (1) youth gangs were not formed on the basis of ethnicity; (2) little or no urban cultural infrastructure was in place in cities where gangs were prevalent; and (3) people working with delinquent youth included police, lawyers, and drug specialists, but no social workers. Youth at risk to join gangs were from single-parent, low-income families, with little education, and histories of domestic violence and drug and alcohol abuse.

Omel'chenko also studied female gang participation in Ul'ianovsk. She found that female gangs wore distinctive clothing, including wide pants, gaudy makeup, and bows in their hair. The female gangs had well-defined leadership and a simple structure, without many organizational levels. They were known to attack males attending a local military communications college. By 1993, Omel'chenko believes, all-female gangs no longer existed in Ul'ianovsk; members were absorbed into male gangs.

United Kingdom

The United Kingdom's experiences with gangs are somewhat similar to those of the United States. According to government and media reports in the United Kingdom, the number of youth gangs is increasing, along with the extent of their criminal activities. However, aside from government reports, little research has been conducted on gangs, their characteristics, and their criminal histories. The lack of a consistent definition of gangs in the United Kingdom also makes comparisons difficult. When studying various youth groups, some researchers refer to "cliques" or "criminal groups," which for their purposes may or may not be the same as youth gangs.

Some studies of gangs throughout the country have been conducted and reported. Using oral reports, Humphries (1981) examined street gangs in the United Kingdom. He determined that members of street gangs were working-class youths who believed they were discriminated against and were oppressed. Youths joined the gangs for friendship, for a feeling of belonging as a means to gain status, and because they had little else to do with their time. Studying patterns of violence, Humphries concluded that an inverse relationship existed between gang violence and the state of the economy, that is, as the economy declined, the amount of gang violence increased. When gang members were unable to purchase various goods because of their lack of income, they resorted to the commission of crime, primarily property crime, to obtain what they needed.

A more recent study was conducted by Stelfox (1998), who surveyed all police forces in the United Kingdom. Most police forces responded to the survey (48 out of 51); 16 forces reported gangs in their areas, and these were sent a second questionnaire requesting additional information. Profiles of 71 gangs were gathered; most gangs consisted of adult males between the ages of 25 and 29. Over one-half of the gang members were white, 25 percent of them were a mixture of ethnicities, and the remaining gangs were generally composed of a single ethnic group. One gang was composed primarily of females. Gangs were generally loosely structured, and many participated in drug distribution and other criminal activities.

Bennett and Holloway (2004) examined the extent of gang membership in England and Wales using data gathered from the New English and Welsh Arrestee Drug Abuse Monitoring program. They found that 15 percent of the arrestees were either current or past members of a gang, 4 percent (92) were current members, and 11 percent (300) were former gang members. Most were male (95 percent), white (75 percent), and under the age of 25 (61 percent). The researchers estimated that, based on their data, approximately 20,000 gang members were in England and Wales during 2000 and 2001.

Mares (2001) examined street gangs in three areas of Manchester between 1997 and 1998—Moss Side, Wythenshawe, and Salford. Moss Side was a poor neighborhood near the center of Manchester, and its gangs were violent, fought with other local gangs, and were deeply involved in the drug trade. They also participated in other crimes, such as car thefts, robberies, and protection rackets. Most members were Afro-Caribbean, between 10 and 30 years old, and saw gang membership as providing social relationships. Gang structures were loose, with little hierarchical structure and no defined leadership.

In Wythenshawe, another poor area of Manchester, Mares found a gang whose 25 members were primarily white, ranging in age from 14 to their early twenties, and including some females. Like the gangs in Moss Side, this gang had no defined organization or leadership. It was territorial and had minimal involvement in drug sales; its primary criminal activities included car theft, shoplifting, and extortion. Meanwhile, gangs in the Salford district, a working-class neighborhood, were territorial and violent. Members ranged in age from 10 to 25 years old and spent a great deal of effort in projecting an image of aggressive and criminal behavior. Their criminal activities included car theft, robbery, and drug sales.

The street gangs Mares observed demonstrated historical class relations throughout the country. As a member of the working class in the United Kingdom, an individual was expected to be "hard," that is, the individual was expected to be strong and tough. Street gangs provided the young working-class individuals in Manchester with an opportunity to establish an image of being hard (Mares 2001).

Another study of gangs in the Manchester area was conducted by Bullock and Tilley (2002). They gathered information from the Manchester police databases, conducted interviews with 23 males who were believed to be gang members, and held a focus group. They determined that Manchester had four major street gangs, each with between 26 and 67 members, most of whom were black and male. These gangs were involved with a variety of criminal activities, ranging from petty offenses, such as property crimes, to more serious criminal offenses.

Female gangs in South London were studied by Archer (1995). Most gang members were from single-parent families, joined when they were between the ages of 13 and 14 years, lived in the inner city, were of Afro-Caribbean ethnicity, and were not enrolled in school. They wore distinctive clothing that set them apart from nongang members as well as from members of other gangs. For example, gold sun visors, hot pink leggings, and red jackets were worn by the Peckham Girls gang.

Archer examined reasons why the girls joined gangs and found that their reasons were similar to many other gang members throughout the world: for a sense of membership or belonging, to earn the respect of their peers, to gain a feeling of power and control, and to control their territories. For example, members of one gang, the Gunners, focused their activities on attacking males who were known to have assaulted females in their neighborhood.

Gangs in Asia

Research on youth gangs has been conducted in some Asian countries, and news reports indicate the presence of gangs in other countries. Information concerning gangs is presented here for China, India, and Japan to provide a brief look at Asian gangs.

China

When we think about gangs in China, we usually think about triads. The term *triad* refers to a variety of criminal groups that began with a tradition of resistance within China, supposedly during the late 1800s and early 1900s, when several Shaolin monks organized a secret society to overthrow the Ch'ing dynasty. The group was referred to as Tiandihui (Heaven and Earth Society) or Sanhehui (Three Harmonies Society). In 1911, the Ch'ing dynasty was overthrown and the Tiandihui were no longer needed. However, they continued to exist and turned to extortion and other illegal activities to support themselves. Once the Communist Party took control of the country in 1949, most of the triad activity was stopped, and many of the groups moved to Hong Kong.

In 2007, more than 57 triad groups in Hong Kong exist; some are highly organized criminal enterprises, while others are little more than local street gangs. Triads also exist in Taiwan, Macau, Europe, South Africa, Australia, and North America. They are usually highly structured, ranging from low-level gang members to officers.

While some gangs identify with the triads, most youth gangs are not the same as triads. They may, however, be organized around traditional triad principles. "Triads often viewed the performance of street gang members as a probationary period before full triad membership" (Matheron 1988). Chu (2000) explained that in China "there is a tendency for youths to group themselves into gangs, whose members profess triad affiliation to achieve recognition of their power and to intensify their illegal activities. . . . However, they have no true allegiance to any triad society" (26).

In studying Chinese gangs, Zhang et al. (1997) found that they were often composed of male youths from 15 to 25 years old, loosely organized, territorial, and often named based on their hometowns. Zhang and his colleagues did find that some gangs were fairly highly structured, with clear leaders and a detailed division of labor for certain criminal activities. The gang-related crime included burglary, larceny, and several other felonies, most often perpetrated by 16-year-olds.

India

Street gangs have a long history in India. From the Thugz, who first appeared around AD 1200, to the Thugees of the 19th and early 20th century, gangs roamed the countryside committing robberies, extortion, and murder. The Thugees claimed they were a religious sect, but they were heavily involved in these criminal activities. During the mid-19th century, other criminal gangs appeared, including the Goondas.

During the 1950s, Srivastava (1955) studied gangs in Bombay and reported that youths joined gangs based on their caste. These gangs were loosely organized; were short lasting; and committed mostly petty crimes, including property crimes. In later research, Sidvha (1997) reported that youth gangs in Bombay were more organized than most Indian gangs and had ties to and support from local police.

Following interviews with 200 street gang members throughout India, Shukla (1982) reported that most criminal gangs were involved in property crimes and occasional violence against rival gangs. Gang members were generally male, between the ages of 16 and 21 years old, and lived in urban areas. They were organized according to the Indian caste system, with members of each gang from the same caste; victims were also generally of the same caste. Gangs included the leader and core members, peripheral members, and fringe/associate members. The gangs fought each other over territory but also cooperated with each other, especially when police tried to intervene in or suppress their activities.

Grennan et al. (2000) observed that youths who joined gangs in India between the ages of 16 and 18 years were frequently unemployed and had a history of participation in criminal activities. Gangs were primarily involved in street-level crimes but also were hired by politicians running for office to influence voters, to help control labor unions, and to intimidate competitors of certain businesses.

Japan

Gangs were first observed in Japan following the attack on Hiroshima in 1945. Groups of orphaned youth joined together for survival, participating in both legal and illegal activities to survive (Jungk 1959). Once World War II ended, gangs of delinquent youths began to appear. Property crimes were the most common type of crime committed by gang members. These gangs were similar to European-style gangs and formed in response to societal stresses placed on them and their families as Japan recovered from the war (Grennan et al. 2000).

Kersten (1993) asserts that modern youth gangs in Japan are similar to street gangs in Western countries. Gang members are usually males between the ages of 14 and 20 years and project images of toughness, masculine power, and rebellion against authorities and conformists. Gangs are fairly loosely organized, primarily for social rebellion against the mainstream society, rather than for economic or criminal reasons. As part of this social rebellion, gang members have distinctive hairstyles and clothing choices.

Gangs in Australia and New Zealand

Australia

While street gangs do exist in Australia, they do not appear to be as prevalent as in other industrialized countries. According to some researchers, juvenile delinquency and gang behavior are not always related. Daniels (1977) reported that juvenile delinquency in Australia was not generally gang based. Groups of youths generally had little or no organizational structure and did not have permanent or continuing membership (Klein 1995).

Gangs have been known about and studied in Australia since at least the 1940s. Street and school gangs from 1946 to 1956 were studied by Bessant and Watts (1992). They found these gangs were focused on territory and honor, and they resorted to violent behavior when either was threatened. Gang members ranged in age from 12 to 18 years, were from the same ethnic groups, and focused on territory. They generally wore distinctive clothing, including tartan shirts, t-shirts, and zoot suits. Gang members believed in honor, toughness, and masculinity. Greek and Italian immigrants were often targeted by the gangs for violence because they were seen as a challenge (Bessant and Watts 1992).

Similar to results from other studies throughout the world, researchers have found that media reports of gang involvement and gang violence may inflame community fears and beliefs about gangs. Australian communities appeared to have overreacted during the early 1990s, when they imposed strict curfews on youth in many areas (Bessant 1994). A small sample of Arabic-speaking young men who immigrated to Australia were interviewed by Poynting, Noble, and Tabar (1999); these youths believed that the public outrage over gangs was created by the media and that the stereotypes they perpetuated only escalated racism throughout the country.

According to most of the literature, research, and law enforcement agency reports on gangs in Australia, most gangs are composed of ethnic minorities and Aboriginal groups, not white Australians. Brisbane gangs include Pacific Islanders, Vietnamese, and Aboriginal homeless young men, along with some white Australians (Haberfield 2000).

Most gangs apparently are not highly structured. After studying gangs and gang activity in Australia, the Australian Bureau of Criminal Intelligence (ABCI) concluded that even though some gangs could be identified and were involved in criminal activity, most of the crime committed by these groups was not highly organized but more opportunistic (ABCI 1991). In other research, the Standing Committee of Social Issues in the New South Wales Legislative Council (1995) could not find any evidence of highly structured gangs in Australia.

White and his colleagues (1999), in a study of gangs in Melbourne, found a great deal of "confusion and ambiguity over the difference between 'gangs' and 'groups'" (White et al. 1999). Most were ethnic-based gangs; their members were primarily male, although some females were engaged in gang-related behaviors; and they were most often involved in muggings and auto theft.

Law enforcement agencies in many areas of Australia are concerned about Vietnamese gangs. These gangs have been involved in drug distribution, gambling, extortion, home invasions, and other criminal activities. Vietnamese gang members in Australia, as in the United States, frequently victimize members of their own communities. Vietnamese gangs, including the 5T and the 108 gangs, in Sydney were often well organized and heavily involved in heroin sales; they also victimized members of their own communities (Covey 2003).

Youths from Hong Kong have also formed or joined gangs in Australia. During 1997, Australia saw an increase in immigrants from Hong Kong once Hong Kong came under Chinese rule. Law enforcement agencies believe that some of the triads that operated in Hong Kong have come to Australia (Goldworthy 1998).

Some researchers have reported the use of the terms *Bodgies* and *Widgies* to identify some youth street gangs in Australia (Bessant and Watts 1992; Short and Strodtbeck 1974). These gangs copied American-style clothing and popular music from American films as their own style.

New Zealand

A variety of street gangs exist in New Zealand, including skin-head, bikie (motorcycle), white power, ethnic, and triad gangs (Winter 1998). While many of the gangs are formed to provide members with friendship and a sense of belonging, some have been formed with a focus on criminal and other antisocial and il-legal activities (Covey 2003).

Gangs began appearing in New Zealand following World War II, when many structural and economic issues arose and metropolitan areas experienced high growth following the mi-gration of rural families to the cities in search of employment (Winter 1998). In the mid-1960s, Maori gangs were seen as a growing crime problem, and by the early 1980s, they were ex-panding their illegal activities. According to Neil Cameron (1983), the Maori gangs were viewed as unified groups challeng-ing traditional and European cultural values and customs. The attention paid to the Maori gangs was fueled by news coverage that fostered negative stereotypes of Maori males, including gang members, who were seen as more likely to commit violent crimes.

The 1960s saw the growth of two major gangs, the Mongrel Mob and Black Power. The Mongrel Mob got its name after a magistrate judge called them "a pack of mongrels." Both gangs have approximately 145 "chapters" that include 2,600 members, primarily Maori youth. Initiation ceremonies require that prospective members prove that they are worthy of joining the gang, and include a wide variety of tests ranging from mild to se-vere, such as drinking urine to committing a specific crime or serving time in jail. Once the individual becomes a gang member, he has earned the right to wear the gang's emblem, known as "patching" (Callinan 2007).

During the 1990s, law enforcement agencies saw another in-crease in gang numbers and illegal activities. Gangs were adopt-ing the names, the characteristics, and many of the activities of American gangs, including drive-by shootings, bombings, and fights between gangs. Law enforcement agencies during this period observed three types of gangs: ethnic, motorcycle, and youth. They have seen a particularly large growth of youth gangs, primarily on the North Island (Macko 1996).

Today, the most prominent gangs include the Mongrel Mob, Black Power, and Nomad; most gang participants are youths from Maori and Pacific Island backgrounds. Many of the gang members wear distinctive patches, gang colors, and tattoos. Their activities include the selling and distribution of drugs, firearm possession, and threatening and intimidating behavior. Local street gangs imitate the behavior of American street gangs, including participating in criminal activities such as robbery and burglary; however, the existence of street gangs often is short, either because the gang members end up in prison or because they decide to get out of the gang life.

In examining female participation in gangs, Eggleston (1997) found that females did participate in gangs in Auckland. Most of the gangs she examined were made up of Maori youth. She determined that many of the male gang members physically abused the female members, raping them, beating them, and generally treating them as sex objects. Male gang members saw the females only as peripheral players in the gang, noting that if a female was the girlfriend of a male gang member, she was considered a member of the gang.

Law enforcement agencies and other community organizations in New Zealand focus their activities on prevention. Programs were established to provide gang members or at-risk youth with jobs. Some gangs, including the Black Power and Mongrel Mob gangs, tried to work with the government by urging cooperation and concessions from law enforcement, although many thought the gangs were manipulating law enforcement and not truly sincere in changing their ways or giving up their criminal activities (Winter 1998).

Gangs in Africa

Although Africa is the least urbanized area in the world, many countries in Africa are experiencing a huge growth in urban areas, as more people are moving to the cities in search of jobs and other economic opportunities not found in the rural areas.

One of the consequences of this rapid urbanization is a growing number of street children and gangs.

In 1992, the Organization of African Unity (OAU) estimated that there were 16 million street children in Africa. The OAU expected this number to double by 2000 (OAU/UNICEF 1992). Approximately one-half of the population in Africa is 18 years old or younger. The impact of this statistic on each country's infrastructure, social services, and economic sector is incredible; as these children become adults, they will hit a job market that is not prepared to handle all, or even most, of them. In the meantime, many of these children may join gangs—for protection and survival.

Extensive research on street gangs has not been conducted in many African countries; with more severe problems facing them, such as drought, famine, civil war, and HIV/AIDS, the study of gangs is not seen as a high-priority issue. This section provides country-specific information on gangs for several African countries.

Kenya

More than 70 different tribes live in Kenya, many of which have subgroups within the main tribe. Recent years have seen the migration of numerous individuals and families to urban areas in search of jobs and other economic opportunities not often available in rural areas. This migration has contributed to the blurring of tribal connections, as has intermarriage. The movement of large numbers of people to the urban areas has also contributed to the growth of youth gangs in those areas.

According to UN-HABITAT, criminal youth gangs are increasing in numbers and influence in Nairobi, a city that has experienced extensive growth in its population and a concomitant increase in violent crime. The majority of crimes are committed by youths; more than half of all convicted criminals are between the ages of 16 and 25 years (UN-HABITAT 2007).

One of the major youth gangs is an outgrowth of the Mungiki movement, which began in the 1980s. It started as a religious movement, reportedly inspired by the Mau Mau rebellion against British rule in the 1950s, and focused on traditional practices. Thousands of Kenyan youth joined the movement, which over time evolved from a group of youths known for tobacco sniffing, dreadlocks, and facing Mount Kenya while praying to groups of youths who committed various violent crimes. The group was banned in 2002, although many authorities believe it is still in existence, with its members wearing business suits and short hair but continuing to commit a variety of crimes, including murder, extortion, robbery, and kidnapping. It is seen as a highly organized underworld gang; according to Ken Ouko, a sociology lecturer at the University of Nairobi, it is a "politically motivated gang of youths. . . . The religious bit is just a camouflage. It's more like an army unit" (BBC News 2003).

In a study of Nairobi street children, Shorter and Onyancha (1999) found that some youths joined gangs for survival; gangs provided protection to the youths from the harsh life on the streets, gave them a sense of belonging, and provided them with the basic necessities of food and shelter. The researchers found that the average age of gang members was 14 years old, they were involved in drug use and robbery, and they were extremely territorial. Initiation rites included teasing, fighting, and tests of endurance. Shorter and Onyancha also noticed that gang members often worked cooperatively by sharing food, shelter, and economic gains with other gang members and by acting as surrogate families for each other.

Females were sometimes allowed to join gangs, but they were likely to be sexually abused by male gang members. They often were involved in prostitution in order to provide income to the gang (Covey 2003).

The Kenyan government's response to street gangs has been limited. Recycling centers have been set up to provide job training and income to gang members, and some local agencies are working to provide street youth with health care, provide job training, and act as surrogate families to gang members and other at-risk youth. The Urban Management Programme of UNICEF has recommended that organizations such as Big Brothers Big Sisters be set up to provide positive role models for the youths and that the government and private agencies attempt to encourage the youths to be part of the solution by involving them in discussions identifying problems and working out solutions (Urban Management Programme 2000).

Similar to youths in other countries, some young Kenyans are able to escape the gang life. Joseph Oyoo is one such youth, who avoided the gang life through his music. Better known as Gidigidi, he lived in the slums of Nairobi before becoming part of one of Kenya's most well-known bands, along with fellow musician Julius Owino. See Chapter 5 for a biographical sketch of Joseph Oyoo.

Nigeria

Following the end of the Nigerian civil war in 1970, Nigerians saw an increasing number of youth gangs. Some researchers attributed this growth to the loss of traditional cultures following the war, while others saw it as a result of lack of economic opportunities for many people and an abundance of weapons that became available after the war (Oruwari 2006). Nigerian organized crime syndicates are fairly well known throughout the world. Many street gangs have participated in organized crime activities since the 1970s (Grennan et al. 2000).

Street gangs, also referred to as "area boys" in Lagos, are involved in petty criminal activities such as theft and drug distribution. Other gangs are recruited by politicians to attack opposing candidates, persuade the public to vote for their candidate, and employ other intimidation tactics, along with rigging elections (Human Rights Watch 2007).

In a study of gangs in Port Harcourt, Oruwari (2006) found that gangs were organized around certain streets or neighborhoods and emerged as a result of ethnic youth groups trying to protect themselves from other ethnic groups. The city attempted to ban many of the 103 gangs and cults that existed in Port Harcourt, but this effort has not been effective. The Niger Delta Vigilante Group is one of the more well-known gangs. It is highly structured, and its members participate in murders and other criminal activities. Female members generally take care of the male members and often provide free sex to male gang members.

Many urban gang members have tattoos that are usually acquired during initiation ceremonies and serve to help identify members of the same gang to each other. Potential gang members join either voluntarily or by being kidnapped. Most gang members are from low-income backgrounds with no job opportunities or experience. They are between the ages of 15 and 35, with the older members acting as consultants and strategists (Oruwari 2006).

Law enforcement agencies have been fairly ineffective in combating these gangs. Some communities are fearful of the police and believe that they will have to protect themselves, because the police will not be able or willing to protect them. Some areas have created their own vigilante groups for protection against gangs. The military has sometimes been brought in to help curb violent gang activity, but this tactic has also proven fairly ineffective.

South Africa

Street gangs have existed in South Africa since at least the beginning of the 1900s, if not earlier. Glaser (2000) has traced the history of many of the gangs from various townships through the 1970s, and has detailed the history of the male South African street gangs known as *tsotsi* or *bo-tsotsi* from the 1930s through the 1950s. Members of these gangs were black males from working-class, urban areas and from the same geographical location. Females were allowed to become members but played a secondary role to the male gang members; they usually were used as spies and sex objects and assisted the males in their criminal activities. These gangs were highly territorial, protecting their turf from rival gangs. They engaged in criminal activities, including pickpocketing, robbery, kidnapping, rape, and murder (Glaser 2000).

The South African apartheid system classified people as either black, white, coloured, or Indian. The coloured group was the most diverse and heterogeneous of all groups, consisting of all the individuals not fitting into one of the other categories. In 1950, the Group Areas Act dismantled a mixed-race area in central Cape Town known as District Six and relocated the residents to areas in Cape Flats that historically were set aside for coloureds. This relocation resulted in young men competing for limited resources and territory and led to the development of several gangs. Crime rates have increased over the years, and in 2003, the highest crime and homicide rates were in Western Cape Province, which includes Cape Town, and the homicide rate among the coloured population was the highest in the country (Beinart 2001; Covey 2003).

Following the Soweto riots in 1976, many black youths found themselves drawn into political causes and the use of violence as a means to gain equality. The national economy, which had been strong during the 1960s, was slowing down. Apartheid was beginning to be challenged by many countries around the world, with anti-apartheid movements growing in the United States and Europe. The liberation struggle was involving more and more blacks, and many young people were postponing their education in favor of joining the struggle for liberation. In 1991, apartheid laws were repealed. Nelson Mandela was freed from prison and become South Africa's president in 1994.

A large division still exists between black and white South Africans in terms of educational, income, and housing opportunities, and many young blacks are frustrated with this division and their lack of opportunity. Some believe that joining a gang and participating in criminal activities that provide income opportunities for them is justified. Many postponed their education to join the liberation struggle and still see little progress toward economic equality. They have grown up with violence, and many see it as a normal solution to their problems. Gangs control neighborhoods in several urban areas through violence, property destruction, and murder. A number of gangs are involved in drug distribution, which led to fights over territory (Naude 2001). According to Pinnock (1997), youth gangs have replaced traditional society's rites of passage for many South African youth.

Conclusion

As can be seen from the material presented in this chapter, many countries have problems with gangs similar to those experienced in the United States. Some countries have a long history of gangs, such as China's triads. Other countries, such as El Salvador, have only recently seen youth gangs appear.

As the world becomes smaller, in the sense that travel is easier and information can be communicated around the globe in a matter of minutes through the Internet, the gang presence will continue to grow in many areas. With immigrants and refugees establishing themselves and their families in new countries, they may bring gang involvement with them, or their children may find the need to form a gang for protection in response to racial discrimination. Ethnic differences and wars may lead to the formation of gangs, along with struggling economies, rural migration into urban areas, lack of education and employment opportunities for young people, and lack of infrastructure in many countries to help these families and individuals escape poverty. A global approach to sharing information may be an effective means of dealing with gang issues throughout the world.

References

Archer, Debbie. 1995. "Riot GRRRL and Raisin Girl: Femininity within the Female Gang—The Power of the Popular." *The British Criminology Conferences: Selected Proceedings,* vol. 1, [Online article; retrieved 5/13/08.] http://www.britsoccrim.org/volume1/002.pdf.

Astwood Strategy Corporation. 2004. *Results of the 2002 Canadian Police Survey on Youth Gangs.* Toronto: Astwood Strategy Corporation.

Australian Bureau of Criminal Intelligence (ABCI), Strategic Analysis Section. 1991. *Australian Youth Gang Assessment.* Canberra: ABCI.

Barron, S. W., and D. Tindall. 1993. "Network Structure and Delinquent Attitudes with a Juvenile Gang." *Social Networks* 15:255–273.

BBC News. 2003. "Profile: Kenya's Secretive Mungiki Sect." [Online article; retrieved 05/13/08.] http://news.bbc.co.uk/2/hi/africa/2745421.stm.

Beinart, William. 2001. *Twentieth-Century South Africa.* New York: Oxford University Press.

Bennett, Trevor, and Katy Holloway. 2004. "Gang Membership, Drugs and Crime in the UK." *British Journal of Criminology* 44:305–323.

Bergman, B. 1995. "Wild in the Streets." *Maclean's* 108:18–19.

Bessant, J. 1994. "The American Juvenile Underclass and the Cultural Colonization of Young Australians under Conditions of Modernity." *Journal of Gang Research* 2:15–33.

Bessant, J., and R. Watts. 1992. "Being Bad Is Good: Explorations of the Bodgie Gang Culture in Southeast Australia, 1946–1956." *The Gang Journal* 1:31–55.

Bing, Leon. 1991. *Do or Die.* New York: HarperCollins.

Bullock, K., and N. Tilley. 2002. *Shootings, Gangs and Violent Incidents in Manchester: Developing a Crime Reduction Strategy.* Crime Reduction Research Series, Paper 13. London: Home Office.

Callinan, Rory. 2007. "Tribal Trouble." [Online article; retrieved 4/16/08.] http://www.time.com/time/magazine/article/0,9171,1640583,00.html.

Cameron, Neil. 1983. "New Zealand." In *International Handbook of Contemporary Developments in Criminology,* edited by E. H. Johnson. Westport, CT: Greenwood Press.

Campbell, Monica. 2007. "The Shadow of War." *Amnesty International* 33 (4): 14–18.

Castillo, Jose Guillermo. 2007. "Violence in Central America: Briefing and Hearing before the Subcommittee on the Western Hemisphere of the

House Committee on Foreign Affairs." Testimony of Jose Guillermo Castillo, Ambassador of Guatemala, to the 110th Congress.

Chu, Y. K. 2000. *The Triads as Business.* London: Routledge.

Covey, Herbert C. 2003. *Street Gangs throughout the World.* Springfield, IL: Charles C. Thomas.

Criminal Intelligence Service Canada (CISC). 2006. *2006 Annual Report on Organized Crime in Canada.* Ottawa: CISC.

Criminal Intelligence Service Saskatchewan. 2005. "2005 Intelligence Trends: Aboriginal-based Gangs in Saskatchewan." *Criminal Intelligence Service Saskatchewan* 1 (1): 1–8.

Daniels, P. 1977. "How Relevant Are Delinquency Theories?" In *Delinquency in Australia: A Critical Appraisal,* edited by P. Wilson. St. Lucia, Australia: University of Queensland Press.

DeFleur, L. B. 1970. *Delinquency in Argentina: A Study of Córdoba's Youth.* Pullman: Washington State University.

Dimenstein, G. 1991. *Brazil's War on Children.* London: Latin American Bureau.

Eddleman, Linda H. 2007. "Violence in Central America: Briefing and Hearing before the Subcommittee on the Western Hemisphere of the House Committee on Foreign Affairs." Testimony of Linda Eddleman, Executive Director of the Trust for the Americas, to the 110th Congress.

Eggleston, E. J. 1997. "Boys' Talk: Exploring Gender Discussions with New Zealand Male Youth Gang Members." *Caribbean Journal of Criminology and Social Psychology* 2:100–114.

Flores, Roberto. 2007. "Violence in Central America: Briefing and Hearing before the Subcommittee on the Western Hemisphere of the House Committee on Foreign Affairs." Testimony of Roberto Flores Bermudez, Ambassador of Honduras, to the 110th Congress.

Glaser, Clive. 2000. *Bo-Tsotsi—The Youth Gangs of Soweto, 1935–1976.* Portsmouth, NH: Henneman.

Goldworthy, T. 1998. "Triad Activity in Australia." *Lawnet Journal,* January 7.

Gordon, Robert M. 1998. "Street Gangs and Criminal Business Organizations: A Canadian Perspective." In *Gangs and Youth Subcultures: International Explorations,* edited by Kayleen and Cameron Hazlehurst. New Brunswick, NJ: Transaction.

Gordon, Robert M. 2002. "Bossing Mom's Big Boy: Gregory Wooley Made It to the Top." *Montreal Gazette,* April 1, A6.

Grennan, S., M. T. Britz, J. Rush, and T. Barker. 2000. *Gangs: An International Approach.* Upper Saddle River, NJ: Prentice-Hall.

Haberfield, I. 2000. "Gangstas in Paradise—Fear of Street Warfare." *Sunday Mail,* February 13, 4.

Huizinga, David, and Karl F. Schumman. 2001. "Gang Membership in Bremen and Denver: Comparative Longitudinal Data." In *The Eurogang Paradox: Street Gangs and Youth Groups in the U.S. and Europe,* edited by Malcolm W. Klein, Hans-Jurgen Kerner, Cheryl Maxson, and Elmar G. M. Weitekamp. Boston: Kluwer Academic.

Human Rights Watch. 2007. *Criminal Politics: Violence, 'Godfathers' and Corruption in Nigeria.* New York: Human Rights Watch.

Human Rights Watch/Americas. 1994. *Generation under Fire: Children and Violence in Colombia.* New York: Human Rights Watch.

Humphries, Stephen. 1981. *Hooligans or Rebels? An Oral History of Working Class Childhood and Youth 1889–1939.* Oxford: Basil Blackwell.

Jungk, R. 1959. *Children of the Ashes.* New York: Harcourt, Brace, and World.

Kersten, Joachim. 1993. "Street Youths, Bosozoku, and Yakuza: Subculture Formation and Social Reactions in Japan." *Crime and Delinquency* 39 (3): 277–295.

Klein, Malcolm W. 1995. *The American Street Gang.* New York: Oxford University Press.

Klein, Malcolm. W. 2001. "Gangs in the United States and Europe." in *The Modern Gang Reader,* edited by J. Miller, C. L. Maxson, and M. W. Klein. Los Angeles: Roxbury.

Kuasñosky, S., and D. Szulik. 1996. "Desde los Márgenes de la Juventud." In *La Juventud es Mas que una Palabra: Ensayos sobre Cultura y Juventud,* edited by M. Margulis. Buenos Aires: Editorial Biblos.

Lamm, Z. 1993. "Life in a Brazilian Slum." *Swiss Review of World Affairs* December: 13–15.

Le Blanc, M., and N. Lanctôt. 1994. "Adolescent Gang Members' Social and Psychological Characteristics, Gang Participation: A Selection or Activation Process." Paper presented at the Annual Meeting of the American Society of Criminology, Miami, November.

Lien, Inger-Lise. 2001. "The Concept of Honor, Conflict and Violent Behavior among Youths in Oslo." In *The Eurogang Paradox: Street Gangs and Youth Groups in the U.S. and Europe,* edited by Malcolm W. Klein, Hans-Jurgen Kerner, Cheryl Maxson, and Elmar G. M. Weitekamp, 165–174. Boston: Kluwer Academic.

Mackenzie, Andrew, and Sara L. Johnson. 2003. "A Profile of Women Gang Members in Canada." Ottawa: Correctional Service of Canada.

Macko, Steve. 1996. "Street Gangs Come to the South Pacific." [Online article; retrieved 4/16/08.] http://www.emergency.com/nz-gangs.htm.

Mares, D. 2001. "Gangstas or Lager Louts? Working Class Street Gangs in Manchester." In *The Eurogang Paradox: Street Gangs and Youth Groups in the U.S. and Europe,* edited by Malcolm W. Klein, Hans-Jurgen Kerner, Cheryl Maxson, and Elmar G. M. Weitekamp. Boston: Kluwer Academic.

Matheron, M. S. 1988. "China: Chinese Triads, the Oriental Mafia." *CJ International* 4 (3): 3, 4, 26–27.

Mathews, F. 1999. *Youth Gangs on Youth Gangs.* Adelaide, Australia: First International Youth Service Models Conference.

Mellor, Brian, Leslie MacRae, Monica Pauls, and Joseph P. Hornick. 2005. *Youth Gangs in Canada: A Preliminary Review of Programs and Services.* Calgary: Canadian Research Institute for Law and the Family.

Moser, Caroline, and Jeremy Holland. 1997. *Urban Poverty and Violence in Jamaica.* Washington, DC: World Bank.

Naude, Beaty. 2001. "South Africa." In *Teen Violence: A Global View,* edited by Allan M. Hoffman and Randal W. Summers, 145–157. Westport, CT: Greenwood Press.

New South Wales Legislative Council. 1995. *A Report into Youth Violence in New South Wales.* Sydney: Standing Committee on Social Issues, Parliament of New South Wales.

Omel'chenko, Elena. 1996. "Young Women in Provincial Gang Culture: A Case Study of Ul'ianovsk." In *Gender, Generation, and Identity in Contemporary Russia,* edited by H. Pilkington. London: Routledge.

Organization of African Unity (OAU) and United Nations Children's Fund (UNICEF). 1992. *Africa's Children, Africa's Future: Background Sectoral Papers,* 25–27. Dakar, Senegal: OAU.

Oruwari, Yomi. 2006. "Youth in Urban Violence in Nigeria: A Case Study of Urban Gangs from Port Harcourt." Port Harcourt, Nigeria: Our Niger Delta.

Pilkington, Hilary. 1994. *Russia's Youth and Its Culture: A Nation's Constructor and Constructed.* London: Routledge.

Pinnock, Don. 1997. *Gangs, Ritual, and Rights of Passage.* Cape Town: African Sun Press.

Poynting, S., G. Noble, and P. Tabar. 1999. "Intersections of Masculinity and Ethnicity: A Study of Male Lebanese Immigrant Youth in Western Sydney." *Race, Ethnicity and Education* 2:59–77.

Reisman, Lainie. 2007. "Violence in Central America: Briefing and Hearing before the Subcommittee on the Western Hemisphere of the House

Committee on Foreign Affairs." Testimony of Lainie Reisman to the 110th Congress.

Ribando, Clare M. 2007. *CRS Report for Congress: Gangs in Central America.* Washington, DC: Congressional Research Service.

Rodgers, Dennis. 1999. *Youth Gangs and Violence in Latin America and the Caribbean: A Literature Survey.* Washington, DC: World Bank.

Rodgers, Dennis. 2003. "From Primitive Socialism to Primitive Accumulation: Gangs, Violence, and Social Change in Urban Nicaragua, 1997–2002." *CERLAC Bulletin* 2 (3): 1–6.

Salazar, A. 1990. *Born to Die in Medellín,* translated by N. Casitor. London: Latin America Bureau.

Shakur, Sanyika. 1993. *Monster: The Autobiography of an L.A. Gang Member.* New York: Grove Press.

Short, J. F., Jr., and F. L. Strodtbeck. 1974. *Group Process and Gang Delinquency.* Chicago: University of Chicago Press.

Shorter, Aylward, and Edwin Onyancha. 1999. *Street Children in Africa.* Nairobi, Kenya: Paulines Publications Africa.

Shukla, K. S. 1982. "Adolescent Criminal Gangs: Structure and Functions." *International Journal of Critical Sociology* 5:35–49.

Sidvha, S. 1997. "Mafia Metropolis." *Far Eastern Economic Review* 160:21, 24, 28.

Srivastava, S. S. 1955. "Sociology of Juvenile Ganging." *Journal of Correctional Work* 2:72–81.

Stelfox, P. 1998. "Policing Lower Levels of Organised Crime in England and Wales." *Howard Journal* 37 (4): 393–406.

Stevns, A. 2001. "Street Gangs and Crime Prevention in Copenhagen." In *The Eurogang Paradox: Street Gangs and Youth Groups in the U.S. and Europe,* edited by Malcolm W. Klein, Hans-Jurgen Kerner, Cheryl Maxson, and Elmar G. M. Weitekamp. Boston: Kluwer Academic.

Tibaijuka, Anna Kajumulo. 2005. "The Emerging Global Order: The City as a Catalyst for Stability and Sustainability." [Online remarks; retrieved 4/16/08.] http://www.unhabitat.org/print.asp?cid=5389&catid=14&typeid=8.

United Nations Children's Fund (UNICEF). N.d. "Through Theatre and Music, Rival Gangs in Guatemala Make Peace." [Online article; retrieved 4/16/08.] http://www.unicef.org/adolescence/guatemala_1943.html.

United Nations Educational, Scientific and Cultural Organization (UNESCO) Institute for Statistics. 2005. *Statistics in Brief: Education in Nicaragua.* Montreal: UNESCO Institute for Statistics.

United Nations Human Settlement Programme (UN-HABITAT). 2007. "Nairobi: Crime and the City." Crime and Violence City Case Studies press release. Nairobi, Kenya: UN-HABITAT.

Urban Management Programme. 2000. *Street Children and Gangs in African Cities.* Nairobi, Kenya: Urban Management Programme, United Nations Centre for Human Settlements.

U.S. Department of State, Agency for International Development (USAID). 2006. *Central America and Mexico Gang Assessment.* Washington, DC: USAID Bureau for Latin American and Caribbean Affairs.

Valenzuela, E. 1984. *La Rebelión de los Jovenes: Un Estudio sobre Anomia Social.* Santiago de Chile: Ediciones Sur.

Van Gemert, Frank. 2001. "Crips in Orange: Gangs and Groups in the Netherlands." In *The Eurogang Paradox: Street Gangs and Youth Groups in the U.S. and Europe,* edited by Malcolm W. Klein, Hans-Jurgen Kerner, Cheryl Maxson, and Elmar G. M. Weitekamp, 145–152. Boston: Kluwer Academic.

Washington Office on Latin America. 2006. *Youth Gangs in Central America: Issues in Human Rights, Effective Policing, and Prevention.* Washington, DC: Washington Office on Latin America.

White, Rob, S. Perrone, C. Guerra, and R. Lampugnani. 1999. *Ethnic Youth Gangs in Australia: Do They Exist?* Overview report. Melbourne: Australian Multicultural Foundation.

Winter, Pahmi. 1998. "Pulling the Teams Out of the Dark Room: The Politicisation of the Mongrel Mob." In *Gangs and Youth Subcultures: International Explorations,* edited by Kayleen and Cameron Hazlehurst. New Brunswick, NJ: Transaction.

Zhang, L., S. F. Messner, Z. Lu, and X. Deng. 1997. "Gang Crime and Its Punishment in China." *Journal of Criminal Justice* 33:359–387.

4

Chronology

This chapter provides a chronology of the significant events, cases, and statutes relevant to gangs, their purposes, and their development.

1200 The word *thug* originates in India. It comes from the name *Thugz*, which refers to a gang of criminals that wandered throughout India pillaging various towns along their route. The Thugz used their own symbols and hand signs to communicate and created their own rituals and slang.

1791 People living in Philadelphia complain about the problems created by young hooligans who travel around together and drink, fight, read sexually oriented material, experiment with sex, and steal.

1820s The first immigrants from Ireland start moving into the Five Points district of Manhattan, New York. Before this time, Five Points had been a relatively quiet and poor residential area. Gangs, composed primarily of young adults or older teenagers, start forming as a result of the poverty, dirty living conditions, and prejudice that these immigrants face. Each gang has its own colors, style of dress, and distinctive name, and each one uses a variety of weapons, including pistols, knives, brass knuckles, ice picks, and brickbats, in its wars with rival gangs.

1854 The New York Children's Aid Society issues its first annual report that discusses crime committed by juveniles

1854 in the city. The report notes that juvenile crime is in-
(cont.) creasing; that juveniles are well organized; and that they
have their own signs, their own language, special places
where they gather, their own special guards, and members who help entice or divert potential victims to their
area.

1870s In New York City, residents and members of the press are
worried about the growth of juvenile gangs who prowl
around, terrorize local citizens, and commit various
crimes. Going by such names as the Nineteenth Street
Gang and the Short Boys, these groups are affiliated with
political parties and local saloons. The gangs help get
their favorite politicians elected by using strong-arm tactics. Adults often lead juvenile gangs.

1898 Henry D. Sheldon, writing in the *American Journal of Psychology,* classifies gangs according to their primary purpose for organizing: secret clubs; predatory organizations;
social clubs; industrial associations; philanthropic associations; athletic clubs; and literary, artistic, and music organizations. Athletic clubs are the most popular, with
predatory organizations a distant second.

1900 Jewish and Chinese gangs move into and establish their
own territories in New York City.

1912 In his book *The Boy and His Gang,* J. Adams Puffer reports
on his study of 66 clubs and gangs. He finds that the two
types of groups are quite similar to each other; in fact, he
uses the two terms almost interchangeably. All clubs and
gangs have a specific purpose, such as to cause trouble,
to play games, to seek adventure, to steal, or to fight
against other gangs. Most gangs have their own territory; it might be a street corner, a club room, or a little
building in the woods. He also believes that most boys
have a deep need to join a group and that gangs are a
normal outgrowth of adolescence.

1926 Paul Furfey examines gangs and their basic characteristics. The gangs he studies are usually composed of juve-

niles between the ages of 10 and 14 years, are organized by local neighborhood, and are loosely structured. He finds that gangs composed of lower-class members are better integrated than other gangs and stay together as a gang longer. He concludes that most boys join gangs for economic reasons; that is, to make or get money.

1927   Frederic Thrasher, a leading authority on gang activity, writes *The Gang*, based on research he has conducted on 1,313 gangs in Chicago.

1931   The 42 Gang of Chicago is considered one of the most menacing juvenile gangs in the United States. Clifford Shaw and fellow University of Chicago sociologist Henry McKay study this gang, whose 42 tough juvenile members are known to murder police officers, stool pigeons, and robbery victims; strip cars; hold up nightclubs; and kill horses. They are described as a typical scavenger gang. Many members graduate into the Capone mob. Shaw and McKay discover that a gang member achieves high status by being sent to the reformatory.

Shaw and McKay write *Social Factors in Juvenile Delinquency: Report on the Causes of Crime,* a monograph on juvenile delinquency and gangs. They discuss the social forces that lead young people to join gangs.

1939   Frank Tannenbaum writes *Crime and the Community,* in which he describes how early members of Chicago gangs graduate into committing more serious criminal acts. Groups that start off as play gangs with members stealing apples or shoplifting may eventually develop into gangs that steal cars, commit robbery, and sometimes murder. Tannenbaum notes the important role the family plays in whether or not a child becomes delinquent.

1940s   Many researchers begin to study juvenile gangs in New York City, primarily in response to growing concern among local citizens that juveniles are joining gangs in increasing numbers and are becoming more violent than in the past.

1942   Many researchers respond to the increasing concern about juvenile crime and the role that gangs play in this crime. Shaw and McKay publish their theory of cultural transmission as an explanation for juvenile delinquency. They believe that living in disadvantaged environments, the lack of social controls, and one group passing on their knowledge to others about crime lead youngsters to participate in criminal activities.

1943   During World War II, many residents of the Mexican American neighborhoods of Los Angeles experience prosperity for the first time. These Mexican Americans develop a sense of ethnic pride and, as a result, begin to see the types and extent of discrimination they face because of their ethnicity. Many children of these families join gangs and develop their own style of dress and language; this pachuco style includes wearing flamboyant zoot-suit clothing and using a hybrid English/Spanish slang. Many of these gangs are nonviolent and do not get into trouble with the law. However, the media focus on the zoot suits that many young men are wearing. As racial tensions increase, fights break out between youths and U.S. sailors. For several nights, groups of sailors bent on vengeance drive through the barrios and attack the youths while the police, some say, look the other way. Because the police do not help, the youths feel the need to protect their territory from the sailors by responding to the violence shown on the part of the sailors.

William Foote Whyte studies juveniles in gangs and believes that gang members are searching for prestige, support from others, and reassurance from other gang members that they are accepted and valuable. These needs, he says, result from a lack of economic opportunity for young gang members. Life for many of these young men is hard, with limited opportunities to succeed in the larger society. Whyte contends that juvenile gangs are not as violent as many people believe and that they do conform in large part to the ideas of society.

1946   New York City is overwhelmed by violent street gang activity such as vicious and apparently senseless murders.

In a special effort known as the detached-worker program, youth workers walk the streets with gang members. In a short time, the mayor of New York City creates a permanent agency, the New York City Youth Board, to reduce gang crime. The board produces a series of manuals and books in which it develops a concept of gang and gang behavior that is accepted by many similar programs throughout the country.

Sophia Robison and her colleagues study juvenile gangs in New York City's Harlem section and find that these juveniles are violent and are hostile toward anyone not in their gang. Not all gang members are involved in delinquent acts, however; usually only a core group of members commit crimes against people not in the gang. Most gang members are between the ages of 10 and 18 years, while the leaders are usually 15 to 20 years old. Gangs fight each other, and they steal, mug people, and extort money.

1947   Trained social workers begin to make contact with gang members in New York City, particularly in central Harlem, with the objective of changing the attitudes and behaviors of these youths. Workers are assigned to several gangs to help stop criminal activities such as fighting, stealing, smoking marijuana, and committing sexual offenses. As alternatives, workers organize athletic activities, block parties, camping trips, trips to the movies, and other positive activities. Paul Crawford, Daniel Malamud, and James Dumpson later publish a report on the results of these programs.

1949   William Bernard studies gangs in New York City and finds that most gangs have between 25 and 200 members, are age graded, and have both core and marginal members. Roles of individual gang members are clearly spelled out. Most gang members carry weapons but spend much of their time just hanging out with other members, not fighting other gangs. Bernard also studies female gang members in New York City and notes that female membership in gangs has increased. He finds that most girl gangs are affiliated with male gangs. Initiation

1949 rites usually require new members to have sex with male
(cont.) gang members.

In his study on gangs and gang behavior, Leonard Dunston finds that Harlem gangs are loosely structured, with the largest having no more than 100 members (Dunston 1990).

1950s Public awareness of gang activity grows. Researchers report that several of the larger gangs, such as the Blackstone Rangers of Chicago and the Latin Kings, have started organizing gang activity in smaller cities throughout the Midwest. Issues of territory, masculinity, and fighting ability become more important. Some gangs start using heroin, and the use of heroin increases in gangs whose members already use it.

Gangs start engaging in big fights, called rumbles, with their own set of rules. War councils meet to determine time, place, and weapons to be used for each rumble. Favorite weapons are bats, bricks, clubs, and chains.

1950 The Welfare Council of New York City publishes a report on its work with male gangs and their female affiliates in Harlem. The council finds that most girls who are involved in gangs and gang activities are sisters or friends of the male members, are sexually promiscuous, and commonly have illegitimate children as a result of their activities. The male gang members are more likely than the females to engage in illegal behavior, although the females admit to encouraging the males to break the law. The report depicts the girls as exploited by the male gang members.

1954 The Boston Delinquency Project is founded in an attempt to reduce juvenile delinquency and crime in a lower-class area. The basic objectives of this program are to shift the focus of street-corner gangs from criminal behavior to law-abiding behavior, improve the coordination of local social service agencies, and strengthen the family system. Agencies involved in these activities include the local government, police department, courts, public schools, recreation department, state youth corrections division, medical clinics, social work agencies, churches, universities, and a variety of special-cause groups. Field workers establish contact with almost 400 youths who are members of 21 street gangs. As a result of this project, coordination among community agencies is improved, although an evaluation of the project concludes that the law-abiding behavior of gang members does not increase significantly.

The movie *The Wild One,* starring Marlon Brando and Lee Marvin, debuts. Featuring an outlaw motorcycle gang, this movie is based on an actual incident in which a motorcycle gang terrorized and vandalized the town of Hollister, California, in 1947. In the movie, the Black Rebel Motorcycle Club enters the town of Carbonville, disrupts a legitimate motorcycle race, steals the race trophy, and moves on to another town, where it settles in. Another gang, the Beetles, once affiliated with the Rebels but now their bitter rivals, arrives in town. The movie creates a major controversy. In the United States, distribution problems arise because some people believe that young viewers will imitate the violence; in England, the movie is banned.

1955   Albert Cohen writes *Delinquent Boys: The Culture of the Gang,* one of the first scholarly monographs to focus on delinquency and gangs. Cohen discusses what juvenile delinquency is, where it can be found, and the conditions within American society that lead to it. He does not see gang behavior as different from general delinquent behavior and examines delinquency within the context of social forces that shape behavior.

The movie *Blackboard Jungle* depicts the difficult life of a high school teacher in a large metropolitan city. It stars Glenn Ford, Anne Francis, Sidney Poitier, Vic Morrow, Margaret Hayes, and Richard Kiley. The plot focuses on one of several gangs at an all-boys vocational school and the battles between delinquent boys and their teachers.

The movie *Rebel without a Cause,* starring James Dean, focuses on troubled and often delinquent youth. The

1955   movie depicts 24 hours in the life of Dean's character, Jim
(*cont.*) Stark, who has just started at a new high school. He en-
          counters a hostile group of students, has a knife fight
          with the leader of the group, and gets involved in a
          "chickie run" (two guys drive stolen cars at fast speed to-
          ward a cliff, and the winner is the last one to jump out).

1957   The Youth for Service program in San Francisco begins.
          It is one of the city's first "detached worker" or "gang
          worker" programs, in which the worker is literally de-
          tached from his or her desk and office and sent out in the
          streets to work with gangs. This particular program also
          employs gang members as workers in a variety of com-
          munity service projects throughout the city, including
          cleanup and repair projects.

1958   Most researchers believe that the Vice Lords have now
          organized in the Lawndale area of Chicago. Various sto-
          ries suggest that a group of boys residing at the Illinois
          State Training School for Boys have dropped their vari-
          ous gang affiliations and banded together to create the
          Vice Lords, which will become one of the toughest gangs
          in the city.

1960s   The Vice Lords incorporate as a nonprofit agency with
          8,000 members in 26 divisions. They initiate a variety of
          economic and community service projects, none of which
          are successful, according to some sources (Short 1990).

          The prevention of delinquency and gangs becomes a na-
          tional priority, as the press and the general public be-
          come more aware of gang activity. The Blackstone
          Rangers, the Devil's Disciples, and the Vice Lords be-
          come well known throughout the country. Many gangs
          become involved in the civil rights movement and in
          politics. Some gangs, such as the Vice Lords, the Black
          Panthers, the Young Lords, and the Black Liberation
          Army, offer a positive alternative to typical gang activity
          by becoming active in politics and civil rights activities.

1960   The New York City Youth Board issues a report on the re-
          sults of a comprehensive study of New York City youth

gangs. It examines a variety of youth groups, including street clubs and gangs, all of which have different structures and activities. Gang members studied range in age from 12 to 22 years and usually have an antagonistic relationship with the communities in which they live and hang out. They all have their own patterns of behavior and their own language.

The Chicago Youth Development Project is organized by the Chicago Boys Club. The project emphasizes aggressive work on the street and through community organization and focuses on groups rather than individuals. Organizers believe that if dedicated street workers take on youths at risk for a variety of gang and criminal behaviors, the number of youths in trouble with the law will decrease.

Richard Cloward and Lloyd Ohlin write *Delinquency and Opportunity: A Theory of Delinquent Gangs*. They say that legitimate and illegitimate opportunities exist in every community, and when young people believe that legitimate opportunities are not available to them, they turn to illegitimate opportunities for financial and emotional support. The researchers point out that being a young person in American society is difficult, and they see job training and job placement as critical elements in helping youths make the transition into adulthood.

1961   The Juvenile Delinquency and Youth Offenses Control Act is passed, in which the federal government becomes an active partner with states and local communities to prevent and control the spread of delinquency. The President's Committee on Juvenile Delinquency and Youth Crime is authorized by this act and is charged with controlling various forms of delinquency, including gangs.

The Los Angeles Group Guidance Project is developed under the auspices of the Los Angeles County Probation Department. As a four-year detached worker project, it emphasizes a group approach to stemming violence by organizing parent clubs and providing group counseling and group activities. The project attempts to change gang

1961   members' values, attitudes, and perceptions of gang par-
(*cont.*)   ticipation. However, gang activity does not decrease.

The movie *West Side Story* is released. It stars Natalie
Wood, Richard Beymer, Russ Tamblyn, Rita Moreno, and
George Chakiris. Highlighting the racial and social tensions of street-gang rivalry in New York City, the story
pits the Sharks against the Jets. Maria, who is Puerto
Rican, arrives in the slums of Manhattan's West Side. Her
brother is leader of the Sharks. Maria falls in love with
the former leader of the Jets, a white gang, and their love
affair provokes racial tension between the two gangs,
which plan a rumble. In the end, Maria's brother stabs
the leader of the Jets to death, then is himself stabbed to
death by her boyfriend, who is subsequently cornered
and killed by one of the Sharks.

1963   Lewis Yablonsky writes *The Violent Gang*. Along with
many other experts, Yablonsky believes that, for the most
part, youths who join gangs are not sociopathic or seriously disturbed, but rather are a product of their social
status; that is, most youths in 1963 join gangs because of
their low social status and their lack of opportunity, including educational, social, and economic, rather than
because they are crazy or unbalanced.

1964   Wah Ching (Youth of China) is the first foreign-born
gang organized by Chinese immigrants to protect themselves from American-born Chinese. By recruiting new
members among recent immigrants, this gang becomes
powerful.

Mobilization for Youth, a project focusing on a 67-block
area in the Lower East Side of New York City, begins. It
is founded on the premise that delinquent and criminal
acts committed by people, including youth, in low-
income groups are primarily a result of obstacles they encounter in trying to improve their social and economic
situation. This program stands out from many others because it helps impoverished residents of low-income
areas to help themselves. However, the program worries
many people because of its political activities; the Fed-

eral Bureau of Investigation (FBI) investigates those who participate in organized action, newspapers charge the project with subversion, project files are confiscated, and the use and effectiveness of federal as well as local funds are questioned. As Richard Quinney (1970) explains, "To provide the poor with services and assistance from above has been the traditional way of doing things. It is regarded as subversive when the poor attempt to change the social pattern of their poverty. Welfare is legitimate oppression, political action by the poor is anarchy" (202).

1965   The United States allows increased Chinese immigration, which adds many Chinese teenagers and their families to the U.S. population. Chinese communities cannot cope with the great influx of immigrants. Newcomers receive little help, and Chinese teenage participation in youth gangs increases.

1967   The Youth Manpower Project of the Woodlawn Organization in Chicago begins. It is a highly controversial project, costing $1 million, developed by the Community Action Program of the U.S. Office of Economic Opportunity. The project's major goals are to provide job training and referral, reduce gang violence, and reduce the risk of riots in gang areas. The staff includes the leaders of two major gangs: the East Side Disciples and the Blackstone Rangers. Members of each gang staff two training centers; with a professional training staff of only four people and approximately 30 young adults and 600 participating youths, the program is not successful in changing youth attitudes and values. The police, local community agencies, local legislators, national legislators, and the news media choose sides in praising or condemning the project, and it becomes so controversial that the government shuts it down.

1969   David "King David" Barksdale is shot in an ambush. He is the leader and founder of the Black Gangster Disciple Nation. The gang adopts the Jewish Star of David, along with upturned pitchforks, as its symbol. This gang is part of the Folk Nation group of gangs formed in response to the conglomerate Black P. Stone Nation, a group of gangs that control the Englewood area of Chicago.

1970   Gang activity and violence in the United States appear to subside. Cities find fewer incidences of gang violence, and studies of gang organization, characteristics, and activities do not appear with the same frequency as they did in the later 1950s and early 1960s. Many youth agencies refocus their attention on other problems, such as status offenses (which include curfew violations and running away from home) and pay less attention to problems with gangs.

About this time, more studies concerning female participation in gang activities are conducted. Several researchers begin to rely on female as well as male gang informants. Several studies show that the girls are primarily seen as sexual objects, that is, they are girlfriends of gang members or provide sex to gang members. Females also provide other services to the gang. A girl might lure rival gang members to an area where her gang members can hurt or kill them, or she might carry drugs or weapons for the male gang members because police officers are less likely to search young girls for these objects.

Current prison gangs, unlike prison gangs of earlier years, start forming in response to the number of street gang members in prison rather than because of conditions within the prison. Gangs gain members and integrate their organization into prison life. Gang rivalries and violence increase as gang leaders gain power and control over young inmates. Disciplining gang members becomes more of a problem than disciplining nongang members.

In the early 1970s, the East Los Angeles Concerned Parents Group forms to combat gang violence. It will become the longest-running grassroots organization as well as one of the most successful in dealing with the youth gang problem. It starts as a support group for the parents of young gang members who have died in gang-related violence. Brother Modesto Leon, who is a monk in the Claretian Order, works with parents to help them actively communicate with each other no matter what gangs their children are in, to learn how to deal with impending gang fights, and to learn effective ways to control their children. Parents learn to trust people in authority positions, to work with probation officers, and to call the police when they think it is necessary. They also involve themselves in mediation meetings between rival gangs.

1971   The Federacion de Barrios Unidos is formed in East Los Angeles. A federation of gangs or barrios, it mediates disputes between rival gangs and gang members, controls gang violence, and works to combat drug use and sales among gang members. The federation forms community improvement associations that use gang members to rehabilitate old buildings, sponsors a boxing program, and mediates rival gang disputes. Many people declare the program successful in combating gang activity and violence.

1972   The U.S. Supreme Court, in *Papachristou v. City of Jacksonville* [405 U.S. 156 (1972)], holds that a Jacksonville, Florida ordinance that criminalizes vagrancy is unconstitutionally vague for failure to define adequately the offending behavior, which encouraged discrimination and arbitrary enforcement by police.

1975   Philadelphia develops the Crisis Intervention Network as a modified street worker program. Street workers travel in radio-dispatched cars responding to calls to a crisis intervention hotline that operates 24 hours a day. They work closely with police to defuse volatile situations, including incidents of gang violence.

1980s   The increased presence of crack cocaine and easy access to guns are believed to be the major factors in the growth of gangs and their institutionalization as major players in the drug trade. Many believe that gang activity has increased and has become more violent and more lethal during this time. Drive-by shootings and gang involvement in the drug trade are increasingly reported in the news.

1980   Los Angeles officials believe that the number of gang homicides is peaking in the city. The gang unit of the

1980 Los Angeles County Sheriff's Department doubles in size,
(cont.) the District Attorney's office initiates Operation Hardcore, and Community Youth Gangs Services (CYGS) is established. CYGS is one of the largest non-law-enforcement, antigang programs in the United States. It integrates prevention, intervention, and community mobilization efforts with support from various justice agencies and uses an interactive, multifaceted program called Target Area Strategy. The Los Angeles County Probation Department authorizes the development of its Specialized Gang Supervision Program, which works with young people who are identified as gang members by themselves or by others, those who participate in gang killings and gang violence, and those on probation who are likely to become involved in gang activity. The primary job of the probation officers is surveillance of gang members.

Teen Angels, a gang rights magazine, makes its debut. The magazine focuses on the Hispanic market and publishes photographs sent in by gangs, along with any personal messages they want to send. Favorite poses include gang members holding guns, showing gang signs, or displaying drawings of their gang symbols. Reprints of articles by the American Civil Liberties Union often appear in the magazine, emphasizing the rights of individuals and groups and demonstrating to gang members that they do have rights.

1982 At least 83 percent of the largest U.S. cities currently have a gang problem, as well as 27 percent of cities with a population of 100,000 or more and 13 percent of cities with a population of 10,000 or more, according to Walter B. Miller, who authors the report *Crime by Youth Gangs and Groups in the United States* for the U.S. Office of Juvenile Justice and Delinquency Prevention.

1983 Gang observers begin to notice an increase in gangs with an interest in the occult. These gangs are organized around a central theme of gaining occult powers and belief in the power of Satan, and they are primarily composed of affluent white youth.

1984   In Chicago, Clark Reid Martell, 25, founds Romantic Violence, considered to be the first neo-Nazi skinhead gang
in the United States. Twelve other young men join
Martell in this gang, and six of these members along with
Martell are convicted of breaking into a woman's apartment, beating her, and drawing a swastika on the wall
with her blood. They commit this act in response to seeing the woman talking with some African Americans.

1985   Another skinhead gang appears, this time in San Francisco. Robert Heick, 20, changes his name to Bob Blitz,
gathers several teenagers together, and forms the American Front. They move into an apartment and call their
neighborhood Skinhead Hill. They paint swastikas on
the sidewalks in their neighborhood and attack people
with long hair, interracial couples, and anyone else they
do not like.

Major news media report that the primary elections in the
26th Ward of Chicago involve gang members. Hispanic
alderman Manuel Torres is supported by the Democratic
Party, and Luis Gutierrez, the challenger, is supported by
the Republican mayor, Harold Washington. Both candidates use gang members to help in their campaigns; activities range from hanging election posters to getting out
the vote. The former leader of one gang is the coordinator
of precinct captains for one candidate.

1987   Many street gangs begin to take on characteristics similar to those of organized crime. They set up systems for
laundering money, put murder contracts out on people,
and have access to unlimited sources of money.

California is the first state to issue an injunction against
a gang. The Los Angeles County Attorney files the first
case arguing for a civil gang injunction against the Playboy Gangster Crips using the public nuisance doctrine.

The Office of Juvenile Justice and Delinquency Prevention, in cooperation with the School of Social Service Administration at the University of Chicago, institutes the

1987   National Youth Gang Suppression and Intervention Pro-
(*cont.*)   gram. This program consists of four parts: assessment of
          the gang problem, development of a model prevention
          program, review of literature, and national survey of
          youth gang problems.

1988   In response to a new high of 387 gang-related homicides
          in Los Angeles County in 1987, the city council provides
          the Los Angeles Police Department (LAPD) with fund-
          ing to conduct a series of 1,000-officer sweeps through
          known gang areas to arrest anyone who dresses like,
          talks like, or acts like a member of a street gang. The po-
          lice believe that without these sweeps the number of
          gang-related homicides will be even higher for this year.
          So many youths are arrested during these sweeps that
          the LAPD has to set up mobile booking units at the Los
          Angeles Coliseum. Some reports indicate that at least
          half of all those arrested are not gang members.

          The California legislature passes the California Street
          Terrorism Enforcement and Prevention Act to help deter
          serious crime. The act "makes it a crime to engage in
          criminal gang activity, [but] subjects persons to sentence
          provision aimed at buildings in which criminal gang ac-
          tivity takes place and permits the prosecution of parents
          under a parental responsibility theory" (Burrell 1990,
          745). "Under the Act, law enforcement officers serve
          personal notices on gang members, who then become el-
          igible for enhanced sentences. The notice ensures that
          the gang member has read and understands the Act and
          that he or she is aware of the gang's illegal activities and
          its legal status as a criminal street gang" (Reiner 1992,
          161).

          The police department in Honolulu, Hawaii, estimates
          that 22 gangs, with 450 members, are active in the city.

1989   Police departments in Ohio (Columbus, Akron, Toledo,
          Cincinnati), West Virginia (Wheeling, Charleston), Vir-
          ginia (Richmond), and Indiana (Indianapolis) begin to
          notice that crack cocaine has infiltrated their cities. The
          sale and use of crack cocaine is spreading to smaller

cities throughout the United States with the help of large corporate gangs in big cities such as Detroit.

An initiative proposed by the Office of Human Services, U.S. Department of Health and Human Services, is another example of projects using community organization and community mobilization to prevent gang violence. Bringing local neighborhood residents and organizations together to work on solving gang problems is the latest approach believed most likely to stem the violence. This approach includes local community agency responsibility, interagency coordination, grassroots citizen participation, community policing, and youth involvement.

1990   The *New York Times* carries one of the first stories about juvenile gang activity moving to the suburbs: "Not Just the Inner City: Well-to-Do Join Gangs" (April 10, 1990, by Seth Mydan). Some of the metropolitan areas mentioned as having suburban gangs include Honolulu, Portland, Seattle, Phoenix, Tucson, Dallas, Chicago, Minneapolis, and Omaha.

1992   The Federal Bureau of Investigation announces the formation of its Safe Streets Violent Crime Initiative, which is designed to encourage individual field offices to focus on violent street gangs and drug-related violence. The initiative establishes FBI-sponsored, long-term, proactive task forces that will focus on violent gangs, violent crimes, and the apprehension of violent fugitives. All federal, state, and local law enforcement agencies work together on the Violent Gang Safe Streets Task Force to address violent crime affecting their communities.

Officials in Albuquerque, New Mexico, notice an explosion of graffiti, at least some of it created by gang members. The city council addresses this problem by appointing the Task Force on Graffiti Vandalism to study the problems associated with graffiti. As a result of the efforts of the task force, Albuquerque enacts the Graffiti Vandalism Ordinance, which creates the Office of Anti-Graffiti Coordination as well as a city program to cover up the graffiti.

1992   On April 29, a jury in Simi Valley, California, decides that
(*cont.*)   four Los Angeles police officers are not guilty of exces-
sive force against Rodney King. Parts of Los Angeles
erupt in riots, and fires destroy several areas of the city.
As a result of these riots, attention is drawn to the problem of gangs in the city. Two of the city's major gangs,
the Crips and the Bloods, in part as a result of the truce
they have in force at the time of the riots, call for a new
city to be built. Instead of rebuilding the liquor stores
and other businesses, they suggest, all abandoned buildings should be gutted; new parks should be built; local
businesses should be encouraged; schools should be re-
built; and, most important, jobs should be created that
pay a decent, living wage for the local citizens. The city's
plans for the area are different; they include rebuilding
the areas and maintaining the status quo without solving
the deeper problems.

1993   The police department in Honolulu estimates that 171
gangs with approximately 1,267 members are active in
the city.

Roman Catholic cardinal Juan Jesus Posada Ocampo and
six other individuals are gunned down in Guadalajara,
Mexico, because their car looked like that of a rival drug
lord, Joaquin "Chapo" Guzman Loera. Several gang
members from San Diego were sent to Guadalajara to kill
Loera, the leader of a rival drug gang, the Arelano Felix
drug gang, but shot and killed Ocampo in a case of mistaken identity.

The Los Angeles Police Department implements the first
injunction that is granted banning gang members from
carrying pagers. The injunction prohibits 100 members
of the Blythe Street gang from using pagers and cell
phones in public.

1994   The Violent Crime Control and Enforcement Act (P.L.
103-322) is signed into law by President Bill Clinton. This
law puts 100,000 new police officers on the street, pumps
nearly $7 billion into prevention programs, and allows

13-year-olds charged with violent crimes (murder, armed robbery, and rape) to be treated as adults. The act also allows existing criminal justice block grants to be used for antigang activities and authorizes $1 million for the U.S. attorney general to use in developing a national strategy to help federal law enforcement agencies coordinate gang-related investigations.

Police in Fort Worth, Texas, having tried every other approach they could think of to reduce gang activity and violence in their city, suggest that six gang leaders should be placed on the police payroll. They believe that these leaders can be trained as mediators in gang disputes and as counselors against violence. City residents complain loudly about paying each of these gang members an estimated $10,000 per year, which they believe will support criminal activity, and the police withdraw their idea.

A *New York Times*/CBS News Poll reports that 18 percent of white youth believe that gangs are a problem in their schools, reflecting a growing belief that gangs are not just a problem in ethnic, primarily African American and Hispanic, neighborhoods.

1995 The U.S. Office of Juvenile Justice and Delinquency Prevention of the U.S. Department of Justice and the Institute for Intergovernmental Research establish the National Youth Gang Center to collect data and be a central repository for gang information (see Chapter 7 for a more detailed description of this program).

The Office of Juvenile Justice and Delinquency Prevention awards grants to five communities in order to implement and test a model program that is supposed to reduce gang crime and violence. The program, known as the Spergel Model, suggests five strategies for dealing with youth involved in gang activities and their communities. Participating communities include Mesa and Tucson, Arizona; Riverside, California; Bloomington and Normal, Illinois; and San Antonio, Texas.

1995   The Violent Gang and Terrorist Organizations File
(*cont.*) (VGTOF) is created to help law enforcement agencies, es-
          pecially in small towns, identify, track, and combat the
          criminal activities of members of gangs and terrorist
          groups. The VGTOF is one part of the National Crime In-
          formation Center and helps to identify known members
          of violent gangs and terrorist groups.

1996   People against Gangsterism and Drugs, established in
          1995, marches against the parliament in South Africa,
          calling on the government to find a solution to the prob-
          lems created by gangs and drugs.

1997   The National Youth Gang Center (1999) estimates that
          30,818 gangs and 846,428 gang members are active in the
          United States.

          The Navajo Nation estimates that approximately 60
          youth gangs exist in Navajo Country.

          President Clinton launches the National Anti-Gang and
          Youth Violence Strategy, based on the approach to gang
          violence developed by the Boston Police Department
          and its collaborative partners, known as Operation
          Cease Fire.

          California enacts a gang information tracking system,
          known as Cal/Gang, which is an automated gang intel-
          ligence database that provides intelligence information
          to local, state, and federal law enforcement agencies to
          help solve gang-related crimes.

          Gustavo "Gino" Colon, a leader of the Latin Kings, is in-
          dicted for running a drug-dealing operation from his
          prison cell; he used the prison's telephone to create a net-
          work of gang members throughout Illinois to deal drugs
          and order hits. He is within 24 hours of being released
          from prison after serving 25 years for murder.

1998   The National Youth Gang Center estimates that more
          than 28,700 gangs and more than 780,000 gang members
          are in the United States (Moore and Cook 1999).

1999 Survey data from the school crime supplement to the National Crime Victimization Survey show a decline in gang presence in schools between 1995 and 1999 (Beres and Griffith 2004).

In Honduras, the homicide rate is 154 per 100,000 inhabitants and is blamed largely on juvenile gangs, organized crime, drug trafficking, and social violence (NAGIA 2005).

The U.S. Supreme Court, in *Chicago v. Morales* [52 U.S. 41 (1999)], rules that a Chicago ordinance that prohibits gang loitering is void based on its vagueness.

2000 The United States begins deporting an average of 50 Salvadoran gang members per week from California to El Salvador (Hayden 2000).

2003 In July, the government of El Salvador declares a state of emergency and enacts an antigang initiative to curb the violence.

Twenty-four members of the Boot Camp gang in Syracuse, New York, are indicted under the Racketeer Influenced and Corrupt Organizations (RICO) Act statute. They are accused of 42 criminal acts, including one homicide, and are viewed as an organized crime enterprise. All members will either plead guilty or will be convicted of crimes.

2004 Massachusetts lieutenant governor Kerry Healey signs into law a bill that allows the police officers in the city of Somerville to arrest purported gang members who appear to be loitering on street corners. This bill is in response to the growth of gang-related crimes in the city.

2005 The U.S. Senate is considering passage of the Gang Prevention and Effective Deterrence Act, which would create new categories of gang offenses, enhance existing penalties, reduce from five to three the number of people required to be together to be defined as a gang, and transfer more juveniles to adult courts and prisons. The bill dies in committee.

2005
(cont.)
Former Homeland Security Deputy Secretary James Loy testifies before the U.S. Congress, claiming that the Mara Salvatrucha, or MS-13, gang is an emerging threat to the United States and groups it with other terrorist organizations, including Al Qaeda.

On June 21, in a police action named Operation Silent Night, 1,300 law enforcement personnel execute 43 search warrants; arrest 36 individuals; and seize 41 guns, more than 12 pounds of narcotics, and $30,000 in cash as part of a crackdown on the Vineland Boys street gang in California. The defendants are charged with violating the federal RICO Act, and the charges include a variety of narcotics, weapons, and violent crimes.

On August 26, the U.S. Bureau of Alcohol, Tobacco, Firearms and Explosives institutes a raid on MS-13 gang members; it arrests 19 individuals and charges them with conspiracy to intimidate the communities of Silver Spring, Langley Park, and Hyattsville, Maryland, through the commission of murders, attempted murders, and kidnappings. The MS-13 suspects are named in a federal indictment alleging that the gang's activities violate the federal criminal racketeering (RICO) statute.

Operation Community Shield is initiated by the U.S. Immigration and Customs Enforcement office. This program targets violent criminal street gangs, which the government views as posing a threat to national security and public safety. Program activities include identification of violent gangs; gathering of intelligence on these gangs; criminal prosecutions of gang members; deportation of illegal immigrant gang members; cooperation with federal, state, and local law enforcement agencies; and public awareness efforts to educate communities concerning violent criminal gangs. The program begins by focusing on the MS-13 gang but quickly expands its focus to include all violent criminal street gangs.

The Alien Gang Removal Act (H.R. 2933) is introduced into the U.S. House of Representatives, which authorizes the Department of Homeland Security to deport those individuals and groups that are designated as "criminal street gangs."

The U.S. Federal Bureau of Investigation centralizes its gang investigations with the opening of its new National Gang Intelligence Center, which will gather intelligence on gangs throughout the country, analyze the data, and share it with law enforcement agencies in order to help develop effective strategies to prevent gang violence.

The Pan American Health Organization holds a conference in Washington, D.C., on "Voices from the Field: Local Initiatives and New Research on Central American Youth Gang Violence," which brings together social service providers, community activists, academics, government officials from the United States and Central American countries, representatives from international organizations, and nongovernmental organizations to discuss strategies for prevention and intervention activities related to gangs.

The FBI launches its National Gang Strategy program, which is set up to target gangs throughout the country that first started in California, including the MS-13 gang.

2006   The Guardian Angels announce an international gang initiative in which they plan to attack gang violence at its source by starting chapters in South America. The group will establish training camps and recruitment centers in Argentina, Peru, and Uruguay.

In March, federal agents from Immigration and Customs Enforcement in the U.S. Department of Homeland Security, working with local law enforcement agencies, arrest 375 gang members in 23 states. As part of Operation Community Shield, an initiative created to disrupt violent transnational street gangs, those arrested are charged with a variety of crimes, including drug and firearms violations, charges of reentering the country after being deported, and other administrative immigration violations.

2006 In December, Michael Coleman, the mayor of Columbus,
(cont.) Ohio, along with 400 law enforcement officials, public
school officials, representatives from the U.S. Attorney's
Office, and other professionals, holds an antigang summit to develop solutions to what they see as a growing
gang problem.

Massachusetts enacts a statute, known as An Act Reducing Gang Violence, that provides law enforcement officials with the tools necessary to combat street-gang
activity by encouraging cooperation between police officers and local neighborhoods and community-based organizations. It includes provisions for witness protection
and increased penalties for possession of illegal firearms.

Alejandro "Bird" Martinez, a member of the Avenues, a
Hispanic gang in Los Angeles, and three other gang
members are convicted of federal hate crimes. They murdered Kenneth Kurry Wilson, a black man, who was
parking his car. Opinions were mixed on whether this
was a race-based crime.

2007 In January, the California Cities Gang Prevention Network is held to work on coordinated efforts to reduce the
effects of gangs in California.

The U.S. Bureau of Alcohol, Tobacco, Firearms and Explosives hosts a gang summit for chiefs of police from
Belize, El Salvador, Guatemala, and Honduras. The participants gather to strengthen their multilateral efforts to
stop the activities of transnational gangs.

A shooting in a Nashville, Tennessee, mall is attributed
to Kurdish Pride, a gang that started out as a group of
Kurdish students who joined together, following the
September 11, 2001, attacks in New York City, for protection from bullies who said they were terrorists. Over
time, the gang started creating trouble, and several members were arrested following the rape of a pregnant
woman committed in the course of a home invasion.
Nashville police believe that the gang is local and only
one of many gangs operating in the Nashville area.

The Fresno, California, police chief proposes using global positioning system monitors to track 20 of the most hard-core, violent gang members. The legality of such a proposal is being debated.

Melvin Murios-Garcia, a member of the MS-13 gang, is sentenced to 188 months in prison, to be followed by five years of supervised release, as a result of a plea agreement with the U.S. Attorney for the District of Maryland. He is one of several MS-13 gang members charged under RICO conspiracy charges.

Oscar Ramos Velasquez, a member of the MS-13 gang, is sentenced to 37 years in prison, to be followed by 5 years of supervised release, following his conviction on charges of conspiracy to commit murder in aid of racketeering; conspiracy to participate in a racketeering enterprise; and conspiracy to commit assaults with a deadly weapon, assault with a deadly weapon in aid of racketeering, and use of a firearm in relation to a crime of violence.

In March, working with local law enforcement agencies, the U.S. Federal Bureau of Investigation completes a two-week nationwide initiative focused on disrupting the criminal activities of neighborhood gangs. Agents from 12 FBI field offices make 108 federal arrests and 47 state arrests, charging those arrested with conspiracy to distribute narcotics and various weapons violations.

The U.S. House of Representatives passes legislation that prohibits members of the armed services from associating with street gangs. The U.S. Senate has not yet voted on the bill.

References

Beres, Linda S., and Thomas D. Griffith. 2004. "Gangs, Schools and Stereotypes." *Loyola of Los Angeles Law Review* 37:935–978.

Bernard, William. 1949. *Jailbait.* New York: Greenberg.

Burrell, Susan. 1990. "Gang Evidence: Issues for Criminal Defense." *Santa Clara Law Review* 30 (Summer): 739–790.

Cloward, Richard A., and Lloyd E. Ohlin. 1960. *Delinquency and Opportunity: A Theory of Delinquent Gangs.* Glencoe, IL: Free Press.

Cohen, Albert K. 1955. *Delinquent Boys: The Culture of the Gang.* Glencoe, IL: Free Press.

Dunston, Leonard G. 1990. *Reaffirming Prevention. Report of the Task Force on Juvenile Gangs.* Albany: New York State Division of Youth.

Furfey, Paul Hanley. 1926. *The Gang Age: A Study of the Pre-Adolescent Boy and His Recreational Needs.* New York: Macmillan.

Hayden, Tom. 2000. "Gato and Alex—No Safe Place." [Online article; retrieved 05/12/08.] http://www.thenation.com/doc/20000710/hayden/print.

Miller, Walter B. 1982. *Crime by Youth Gangs and Groups in the United States.* Report for the National Institute for Juvenile Justice and Delinquency Prevention, U.S. Department of Justice. Washington, DC: Office of Juvenile Justice and Delinquency Prevention.

Mobilization for Youth. 1964. *Action on the Lower East Side, Program Report: July 1962–January 1964.* New York: Mobilization for Youth, Inc.

Moore, J. P,. and I. L. Cook. 1999. "Highlights of the 1998 National Youth Gang Survey." OJJDP Fact Sheet No. 123. Office of Juvenile Justice and Delinquency Prevention. Washington, DC: U.S. Department of Justice.

National Alliance of Gang Investigators Associations (NAGIA). 2005. *2005 National Gang Threat Assessment.* Washington, DC: Bureau of Justice Assistance.

National Youth Gang Center. 1999. *1997 National Youth Gang Survey.* Washington, DC: Office of Juvenile Justice and Delinquency Prevention.

Puffer, J. Adams. 1912. *The Boy and His Gang.* Boston: Houghton Mifflin.

Quinney, Richard. 1970. *The Social Reality of Crime.* Boston: Little, Brown and Company.

Reiner, Ira. 1992. *Gangs, Crime and Violence in Los Angeles.* Los Angeles: Office of the District Attorney of the County of Los Angeles.

Robison, Sophia. 1960. *Juvenile Delinquency: Its Nature and Control.* New York: Holt, Rinehart and Winston.

Shaw, Clifford R., and Henry D. McKay. 1931. *Social Factors in Juvenile Delinquency: Report on the Causes of Crime,* vol. 2. Report for the National Commission on Law Observance and Enforcement. Washington, DC: U.S. Government Printing Office.

Shaw, Clifford R., and Henry D. McKay. 1942. *Juvenile Delinquency and Urban Areas.* Chicago: University of Chicago Press.

Sheldon, Harry D. 1898. "The Institutional Activities of American Children." *The American Journal of Psychology* 9:424–448.

Short, James F. 1990. "New Wine in Old Bottles? Change and Continuity in American Gangs." In *Gangs in America,* edited by C. Ronald Huff. Newbury Park, CA: Sage.

Tannenbaum, Frank. 1939. *Crime and the Community.* Boston: Ginn and Company.

Thrasher, Frederic M. 1927. *The Gang: A Study of 1,313 Gangs in Chicago.* Chicago: University of Chicago Press.

Welfare Council of New York City. 1950. *Working with Teenage Groups: A Report on the Central Harlem Project.* New York: Welfare Council of New York City.

Whyte, William Foote. 1943. *Street Corner Society: The Social Structure of an Italian Slum.* Chicago: University of Chicago Press.

Yablonsky, Lewis. 1970. *The Violent Gang,* rev. ed. Baltimore: Penguin.

5

Biographical Sketches

This section provides short biographical sketches of individuals who play or have played a key role in working with gangs and conducting research in areas of vital interest to those who are concerned with understanding and working with gangs. Also included are profiles of several gang members and former gang members.

Daniel "Nane" Alejandrez (dates unknown)

Nane Alejandrez was born in Mississippi; his parents were migrant workers from Texas. He spent much of his childhood traveling to locations where his parents were most likely to find work. When Alejandrez returned from the Vietnam War addicted to heroin, he came back to a community that was involved in drugs and gang violence, and he joined in. He lost several family members, including two brothers, to what he refers to as the madness of inner-city America, but he was able to turn his life around with the help of a friend who was a former addict.

He is an experienced activist within the Latino community in California. He formed Barrios Unidos in 1977 in Santa Cruz, California, which is one of the most significant gang prevention and intervention programs in the state. Working with youths and adults, using educational activities, dances, and music, Alejandrez and his organization have established the César Chávez

151

School for Social Change as an alternative high school for at-risk youth.

David Barksdale (1947–1974)

As leader of the Black Disciple Nation, David Barksdale was well known among Chicago street gangs, especially for his street-gang organization skills. By 1969, Barksdale was tired of the senseless violence he believed was destroying the African American communities in Chicago. He approached Larry Hoover, the leader of the Gangster Nation, and proposed that the Disciple Nation and the Gangster Nation merge to become the Black Gangster Disciple Nation. Hoover agreed. Barksdale and Hoover shared the leadership of the new gang. In 1974, Barksdale died of kidney failure, a result of complications from a gunshot wound he suffered in 1968.

Leon Bing (b. 1950)

It might seem surprising that Leon Bing, a female journalist from a wealthy family in Pasadena, California, would want to write about gang members and would be willing to work to gain the trust of many of these tough young boys. She had written about youth issues and had talked with several youngsters who mentioned gangs and gang activity before she started to focus on gangs herself. Her first contact with gang members occurred in 1986, when she was writing an article for the *L.A. Weekly*. Not knowing how to make contact with them, she asked a ticket taker at a local movie theater if he knew any gang members or knew where she could find some. He told her that many members of the Bloods met every Sunday afternoon in a certain park in South Pasadena. Along with Howard Rosenberg, a photo editor from the *L.A. Weekly,* she went to the park, where they saw plenty of red, the Bloods' color, worn by teenagers and young men. That day marked the beginning of her relationship with several gang members. She wrote *Do or Die,* a book about young gang members and their lives, and for four years following the book's publication, she wrote articles about gangs for the *L.A. Weekly.*

Anne Campbell (b. 1951)

Anne Campbell was one of the first scholars to explore the participation of females in gangs. She is currently a principal lecturer in the School of Health, Social and Policy Studies at Teeside University in England and is the author of *The Girls in the Gang* (1984) and *Girl Delinquents* (1981). Formerly an associate professor in the School of Criminal Justice at Rutgers University, she has spent nearly 20 years investigating aggression and violent behavior. She spent two years as a participant-observer with New York female gangs and reported the results of this research in *The Girls in the Gang*. Her current research concerns theories about the similarities and differences in aggressive actions of women and men.

Her research and writing grew out of her frustration with the lack of information on female delinquency. As a residential social worker in her first job after graduating from Oxford University in 1972, she worked with delinquent girls. The girls were divided into two groups. One group was boisterous and aggressive and, according to the terminology of the day, they were "acting out"; the girls in the other group were more withdrawn and more complex, displaying self-injurious behavior and other less overt means of gaining attention. Campbell chose to work with the boisterous and aggressive group but found no research in the literature that could help her understand the behavior of these girls. As she struggled to help them, she realized that "without some coherent conceptual framework with which to approach these girls' problems" she would not succeed (Campbell 1984, vii).

Campbell returned to Oxford University to work on a doctorate focusing on female delinquency. She became convinced that delinquent and aggressive behavior expressed by women was not understood by men. Most men viewed these girls as maladjusted, because they seemed to be acting like men. Aggressive behavior is considered a male characteristic, and women who are aggressive are seen as unfeminine and not totally sane.

Richard Cloward (1926–2001)

Richard Cloward received his BA from the University of Rochester in 1949, a master's in social work from Columbia University in 1950, and his PhD from Columbia in 1958. He taught social work at Columbia from 1954 until his death in 2001. In 1960, along with Lloyd Ohlin, he wrote *Delinquency and Opportunity: A Theory of Delinquent Gangs,* in which they explain their belief that social strain accounts for juvenile and gang delinquency. He was awarded the Dennis Carroll Award by the International Society of Criminology in 1965 as a result of writing this book, one of the first to connect social strain and delinquency. He later won the C. Wright Mills Award from the Society for the Study of Social Problems in 1971 for his book *Regulating the Poor.* His other books include *Social Perspectives on Behavior* (1958), *The Politics of Turmoil* (1974), and *Poor People's Movements* (1977).

Albert K. Cohen (b. 1918)

Albert Cohen received a BA from Harvard University in 1939 and his master's degree from Indiana University in 1942. After working for one year at the Indiana Boys School (a state institution for male juvenile delinquents), he returned to Harvard for a year of graduate study in 1946. Cohen joined the sociology department at Indiana University in 1947. He received his PhD in sociology from Harvard in 1951 and, after 17 years at Indiana University, joined the faculty at the University of Connecticut, where he taught for 23 years until his retirement in 1988. His best-known work is *Delinquent Boys: The Culture of the Gang* (1955). Another book, *Deviance and Control* (1966), was one of the first comprehensive textbooks in the field of deviance. His published works have focused primarily on issues relating to the many theories of deviance. He has been a visiting professor at the University of California (Berkeley and Santa Cruz), Cambridge University, John Jay College of Criminal Justice, and the University of Haifa (Israel), and a visiting scholar at Arizona State University and Kansai University in Osaka, Japan. He spent one year at the Center for Advanced Study in the Behavioral Sciences at Stanford University. He has contributed articles on gangs and delinquency to several professional journals.

G. David Curry (b. 1948)

David Curry is a professor of criminology at the University of Missouri. He was previously an associate professor in the Crime and Justice Program in the Department of Sociology and Anthropology at West Virginia University. He completed National Institute of Mental Health (NIMH) postdoctoral work with the Methodology Committee in the Department of Behavioral Sciences at the University of Chicago in 1987–1988. He has worked for SPSS Inc. as a statistical writer and as a senior research associate at the University of Chicago for an evaluation of a gang-intervention program targeting minority students in inner-city African American and Hispanic schools. His publications include *Sunshine Patriots: Punishment and the Vietnam Offender* (1985), "Gang Homicide, Delinquency, and Community," written with Irving A. Spergel and published in *Criminology* in August 1988, and *Survey of Youth Gang Problems and Programs in 45 Cities and 6 Sites* (1990), written with Spergel and others and published by the National Youth Gang Suppression and Intervention Project at the University of Chicago School of Social Service Administration. Curry and Spergel often work together on research concerning gang delinquency among youths. Curry also conducts research on women, violence, and crime.

Sandra Davis (dates unknown)

Sandra Davis was a gang member during the 1980s. Her son, also involved in gang activities, was shot and killed in 1982. She became more deeply involved in gang activities in the search for her son's killers and was eventually imprisoned for unrelated gang crimes. During her time in prison, she decided to change her life and leave the gang. When she was released from prison, she founded Mothers Against Gang Wars (see program description in Chapter 7) in 1991. She speaks to various audiences about what gang life is like and describes the dangers and realities of being in a gang. She provides presentations to school districts as well as private organizations.

Jeffrey Fagan (dates unknown)

Jeffrey Fagan is a professor at Columbia Law School and codirector of the Center for Crime, Community and Law. He has written profiles of violent delinquents, and his research interests and other publications concern youth gangs, the transfer of violent delinquents to adult court, the relationship between drug abuse and criminality, and conflicts and abuse within the family. He is currently principal investigator on a research and development program focusing on the treatment of violent delinquents. He recently completed a study of drug use, drug selling, and other criminality among people who use crack cocaine and other drugs in New York City. Along with Ko-Lin Chin and Robert Kelly, he is conducting research on the patterns of extortion and victimization used by Asian gangs in New York City. He is coauthor with Joseph Weis of *Drug Use and Delinquency among Inner City Youths* and is editor of the *Journal of Research in Crime and Delinquency.*

In his research, Fagan has found that substance abuse plays a larger role in a juvenile's participation in gang activities than the degree of integration the juvenile exhibits with his or her family. He has also found that when asked why they joined a gang, many gang members answer that they joined to protect their neighborhood.

Antonio "King Tone" Fernandez (dates unknown)

Antonio Fernandez became the leader, or Inca, of the Almighty Latin King Queen Nation (ALKQN), also known as the Latin Kings, in New York City in 1995. He took over from Louis Felipe, the founder of ALKQN, when Felipe was arrested for and tried and convicted of various murder and racketeering charges. Fernandez was well known by local authorities for his participation in various marches and rallies protesting the government's housing policies, welfare cuts, and police brutality. The gang originated as a prison gang, but Fernandez claimed to have changed it into an organization focused on community action. In 1999, he pleaded guilty to selling 700 grams of heroin along with 3.5 kilos of cocaine and was sentenced to twelve-and-a-half years in prison.

Jeff Fort (b. 1947)

By the time he was 13 years old, Jeff Fort had dropped out of school and helped organize a local street gang, the Blackstone

Raiders, in Chicago. He applied to the State of Illinois for a charter for a political organization known as the Grassroots Independent Voters of Illinois that would support candidates in local elections. Once he received the charter, he applied for federal funds and received a $1.4 million grant for job training. However, instead of spending the money on training, the group bought cars and houses with it. The government began an investigation into the use of the grant money, and in 1972, Fort and some of his friends were convicted of embezzlement of the $1.4 million government grant. Fort was sentenced to four years in prison for embezzling funds and for lying to government agents.

During his time in prison, he converted to Islam and changed his name to Chief Prince Malik. When he was released in 1978, he returned to Chicago and changed the name of the Blackstone Raiders to El Rukn. The gang was involved in illegal drug sales, extortion, and other illegal activities. In 1983, Fort was sentenced to 13 years in prison after a drug conviction, but still maintained his leadership position with El Rukn.

In 1986, four members of El Rukn flew to Libya and brokered a deal with Muammar Qaddafi, who agreed to pay El Rukn $2.5 million in exchange for certain acts of terrorism. Qaddafi called the Chicago headquarters of El Rukn and was transferred to Fort in prison to seal the deal. Following the purchase of an antitank missile from undercover Federal Bureau of Investigation (FBI) agents, the four members of El Rukn moved the missile to their armory and were arrested by the FBI. All four, along with Jeff Fort, were indicted for conspiring to transport explosives and commit violent acts on behalf of the government of Libya. Fort was convicted and sentenced to 80 years in prison and fined $225,000.

Arnold Goldstein (1933–2002)

Growing up in Brooklyn, Arnold Goldstein joined a street gang and participated in some activities that could have gotten him in trouble with the legal system. Ultimately, he was able to avoid trouble and stay in school. He earned his bachelor's and master's degrees at City College of New York and his doctorate in psychology at Pennsylvania State University. Goldstein joined the psychology department at Syracuse University as a professor of clinical psychology in 1963; he taught at Syracuse and directed the university's Psychotherapy Center until 1980. He founded the Center for Research on Aggression at Syracuse in 1981.

In 1985, he joined the Division of Special Education at Syracuse. As a researcher and theoretician, he was interested in working with subjects who were difficult to reach and understand. He focused most of his research efforts on juvenile offenders and parents who abuse their children. He developed psychoeducational programs and curricula that are designed to teach prosocial behavior to people who are chronically antisocial.

Goldstein developed art replacement training in 1987 as a comprehensive program to help aggressive adolescents deal with their anger, enhance their interpersonal skills, and develop an awareness of and concern for the rights and needs of others. Students would leave the program with the skills needed to behave in socially responsible, nonaggressive ways at home, in school, and in their communities. This program has been successfully introduced in several other countries, including Australia, New Zealand, Canada, the United Kingdom, Germany, Norway, Sweden, Italy, Peru, Taiwan, and Japan.

Much of his writing focused on young gang members who face more than the normal amount of tension and stress in the process of developing their identity. He believed that many young people join a gang primarily for the status that being a gang member confers on them, rather than for the economic opportunities that the gang provides. In his book *Delinquent Gangs: A Psychological Perspective,* Goldstein explored the characteristics of the contemporary gang and suggested strategies for successful intervention. In *The Gang Intervention Handbook,* Goldstein and Ronald Huff present the work of a group of experts on gang research and intervention strategies.

John Hagedorn (b. 1947)

John Hagedorn is an associate professor of criminology, law, and justice at the Great Cities Institute at the University of Illinois at Chicago. As a social scientist who also has been a community organizer, journalist, and gang program director, Hagedorn has broad experience in a variety of situations. Instead of asking the local police department to provide him with the names of gang members to contact for his research, Hagedorn gained access to Milwaukee's gangs through the contacts he made as a program director of a gang project. He coordinated an effort to reform Milwaukee County's social welfare system while completing his PhD dissertation on that topic.

He is the author (with former gang leader Perry Macon) of *People and Folks: Gangs, Crime, and the Underclass in a Rustbelt City* (1988), published by Lake View Press. The book portrays gang members as racially oppressed minorities and suggests that white sociologists who study gangs offer too much theory and too little fact. As editor of *Gangs in the Global City: Alternatives to Traditional Criminology,* Hagedorn brought together international scholars to explore the development and growth of gangs throughout the world. His research interests include the relationship of gangs and the people in lower-class and urban neighborhoods, changing public policy toward gangs and the underclass, organizational change in social welfare, and the impact that welfare has on lower-class communities.

Larry Hoover (b. 1950)

Larry Hoover was born in Mississippi and moved to Chicago with his parents when he was four years old. By the time he was 13, he had joined the Supreme Gangsters. In 1965, he was expelled from school after being shot by a rival gang. He became leader of the Supreme Gangsters shortly thereafter. In 1969, he and David Barksdale merged their gangs into the Black Gangster Disciple Nation. In 1973, Hoover was convicted of murder and began serving a life sentence.

Ruth Horowitz (b. 1947)

Ruth Horowitz, a professor of sociology at New York University, has made important contributions to the scholarly study of gangs. She received her PhD from the University of Chicago and has written several articles on gangs in Chicano communities. Her book *Honor and the American Dream: Culture and Identity in a Chicano Community* was published by Rutgers University Press in 1983. She authored, with James Inciardi and Anne Pottieger, *Street Kids, Street Drugs, Street Crime: An Examination of Drug Use and Serious Delinquency in Miami,* a study of seriously delinquent and drug-abusing youth. Horowitz has studied the relationships that develop between gang members and the communities in which they live, and how community residents are able to reconcile their feelings about violent acts committed by gang members and the relationship between themselves and the gang members.

C. Ronald Huff (dates unknown)

As dean of the School of Social Ecology and a professor of criminology, law, and society at the University of California, Irvine, C. Ronald Huff has extensive experience in the areas of gangs, youth violence, and public policy. Previously, he was director of the Criminal Justice Research Center and professor of public policy and management at The Ohio State University, where he began teaching in 1979. Prior to joining the Ohio State faculty, he taught for five years at the University of California, Irvine, and Purdue University, where he coordinated the applied sociology program and designed the program and curricula for students majoring in criminology and criminal justice. His previous professional positions have been in correctional, mental health, and children's services agencies and institutions.

His publications include more than 40 journal articles and book chapters, numerous research reports and monographs, and six books. He has completed his seventh book, *Convicted but Innocent: Wrongful Conviction and Public Policy* (with Arye Rattner and the late Edward Sagarin). As editor of *Gangs in America* (1990), Huff pulled together other leading experts in the field of gang research and provided important data to researchers and others interested in this field. He has served as a consultant on gangs and youth violence to the U.S. Senate Judiciary Committee, the U.S. Department of Justice, and the FBI Training Academy.

Malcolm Klein (dates unknown)

As professor of sociology at the University of Southern California (USC) and senior research associate with the Social Science Research Institute, USC, Malcolm Klein has conducted research on a variety of topics concerning gangs and gang characteristics. He has been involved in gang research for more than 30 years. From 1962 to 1968, he directed evaluation of and basic research projects on juvenile gangs. Since 1969, his research has focused on comprehensive criminal justice planning, evaluation of dein-stitutionalization programs (that is, programs that focus on get-ting criminals back into society rather than incarcerating them), and assessment of the legislative impact on major criminal justice issues. His current research involves police handling of juvenile offenders and police investigation of gang-related homicides.

Klein received the Edwin H. Sutherland Award in 1990 from the American Society of Criminology for his research efforts. He believes that no simple solutions exist to understanding gangs or solving the problems created by gangs. He contends that many criminal justice agencies wrongly tend to stereotype gang mem-bers, blame them for all sorts of problems, and label gang members and other youths in gang neighborhoods as delinquents.

Klein continues to provide consulting services to a variety of gang programs and is an expert witness and a consultant in nu-merous criminal court cases. In 1997, he initiated the Eurogang Program, a consortium of more than 100 U.S. and European gang researchers and policy makers involved in understanding the emerging street-gang problems in Europe. This program contin-ues to engage his time as six international conferences and a half-dozen study proposals have moved the program forward.

George W. Knox (dates unknown)

George Knox currently teaches in the Department of Corrections and Criminal Justice, Chicago State University, where he heads the National Gang Crime Research Center. His publications in-clude research on teenage and adult offenders and rehabilitation programs. He is the editor of the *Gang Journal*. His research ef-forts focus on the national and international nature of gangs and their characteristics, activities, and patterns of violence. Knox re-ceived his BA from the University of Minnesota in 1974, his MA from the University of Texas at Arlington in 1975, and his PhD from the University of Chicago in 1978.

Cheryl L. Maxson (dates unknown)

Cheryl Maxson is currently an assistant professor in the Depart-ment of Criminology, Law and Society at the University of Cali-fornia, Irvine (UCI). She spent more than 10 years as a research associate and director of the Social Science Research Institute at the University of Southern California. She is currently working with other well-known researchers, including Ronald Huff, at UCI's School of Social Ecology, one of the leading centers for gang research. Her recent research and publication activity focused on the nature of gang violence, gang-identification practices used by police, and police response to gang-related crime. Previous research topics have included predicting legislative change and evaluating the implementation and impact of legislative initiatives.

Walter B. Miller (1920–2004)

Walter Miller was interested in youth gang problems since 1954, when he joined the staff of the Special Youth Program in Roxbury, Massachusetts. This program was one of the country's first detached-worker programs, in which social and other youth workers were sent out into the streets to meet and work with youngsters who were in trouble with the law or at risk of becoming involved in illegal activities. He published more than 40 papers and books on youth gangs, juvenile delinquency, and lower-class subcultures. One of his papers, "Lower Class Culture as a Generating Milieu of Gang Delinquency" (1958), is the single most frequently cited journal article in the literature on criminology. He was project director of the National Youth Gang Survey for the U.S. Department of Justice, Office of Juvenile Justice and Delinquency Prevention, from 1974 to 1980. He retired in 1982 from the Center for Criminal Justice at Harvard Law School but continued to write, lecture, and consult on youth gangs and related issues until his death.

Joan W. Moore (dates unknown)

Joan Moore is a professor in the sociology department at the University of Wisconsin at Milwaukee. She has worked for several years on a series of studies concerning gangs in the East Los Angeles area. These studies have provided material for her two books, *Homeboys* (1978) and *Going Down to the Barrio* (1991). She also has been concerned with the relevance to gangs and gang behavior of many of the popular theories of poverty in Latino communities, and she coedited a study focused on impoverished communities. She is a strong advocate for young men and women who have joined gangs, believing that locking up these offenders in prison is not the most cost-effective or best treatment for them. She believes that education and drug counseling programs are most effective in helping these young people turn around their lives.

Moore has recently teamed up with John Hagedorn to study female gang members. They have encouraged former gang members to join their research staff; these staff members are effective liaisons between the researchers and the gangs. These former gang members are provided with basic training in research, and they have lent valuable insights into the inner workings of gangs.

Lloyd Ohlin (b. 1918)

Sociologist Lloyd Ohlin received his BA from Brown University in 1940, his MA from Indiana University in 1942, and his PhD in 1954 from the University of Chicago. He has been a sociology instructor at Indiana University, a sociologist and actuary at the Illinois Parole and Pardon Board in Joliet, a supervising research sociologist, and a director at the Center for Education and Research in Corrections at the University of Chicago. In 1960, with Richard Cloward, he wrote *Delinquency and Opportunity: A Theory of Delinquent Gangs.* In this book, they discuss their belief that juvenile and gang delinquency can best be explained by theories of social strain. He joined the faculty at Columbia University as a professor of sociology in 1956 and became director of the Research Center in 1962. He spent one year as a special assistant to the secretary for juvenile delinquency in the Office of the Secretary of the U.S. Department of Health, Education, and Welfare. In 1967, he became the Roscoe Pound Professor of criminology at Harvard University. In addition to his teaching duties, he has been a member of the research council of the Division of Youth for the State of New York; associate director of the President's Commission on Law Enforcement and Administration of Justice; chairman of the advisory board of the Massachusetts Department of Youth Services; chairman of the advisory board of the National Institute of Law Enforcement and Criminal Justice; and a consultant to the Ford Foundation, the National Institute of Mental Health, and the American Bar Foundation.

Joseph Oyoo (dates unknown)

In the late 1990s, Joseph Oyoo was living in the slums of Nairobi, Kenya, with his father, mother, and nine siblings. He was young, with little hope of gaining an education or finding a job. One of his few options was to join one of the gangs that roamed the slums of Nairobi. However, he avoided the temptation of joining a gang and, instead, turned to music to keep him out of the gang and get him out of the slums. He joined with Julius Owino and formed one of Kenya's most popular and successful hip-hop bands, Gidigidi Majimaji.

In 2002, during the campaign for president of the country, one of Gidigidi Majimaji's songs, *Unbwogable* (Unbeatable), became the song for the National Rainbow Coalition, which went on to win the election. The song propelled the band to the top of the music charts in Kenya. In 2004, Oyoo and Owino were named Messengers of Truth by the United Nations Human Settlements Programme, or UN-HABITAT. They appeared at the World Youth Forum in Vancouver, Canada, in 2006, in part because of their nongovernmental organization, Street Expression, which was formed to work with youth in Nairobi to encourage them to stay out of gangs and improve their lives.

Omar Portee (dates unknown)

In 1993, while at Rikers Island serving time for a weapons offense, Omar Portee founded the United Blood Nation (also known as the East Coast Bloods), which would become one of the most violent street gangs in New York. He created it because he believed he needed protection and to have power over other inmates. Also known as O. G. Mack, Portee, along with other members of the Bloods, created elaborate systems of hand signals to communicate with each other while in jail. Portee was released from jail in 1999 and returned to the streets to build the Bloods into a powerful street gang.

In 2002, he was convicted on 10 counts, including racketeering, racketeering conspiracy, conspiracy to commit murder in aid of racketeering, being a felon and possessing an AK-47 semi-automatic assault weapon, conspiracy to distribute cocaine and marijuana, conspiracy to commit credit card fraud, and conspiracy to commit identity theft. Following a two-and-a-half month trial in federal court, he was sentenced to 50 years in prison.

Luis J. Rodriguez (b. 1954)

Luis Rodriguez was born on the border of the United States and Mexico and grew up in South Central Los Angeles, joining a gang by the time he was 11 years old. He was also active in the Chicano movement during the 1960s and 1970s, and in 1970, when he was 16 years old, he was beaten and arrested during the Chicano Moratorium Against the War, known to many as the East L.A. Riot. The riot resulted when sheriff's officers and police attacked demonstrators, leaving at least three dead and much of Whittier Boulevard in flames. Members of his gang traveled into the San Gabriel Mountains to learn how to shoot guns, taught by veterans returning from the Vietnam War.

Rodriguez was arrested for a variety of crimes committed between the ages of 13 and 18, including stealing, rioting, assaulting police officers, and attempted murder. By the time he was 18 years old, Rodriguez was hooked on heroin and facing a six-year prison sentence. Because of his positive work in his community, many community members wrote letters on his behalf and his sentence was reduced to county jail time. As a result of the community's response to him and support for him, he quit using drugs and committed his life to revolutionary thinking and community organization.

He spent more than 10 years with Mosaic Multicultural Foundation, which was founded to help men who had experienced or perpetrated serious violence. Rodriguez is now an award-winning poet, journalist, and critic whose works have appeared in *The Nation, Chicago Reporter, Playboy,* and the *Los Angeles Weekly.* He also is the publisher of the Tia Chucha Press, which has published poetry by African American, Puerto Rican, Chicano, and Native American writers. *Always Running: La Vida Loca: Gang Days in L.A.,* his poignant book about growing up in Watts and East Los Angeles, was published in 1992.

James F. Short (b. 1924)

James Short was one of the first scholars to write about gangs. He is a professor emeritus of sociology at Washington State University, where he has also served as dean of the graduate school (1964–1968) and director of the Social Research Center (1970–1985). He received his PhD from the University of Chicago in 1951.

His books include *Suicide and Homicide* (1951), written with Andrew F. Henry; *Group Process and Gang Delinquency* (1965), written with Fred L. Strodtbeck; and *Delinquency and Society* (1990). He has contributed to many books, including *Juvenile Gangs in America* (1967), edited by Malcolm W. Klein. He is a former editor of the *American Sociological Review* and an associate editor of the *Annual Review of Sociology*. A former president of the Pacific Sociological Association and the American Sociological Association, he has participated as a fellow at the Center for Advanced Study in the Behavior Sciences; the Institute of Criminology at Cambridge University; the Rockefeller Center in Bellagio, Italy; and the Centre for Socio-Legal Studies at Oxford. He has received numerous honors, including NIMH and Guggenheim fellowships, the Edwin H. Sutherland Award from the American Society of Criminology, the Bruce Smith Award from the Academy of Criminal Justice Sciences, and the Paul W. Tappan Award from the Western Society of Criminology. He is the 1990 Beto Chair Professor of Criminal Justice at Sam Houston State University.

Curtis Silwa (dates unknown)

Born in Brooklyn, New York, Curtis Silwa learned about social responsibility at an early age. Offered a partial scholarship to Brown University, he was a student activist at Brooklyn Prep School and was expelled during his senior year for these activities. During a stint as night manager of a local McDonald's, Silwa created a program to clean up the community; activities included cleaning up vacant lots, painting over graffiti, boarding up vacant buildings, and planting trees and gardens. This program was expanded to include patrolling one of the worst subway lines in New York City, with the help of volunteers known as the Magnificent Thirteen. As this group grew in numbers and in popularity, Silwa realized he needed an organization with more structure, and the Guardian Angels were created in 1979.

As of 2007, the organization has more than 90 chapters throughout the United States, Canada, Europe, South Africa, Brazil, Japan, New Zealand, and the Philippines. Volunteers patrol streets, subways, and other public areas; they attend community events and offer educational programs for students and teachers through the Guardian Angels Education Academy. Young people from the inner city are encouraged to join as volunteers, teaching them to take pride in their communities and keeping them out of trouble.

Irving Spergel (b. 1924)

One of the major researchers in the field of gang studies, Irving Spergel received his BS in 1946 from the City College of the City University of New York, an MA from Columbia University, a master's degree in social work from the University of Illinois in 1952, and a doctorate in social work from Columbia University in 1960. He has been a professor in the School of Social Service Administration at the University of Chicago since 1960 and is a principal investigator for the National Youth Gang Suppression and Intervention Research and Development Program, a long-term evaluation of a gang-intervention program. This program, funded by the Office of Juvenile Justice and Delinquency Prevention of the National Institute of Justice, targets minority students in African American and Hispanic inner-city schools. As a street-gang worker, supervisor, and court worker in the 1950s in New York City, Spergel learned firsthand about gangs and the problems they cause as well as the problems these youths face while growing up.

His major research interests are youth gangs, community organization, and the evaluation of programs for youth services. He has completed a statewide evaluation of the Comprehensive Community Based Youth Services program of the Illinois Department of Children and Family Services, a diversion program for status offenders, those found guilty of curfew violations, or youths who have run away from home. This program attempts to keep status offenders from being sent into the juvenile justice and the child welfare systems. Spergel has been a consultant for the B'nai Brith Youth Organization; the U.S. Departments of Justice, Labor, and State; the American Social Health Association; and the Illinois Department of Corrections. He has received awards from a variety of organizations and agencies, including the National Institute of Mental Health, the Ford Foundation, the President's Committee on Juvenile Delinquency and Youth Development, the Office of Economic Opportunity, the Law Enforcement Assistance Administration, the U.S. Department of Justice, and the Illinois Law Enforcement Commission. His major publications include *Street Gang Work* (1966), *Community Problem*

Solving: The Delinquency Example (1969), *Community Organizations: Studies in Constraints* (1972), and *Social Innovation: Politics, Program, Evaluation* (1982). His most recent publication is *The Youth Gang Problem: A Community Approach,* an excellent and comprehensive resource book. He has also contributed to several books and has written many journal articles, organizational publications, and research reports.

Carl S. Taylor (b. 1949)

After receiving his bachelor's degree at Michigan State University (MSU), Carl Taylor was hired by the MSU Office of Student Affairs to run its Minority Aid Program, which he developed into a successful program that was copied by many other campuses. After earning his master's degree in criminal justice in 1976 at Michigan State, he worked as a manager for a security company in Detroit, where he became interested in gangs and gang behavior. Taylor received his PhD in the administration of higher education in 1980 from MSU. He became director of Criminal Justice Programs at Jackson Community College in Michigan in 1989 and adjunct professor in the School of Criminal Justice at MSU. He is currently professor of criminal justice and clinical professor at Grand Valley State University in Allendale, Michigan, and director of the Youth Culture Studies Center. At the University of Michigan, he was a member of the Public Health Think Tank on Substance Abuse in 1990. He also was an instructor for the National Institute for Corrections, a guest lecturer at the FBI Academy, a member of the Black Community Crusade for the Children's Task Force on Violence sponsored by the Children's Defense Fund, a member of the Michigan Governor's Committee on Juvenile Justice, and a consultant to the National Institute of Justice.

He has spent the past 14 years conducting extensive research on the subculture of gangs and their impact on society. He also has lectured throughout the United States and has appeared on national television programs discussing urban gangs and prisons, gangs and school environments, youth gangs and law enforcement, and drug abuse and gangs. He wrote about his research on Detroit youth and gangs in *Dangerous Society* (1990). In 1993, he wrote *Girls, Gangs, Women and Drugs,* a provocative study of female gang members and the effects of poverty, teen

pregnancy, drugs, and illiteracy on young girls and gang participation. He has contributed to several anthologies and professional journals.

Frederic M. Thrasher (1892–1962)

One of the prominent members of the Chicago School of Sociology at the University of Chicago in the 1920s, Frederic Thrasher
received his PhD in sociology in 1926 from the University of
Chicago; his dissertation was on gangs. Thrasher wrote *The Gang:
A Study of 1,313 Gangs in Chicago* (1927), which was one of the ear-
liest published studies of gangs. Although the book is not heavily statistical, it provides a natural history of gangs. It traces gang
development and includes many photographs that help the
reader imagine life in the early 1900s. He gathered most of his
knowledge about gangs from social workers, court records, personal observation, census data, and others who had studied
gangs.

James Diego Vigil (b. 1938)

As a young man growing up in East Los Angeles, James Vigil was
well acquainted with street gangs. Later, as a high school teacher,
he worked closely with many Chicano youth groups, and as an
anthropologist, he has studied street gangs in the barrios of East
Los Angeles. Vigil is currently associate professor of anthropology and director of the Center for Urban Policy and Ethnicity at
the University of Southern California. He received his BS in
1962 from California State University (CSU), Long Beach; an
MA in social science from CSU, Sacramento; and an MA and a
PhD in anthropology from the University of California, Los Angeles (UCLA). Prior to his current position, he was chair of Chicano Studies at the University of Wisconsin at Madison, was a
professor at UCLA and Chaffey Community College, and has
taught part time at Whittier College and CSU's Sacramento and
Los Angeles campuses. He concentrates mainly on urban anthropology, and his interest in youth issues comes from his experience as an educator and counselor. He has often focused his
research on street gangs, especially the role of street socialization
and the development of gangs. He has conducted fieldwork in a

variety of urban, rural, and suburban barrios, and this research is documented in his book *Barrio Gangs* (1988). His other publications include *From Indians to Chicanos: The Dynamics of Mexican American Culture* (1984); contributions to *Violence and Homicide in Hispanic Communities* (1988), edited by Jess Kraus and associates and published by the National Institute of Mental Health; and articles in journals such as *Social Problems, Human Organization, Aztlan,* and *Ethos.* He is currently conducting cross-cultural research on gangs, studying African American, Asian American, and Latino American youth.

Raymond Lee Washington (1953–1979)

Born in Texas, Raymond Washington moved with his family to South Central Los Angeles when he was three years old. While a student at John C. Fremont High School, he organized a group of his friends into the "Baby Avenues" gang. Washington, along with Stanley "Tookie" Williams, who joined the gang in 1971, wanted to develop the gang into a more forceful unit, based on their knowledge of and fascination with the Black Panthers. The gang changed its name to the "Avenue Cribs" and became the "Crips" in 1971. Other neighborhood youths created their own gangs as a set of the Crips. Washington and Williams played key roles in the expansion of the Crips throughout California. In 1979, Washington was shot and killed by a rival gang.

Stanley "Tookie" Williams (1953–2005)

In 1971, Stanley "Tookie" Williams and Raymond Lee Washington founded the Crips as a way of protecting the community from several small gangs. By 1979, the Crips had become a large organization with members throughout the state of California. That same year, Williams was arrested and charged with the murder of four people; he was convicted in 1981 and sentenced to death. While he was in prison, in solitary confinement in 1989, he examined his life, realized his mistakes, and committed himself to becoming a better person, regretting the violent actions of the Crips. He decided to help encourage young people to stay out of gangs. His autobiography, *Blue Rage, Black Redemption,* tells the story of his transformation from gang leader to antigang advocate. His appeal for clemency was supported by many well-known celebrities, including Jesse Jackson and Jamie Foxx, but his appeals were turned down and he was executed in December 2005.

Lewis Yablonsky (b. 1924)

Probably best known for his book *The Violent Gang*, first published in 1962, Lewis Yablonsky has also written *Crime and Delinquency* (1970), *Gangsters: 50 Years of Madness, Drugs and Death on the Streets of America* (1997), and *Gangs in Court* (2005). Along with many other experts, Yablonsky believes that most young people who join gangs are not sociopathic or seriously disturbed, but are a product of their low social status and lack of opportunity.

He received his BS from Rutgers in 1948 and his MA and PhD from New York University in 1952 and 1958, respectively. His first job, while he was working on his master's degree, was as a supervisor for the Essex County Youth House in Newark, New Jersey. He became a lecturer in sociology at the City College of City University of New York in 1951 and went on to lecture at Columbia University, Harvard University, and Smith College. He was an associate professor of sociology at the University of Massachusetts, then at UCLA, and retired as a professor at California State University, Northridge. He was a consultant to the Rockefeller Brothers Organization on Delinquency in 1957 and to Columbia Broadcasting System in 1958.

He has been approved as an expert witness concerning violent gangs, homicide, and domestic violence in several state and federal courts. He has testified on violent gang structure, characteristics of gang behavior, and other aspects of gang participation in more than 80 cases concerning gang violence and homicides.

Reference

Campbell, Anne. 1984. *The Girls in the Gang: A Report from New York City*. Oxford: Basil Blackwell.

6

Data and Documents

This chapter presents general facts and statistics on the prevalence and demographics of American youth gangs, descriptions of gang databases, gang alliances, descriptions of several of the major gangs in the United States, and signs that parents can look for indicating their children might be involved in gangs. State and federal statute definitions of the terms *street gang, gang member,* and *gang activity* are provided. Federal laws are described. The final section summarizes selected U.S. Supreme Court and lower court decisions that pertain to a variety of issues that have come before the courts concerning gangs and gang activity.

Prevalence

As with other social problems, statistics on the number of gangs in the United States, the total number of gang members, and the number of crimes they commit annually are difficult to obtain. The major problem is in defining the terms *gang, gang member,* and *gang-related crime.* Many researchers agree that estimates of the number of gangs and individual gang members are not always reliable or comparable because definitions vary. Gangs may have core members, fringe members, and "wannabes"—those who may claim to be gang members but are not considered as such by core members. These distinctions usually are not made in any jurisdiction's statistics on gangs. Law enforcement personnel usually take either a member-defined or a motive-defined approach to classifying crime as gang crime. *Member-defined* means that any offense committed by a gang member is gang related. Under *motive-defined* classification, only those crimes committed in the name of the gang, such as defense of territory, retaliation, or witness intimidation, are considered gang crimes. Because no consensus is found among law enforcement agencies about how to identify gang-related crime, comparisons of data from different cities and states are difficult. However, national surveys have been conducted in an attempt to estimate the depth and breadth of the gang phenomenon in this country.

History of Major National Surveys (prior to 2000)

In 1982, Walter Miller published one of the first studies to examine the extent of gang activity throughout the United States. It was supported by the U.S. Department of Justice's Office of Juvenile Justice and Delinquency Prevention (OJJDP). He identified 12 types of youth groups that violate the law, including three types of youth gangs (turf gangs, gain-oriented gangs, fighting gangs). He examined gang problems in 26 of the largest U.S. cities and later expanded his study to include 36 major metropolitan areas. In 18 of the 36 metropolitan areas examined, respondents reported having some type of gang problem. Approximately 2,300 gangs with 98,000 members existed during the 1970s, most of them located in the largest cities, primarily Los Angeles, Chicago, New York, Philadelphia, Detroit, San Diego, San Antonio, Phoenix, San Francisco, and Boston. Gang members ranged in age from 10 to 21 years, and they accounted for approximately 42 percent of arrests for serious and violent crimes (Miller 1982).

Other studies during the 1980s also attempted to measure the extent of the gang problem. In 1983, Needle and Stapleton estimated that 39 percent of cities with populations between 100,000 and 249,999 had a gang problem. Irving Spergel, David Curry, and Ronald Chance conducted the first comprehensive national survey of organized responses to gang activity in 101 cities in the late 1980s. Police departments in these cities were contacted, and the researchers determined that 74 of the cities reported some type of gang problem (Spergel and Curry 1990).

The OJJDP's Program of Research on Causes and Correlates of Juvenile Delinquency supported three in-depth studies of high-risk, inner-city youth in Denver, Pittsburgh, and Rochester, New York. In 1993, Esbensen and Huizinga conducted the Denver Youth Survey. Also in 1993, Thornberry and colleagues examined gang involvement with their Rochester Youth Development Study. Researchers found no gang activity in Pittsburgh. The Denver study found that 7 percent of the sample group were involved in gangs; male gang members were more involved than nongang males in all types of delinquent activities; gang members did not remain in the gang for long (67 percent reported staying in the gang for only one year); and almost 75 percent reported that their gang was involved in fights, robberies, assaults, theft, and drug sales. The Rochester study found that 55 percent of the gang members were members for only one year, although 21 percent remained in the gang during the three years covered by the study. Thornberry and his colleagues also found that their social facilitation model best explained gang participation; this model suggests that the group processes occurring within the gang lead to high rates of delinquency among gang members.

In 1992, Curry and colleagues conducted the National Assessment Survey of law enforcement agencies in the 79 largest U.S. cities and 43 smaller cities. Survey results suggested that 4,881 gangs with 249,324 members existed in 1991. Law enforcement personnel in 91 percent of the 79 large cities reported the presence of gang problems in their cities, and 27 of these cities reported the existence of female gangs. Sixty-four percent of the police departments reported that they believed suppression activities were the most effective in stemming gang activity, 63 percent thought case management of gang member files was an effective means of preventing gang activities, 60 percent thought increased enforcement against gang members was effective, and 55 percent thought increased law enforcement liaison activities were effective in preventing gang activity. Between 1988 and 1992, the percentage of cities reporting gang crime problems increased; in all cities crime rose from 72 percent to 85 percent; in the large cities, 75 percent of the cities in 1988 and 89 percent in 1992 reported gang problems; and in smaller cities, 70 percent in 1988 and 86 percent in 1992 reported problems.

In 1994, another National Assessment Survey was conducted, which expanded the 1992 survey to include all cities with populations between 150,000 and 200,000 and a random sample of cities with populations between 25,000 and 150,000. Eighty-seven percent of cities with populations between 150,000 and

200,000 reported gang crime problems in 1994. The authors estimated that 8,625 gangs, with 378,807 gang members, existed in
the United States in 1993 (Curry, Ball, and Decker 1996).

In a 1994 survey of 368 prosecutors' offices, the Institute for
Law and Justice studied the extent of gang problems in the
United States. The Institute surveyed all 175 U.S. counties with
populations over 250,000 as well as 193 prosecutors randomly selected from counties with populations between 50,000 and
250,000. Of the 175 largest counties, 84 percent reported gang
problems within their counties, while 46 percent of the smaller
jurisdictions reported some type of problem with gangs in their
areas.

Scope of the Problem since 2000

The National Youth Gang Center (NYGC) annually surveys law
enforcement agencies throughout the United States to determine
the extent of gang activity in various jurisdictions. The 2004
study surveyed a sample of police departments in cities with
50,000 or more residents, all suburban county police and sheriff's
departments, a random sample of police departments in cities
with between 2,500 and 49,999 residents, and a random sample
of rural county police and sheriff's departments. Almost 2,300
survey recipients responded to the survey (out of 2,554 total recipients). Highlights of the study include the following:

- Approximately 760,000 gang members were active in
  24,000 gangs in 2,900 jurisdictions in 2004, compared
  with 731,5000 gang members and 21,500 gangs in 2002.
- 85 percent of the estimated gang members were found
  in larger cities and suburban counties.
- More than half of the homicides in Los Angeles and
  Chicago were believed to be gang related.
- Thirty-six percent of law enforcement agencies had specialized gang units that involved at least two officers
  dealing with gang-related activity.
- Fifty-three percent of the law enforcement agencies believed that the gang problem in their jurisdiction was
  getting better or staying about the same as the year before, while 47 percent saw their gang problems as getting worse (OJJDP 2004).

In a study of violence by gang members between 1993 and 2003 by the Bureau of Justice Statistics, Harrell (2005) reported that the percentage of violent crime perceived by the victim to have been committed by a gang member dropped from more than 8 percent in 1993 to less than 6 percent in 2003. Hispanics were more likely to be victims of gang violence than were non-Hispanics. Younger people were more likely than older people to be victims of gang violence.

The 2005 National Gang Threat Assessment study gathered information from 455 law enforcement agencies throughout the United States regarding gangs and gang activity in their jurisdictions. Highlights of the study include the following:

- Almost 32 percent of respondents reported gangs in their jurisdictions were highly involved in drug distribution.
- Approximately 26 percent believed that gangs in their jurisdictions were associated to some degree with organized crime.
- Gang use of advanced technology, including the Internet, computers, and cell phones, was reported by 45 percent of the respondents. This use includes communications with other gang members over the Internet and gang Web sites and electronic bulletin boards.
- Very few (5.7 percent) respondents believed that local gang members were involved in terrorist activities (NAGIA 2005).

The New Jersey State Police have conducted three surveys of gang activity throughout the state between 2001 and 2007. Results from the most recent survey indicate that 43 percent of New Jersey municipalities reported the presence of gangs in their jurisdictions during 2006, compared with 33 percent that reported a gang presence during 2004. More than one-half of the municipalities reported the presence of Bloods, Latin Kings, Crips, Mara Salvatrucha (MS-13), and Pagans motorcycle club gangs; the Bloods were reported in 87 percent of the jurisdictions. More than half (51 percent) of the respondents reported a gang presence in their schools (New Jersey State Police 2007).

The U.S. Department of Justice estimated that approximately 800,000 gang members were active in 30,000 gangs in 2,500 communities throughout the United States in 2005 (Swecker 2005). In January 2007, the Federal Bureau of Investigation (FBI) estimated that approximately 700 gangs existed in Los Angeles alone, with total membership of approximately 40,000 individuals (FBI 2007).

Demographics

Participation in gangs varies with a number of demographic characteristics, including age, sex, and race/ethnicity. These variations are discussed below.

Age

Based on reports in newspapers and on television, most people believe that the age at which children join gangs is getting younger and that most gang members are teenagers. In Frederic Thrasher's 1927 study of gangs, he found that members ranged in age from 6 to 50 years, but most members were between the ages of 11 and 25. In a study of New York gangs in the 1970s, H. Craig Collins (1979) found that the age of gang members ranged from 9 to 30, with many more members at both extremes than were found in earlier years. Using police department data, Ko-Lin Chin (1990) studied New York gangs in the 1980s and found that the range in age of Chinese gang members was from 13 to 37 years, and the mean age was 22.7 years. Walter Miller's 1982 study found that gang members ranged in age from 10 to 21 years with the peak age for membership at 17 years.

Most gang homicides appear to be committed by gang members who are in late adolescence or early adulthood. Maxson, Gordon, and Klein (1985) studied gang homicide statistics in Los Angeles in the 1980s and found that the mean age of gang homicide offenders was 19 years in the city and 20 years in the county. Spergel (1983) studied gang homicide offender statistics in Chicago from 1978 to 1981 and found that 2.2 percent of these offenders were under the age of 14; 50 percent were between the ages of 15 and 18; 21.7 percent were ages 19 or 20; and 25.9 percent were more than 21 years of age.

In more recent surveys, the number of adult (18 years old and older) gang members appears to be increasing, while the number of juvenile (under the age of 18 years) members appears to be decreasing. For example, the NYGC estimates that the average number of adult gang members increased from just under 60 percent during 1996–1999 to more than 60 percent in the years

2002–2004. Meanwhile, the average number of juvenile gang members decreased from 42 percent to 38 percent (NYGC 2007). In the same survey, the NYGC found that adult gang members are more likely to be reported in larger cities and suburban counties, while juvenile gang members are more likely to be found in smaller cities and rural counties.

Sex

Data on females who become gang members are difficult to obtain because many jurisdictions do not believe that female gang membership is a serious problem and do not track gang members by sex. The National Youth Gang Center (2007) reported that in the national youth gang surveys conducted between 1996 and 2004, many agencies were not able to provide information concerning the prevalence of female gang members; they conclude that law enforcement does not consider female gang membership to be a significant issue to most agencies.

However, many researchers have attempted to measure female gang participation using a variety of resources. In 1975, Miller estimated that 10 percent of all gang members were female. In 1979, Collins estimated that, while males outnumbered females in gangs in New York City by 20 to 1, he believed that approximately one-half of all gangs in the city had some type of female auxiliary. Like Miller, researchers such as Campbell (1984) and Lee (1991) have estimated female participation at 10 percent of all gang members. More recent research has found similar rates for female participation in gangs. For example, Curry, Decker, and Egley (2002), in a study of poor and middle-class neighborhoods in St. Louis, found a female participation rate of 8 percent. Esbensen and Weerman (2005), in their study of 11 American cities and counties, found a female participation rate in gangs of 6 percent.

Other researchers, such as Jeffrey Fagan (1990) and Joan Moore (1991), who primarily used self-reports and observations in the field, estimated that female participation in gangs may be as high as 33 percent. Thornberry and his colleagues (2003) found a prevalence rate of 29 percent in their Rochester Youth Development Study, and Regoli and Hewitt (2003) suggest that female participation in gangs may range from 4 to 28 percent of all gang members.

Police data on the number of females in gangs can only reflect the number of female gang members who have committed some sort of crime. These statistics suggest that females commit a relatively small amount of serious gang crime. Using data from the Chicago Police Department, Spergel (1986) found that males comprised 95 to 98 percent of offenders who were involved in serious gang incidents between 1982 and 1984 in four Chicago police districts. In a more recent study of Chicago police records, Bobrowski (1988) found that 12,602 males and only 685 females were arrested for commission of some type of street-gang crime.

Many researchers believe that female involvement in criminal activity is on the rise, and some conclusive evidence indicates that females are becoming more involved in violent criminal activity. However, surveys of gang participation suggest lower delinquency rates for female gang members than those for male gang members, but higher than those of nongang females and even nongang males. In 1983, Spergel examined gang homicide statistics and found that only 1 out of 345 gang homicides in Chicago between 1978 and 1981 was committed by a female. A study in Rochester, New York, reported 66 percent of female gang members and 82 percent of male gang members claimed they were involved in at least one serious delinquent act, compared with only 7 percent of nongang females and 11 percent of nongang males (Moore and Hagedorn 2001).

Some jurisdictions have studied the extent of female participation in gang activity, and results suggest higher rates of participation in certain areas of the United States. For example, the New Mexico Department of Public Safety (1994), in a survey of law enforcement personnel from around New Mexico, reported fairly high rates of female gang activity. In Farmington, police reported that a female gang had recently been organized and had started to paint graffiti all over the town; the gang dissolved shortly after the police arrested several gang members. Sources estimated that gang membership in Farmington ranged from 180 to 220 members and that approximately 20 percent of these members were female. Females had joined male gangs in Las Cruces; in Santa Fe, between 15 and 20 percent of all gang members were female, and one all-female gang was identified; and gangs in Roswell were approximately 25 percent female, and two small all-female gangs were found.

The 2000 National Youth Gang Survey found that only 6 percent of all gang members are female (OJJDP 2002). The 2005 National Gang Threat Assessment study found very few all-female gangs; 10 percent of respondents reported the existence of all-female gangs in their communities (NAGIA 2005).

The National Youth Gang Center (2007) reported that female participation in gangs had not changed much from 1996–1999 to 2001–2004—female participation may have dropped slightly and remains under 10 percent. The NYGC (2007) also reported that female gang members are found more frequently in smaller cities and rural areas. Data from large cities indicated that slightly more than 5 percent of gang members were female, while in smaller cities the rate was 10 percent, and rural counties reported that slightly more than 10 percent of all gang members were female.

Race/Ethnicity

In the first national survey detailing race and ethnicity in gangs, conducted by Walter Miller (1975), he estimated that 48 percent of gang members in the six largest cities were black, 36 percent were Hispanic, 9 percent were white, and 7 percent were Asian. A few years later, in a more extensive survey in nine of the largest U.S. cities, Miller (1982) found that 44 percent of all gang members were Hispanic, 43 percent were black, 9 percent were white, and 4 percent were Asian. Based on these statistics, he speculated that illegal Hispanic immigrants may have contributed to the increasing number of gangs in California.

Spergel and Curry studied gang problems in 1989 and 1990 and surveyed programs developed to deal with gang problems in 45 cities and six special jurisdictions. They found that 53 percent of all gang members coming into contact with police were black, while only 28 percent were Hispanic. Curry and Spergel (1990) noted that "law enforcement agencies were defining and contacting blacks more often as gang members than were other justice agencies" (64). In the same study, Spergel and Curry also found that whites and Asians were among the least-mentioned gang members in police statistics as well as other non–law enforcement agencies. Whites comprised only 2.2 percent of all gang members in law enforcement agencies' reports, and 1.6 percent of gang members were Asian, while in statistics on gang members from non–law enforcement agencies, only 14.2 percent were white and 2.2 percent were Asian.

The average number of African American and Hispanic gang members grew from between the 1996–1999 survey period and the 2001–2004 survey period, according to the National Youth Gang Center's annual surveys, while during the same periods, the number of white members declined slightly. During the 2001–2004 survey period, the distribution of gang members by race was approximately 47 percent Hispanic/Latino, 35 percent African American, 10 percent caucasian, and 7 percent other races/ethnicities (NYGC 2007).

According to the 2005 National Gang Threat Assessment study, the number of Hispanic youths in gangs has grown over the years. Fifty-three percent of the respondents reported Sureño 13 gangs in their communities, 45 percent reported the presence of Latin Kings, 32 percent reported an MS-13 gang presence, 31 percent reported an 18th Street gang presence, 27 percent reported the presence of the Norteños, and 17 percent reported La Raza gangs in their communities (NAGIA 2005).

In 2001, the National Youth Gang Center conducted a survey of 577 federally recognized tribal communities to determine the extent of youth gang activities among Native Americans. Three hundred tribal leaders and law enforcement agencies responded to the survey. Seventy percent of the tribal communities reported no youth gang activity, 23 percent reported active youth gangs, and 7 percent could not determine the existence of youth gangs in their communities. Respondents in the 69 communities reporting gang activity reported from 1 to 40 gangs in the community and 4 to 750 gang members in the community (32 percent reported fewer than 26 gang members, 12 percent reported 12 to 25, 16 percent reported more than 50, and the remaining respondents were not sure of the number of gang members). Eighty percent of the gang members were male, meaning the remaining 20 percent were female, and 74 percent were under the age of 18 years (Major and Egley 2002).

Gang Databases

Several states and local jurisdictions have set up gang databases to track gang members and their activities. In some states, statutes have mandated that they have their own gang databases or exercise the legislative prerogative for creating a centralized database. These states include Colorado, Florida, Illinois, North Dakota, and Texas. Colorado's database is operated by the Colorado Bureau of Investigation; however, as of 2007, fewer than half of Colorado's law enforcement agencies participated in the program.

At the national level, the Federal Bureau of Investigation is currently exploring the possibility of setting up a database system that would coordinate information from the approximately 20 databases currently in existence in 2008. However, the databases differ in form and function and may be difficult to coordinate. In addition, many questions remain concerning the comparability of the information and the ability to share information with other agencies without the permission of the agency or organization that initially provides the information to the FBI.

Described below are some of the more well-known databases, set up by individual states or groups of states.

Cal/Gang

Developed by the California Department of Justice, law enforcement agencies, and SRA International's Orion Center for Homeland Security, the Cal/Gang database records and tracks gang members and their activities. Specifically, it helps law enforcement agencies identify and track individual gang members, their street names, known associates, hand signals, tattoos, and other valuable information.

GangNet

First developed in 1997 for California (known as Cal/Gang in California), as of 2007, GangNet was operational in Maryland, Minnesota, Nevada, New Mexico, North Carolina, Ohio, Texas, Virginia, the District of Columbia, and parts of Canada. It is a user-friendly system that gathers data from gang units, patrol officers, corrections officers, and other law enforcement personnel.

Gang Reporting, Evaluation, and Tracking (GREAT) System

The Law Enforcement Communication Network (LECN), a nonprofit organization for the criminal justice community, operates the GREAT System. This database system tracks more than 150 characteristics of individual gang members, such as age, aliases, addresses, and tattoos, and it includes a color photo system and an imaging system that can support fingerprint, graffiti, and tattoo images. The system is used by law enforcement agencies in 21 states. LECN hopes to have nationwide coverage eventually.

Regional Information Sharing Systems (RISS) Program

The Regional Information Sharing Systems Program links law enforcement agencies throughout the United States in order to share information they have concerning gangs, along with other criminal activities, including drug trafficking, terrorism, cybercriminal activity, and other organized crime. Six regional centers share intelligence and coordinate efforts. RISS utilizes a specialized database, the RISS National Gang Database, or RISSGang, to collect and disseminate information on gangs and gang members. The database provides law enforcement agencies with access to a variety of topics regarding gangs, including suspects, organizations, weapons, locations, and vehicles, along with images of gang members, gang symbols, and gang graffiti. Currently, access to the database includes member as well as nonmember criminal justice agencies.

U.S. Bureau of Alcohol, Tobacco, Firearms and Explosives

The Bureau of Alcohol, Tobacco, Firearms and Explosives (ATF) operates several databases; some of them contain information on gangs, including Bloods, Crips, prison gangs, and motorcycle gangs. The information is available to law enforcement agencies.

Gang Alliances

Three major gang alliances are found throughout the United States: the People Nation, the Folk Nation, and the United Blood Nation.

People Nation

The People Nation alliance was created primarily to protect its members who were in state and federal prison systems from Folk

Nation members. Gangs within the People Nation include the West Coast Bloods, Latin Kings, Vice Lords, Black Peace Stone Nation (formerly El Rukn), Bishops, King Cobras, and Gaylords. The gang's symbols include a five-point star, a pyramid with an eye over it, a crescent moon and star, a five-pointed crown, and a cane. Gang members emphasize the left side, wearing an earring in the left ear, left pants leg rolled up, or baseball cap with the brim to the left. Their graffiti often includes the above-mentioned symbols, such as a five-pointed star, a die with five dots, a crescent moon, or a five-pointed crown.

Folk Nation

The Folk Nation was created in Chicago in 1978 by Larry Hoover. Major gangs in the Folk Nation include the Crips, Black Gangster Disciples, Black Disciples, Gangster Disciples, Latin Disciples, and La Raza.

The gang's symbols and tattoos include a six-pointed star, upright pitchforks, a winged heart, a devil's tail in the form of the number 6, a playboy bunny with one ear bent (a show of disrespect for the People Nation), a sword, and a backward swastika. The six-pointed star was adopted following the death of David Barksdale, the founder of the Black Gangster Disciple Nation. Gang members emphasize the right side by wearing a baseball cap with the brim to the right, rolling up the right pants leg, hanging a bandanna out of the right pocket, or wearing an earring in the right ear.

United Blood Nation

The United Blood Nation was formed on the East Coast of the United States in 1993 by Leonard MacKenzie and Omar Portee (see Chapter 5 and below) in response to the need for protection from Hispanic gangs in the Rikers Island prison system. As member-inmates were released back into society, they returned to their communities and expanded the gang to most communities throughout New York City. Over time, the gang has expanded throughout the East Coast. The United Blood Nation, also known as the East Coast Bloods, includes the Mad Stone Villains; Valentine Bloods; Nine Trey Gangsters; Gangster Killer Bloods; One Eight Trey (183) Bloods; Blood Stone Villains; and Sex, Money, Murder Bloods. According to the U.S. Department of Justice, some

Blood gangs, or sets, as they are commonly referred to, are connected to Norteños gangs, including La Nuestra Familia (NDIC 2003a).

Descriptions of Specific Gangs

Several large, well-known gangs exist in the United States, including the Crips, Bloods, Gangster Disciples, Almighty Latin King and Queen Nation, Black Peace Stone Nation, 18th Street, Norteños, Sureños, Vice Lords, and Mara Salvatrucha. A brief summary of each gang's basic characteristics is provided below.

Crips

One of the oldest gangs in the United States, the Crips started in Los Angeles in the late 1960s. Some researchers, law enforcement personnel, and social service workers believe the Crips came into existence as a result of the FBI's attempt to crack down on the activism of the Black Panther Party. By the end of the 1960s, police had reportedly killed 28 members of the Black Panthers in Los Angeles. Young African Americans, including Raymond Washington and Stanley "Tookie" Williams (see Chapter 5), believed they could continue the social activism of the Black Panthers through the gang, which they formed in the late 1960s. However, the Crips were never able to establish a focus on social and political activism.

Crips sets are fairly loosely organized. They are associated with the Folk Nation. Their primary enemies are the Bloods and other gangs associated with the People Nation. Crips gang colors are blue and purple. East Coast Crips wear blue and white bead necklaces and, usually, white shirts and blue jeans. Their symbols and tattoos include a "B" or a "P" crossed out, showing disrespect for Bloods, also known as Pirus; the number 187, which is the California penal code section number for murder; the word "Cuz," which is a word Crips use when greeting other Crips gang members; and the initials "BK," for Blood killer.

During the late 1960s and early 1970s, guns became more readily available to gang members, and violence between gangs increased. The Crips were a formidable force in Los Angeles, and several other neighborhood gangs joined together and formed the Bloods to fight the Crips. In the 1980s, many Crips-affiliated gangs started selling crack cocaine; over time, these sales provided them with large profits. Realizing the potential of other illicit markets, the Crips used some of their profits to expand. The importance of territory was emphasized, as certain street corners and neighborhoods became big drug dealing locations, and therefore more lucrative to the gang. This focus on drug territory also led to increased violence, between individual Crips gangs as well as with other gangs, including the Bloods, as individual gangs tried to maintain their territories and expand into other promising locations.

Bloods

The Bloods are one of the largest and most violent gang associations in the United States. They were organized in response to the power and violence of the Crips in Los Angeles in the early 1970s. Leaders from two local Los Angeles gangs, Silvester Scott from the Piru Street gang and Benson Owens from the Westside Pirus, united their efforts with several other gangs and formed a larger gang association. They adopted red as their color; members referred to each other as Blood; and they referred to their gang association as the Bloods. According to the National Drug Intelligence Center (NDIC), 15 Bloods sets had been established in Los Angeles by 1978, but they were still outnumbered by the Crips by three to one (NDIC 2003a).

The Bloods became involved in the distribution of crack cocaine during the 1980s; the profits from this drug distribution fueled the expansion of the Bloods to other states. Bloods gangs are also involved in money laundering, assaults, automobile theft, carjacking, drive-by shootings, extortion, homicide, and burglary. Bloods are considered by the U.S. Department of Justice to be one of the most violent street gangs in the United States (NDIC 2003a).

Organizational structure in gangs affiliated with the Bloods can range from loosely to highly structured, depending on the individual gang leadership. In 2003, the U.S. Department of Justice estimated that more than 600 Bloods sets existed in the United States, with between 15,000 and 20,000 total members. The number of members in individual gangs can range from three to several hundred, most often between the ages of 16 and 22 years old but ranging in age from 10 to 40 years old (NDIC 2003a).

Tattoos can include a five-point star, indicating a relationship with the People Nation; the words "Piru" (from a street in

Los Angeles) and "Damu," which is Swahili for blood; or the letters "CK," for Crip killer. Team jerseys worn by gang members include those of the Philadelphia Phillies (baseball), San Francisco 49ers (football), and Chicago Bulls (basketball). They also wear a baseball cap with the brim to the left, wear red shoelaces on the left shoe, and fold up the left pants leg. Some gang members also choose to wear the color of their local set, which may be different from the primary Bloods color.

The East Coast Bloods were organized in New York City in 1993 by Leonard "Deadeye" MacKenzie while in his cell at Rikers Island, while Omar Portee, also known as O. G. "Original Gangsta" Mack, formed the United Blood Nation from his cell at Rikers Island.

Gangster Disciples

The Gangster Disciples gang started out as the Devil's Disciples in 1960 in Chicago, then became the Black Disciples, led by David Barksdale, sometime around 1966. Its biggest rival was the Black P. Stone Rangers gang, led by Jeff Fort. When Barksdale died in 1974, Jerome Freeman became leader of the Black Disciples, while Larry Hoover created a new gang known as the Black Gangster Disciples, which was the primary organization for all the Disciples gangs. In 1978, the gang split into the Black Disciples, Black Gangsters, and Gangster Disciples (Knox 2001). By 1995, the Gangster Disciples had expanded into a well-organized criminal operation with members in 35 states (Knox 2001). While in prison, Larry Hoover urged his gang members to work on their General Educational Development (or GED) diplomas, learn whatever they could about the law and legal appeals, and exercise to keep their bodies strong. All of these activities would benefit the gang when the individual members were released.

Gang colors are black and blue. Symbols used by the gang include the six-pointed star; pitchforks; a heart with wings, tail, and horn; a crown; and a sword. The points of the six-pointed star, referred to as the Star of David, in this case named for David Barksdale, represent life, love, loyalty, wisdom, knowledge, and understanding. Gang members also "sign to the right," meaning that they wear a baseball cap with the brim to the right, roll up the right pants leg, or wear a distinct shoelace in the right shoe. They also may use the number 74 (G is the seventh letter of the alphabet, and D is the fourth—indicating GD, or Gangster Disciples).

They have a written constitution and specific rules and regulations that members must obey. The gang is affiliated with the Folk Nation and, according to Knox (2001), also affiliated with the Crips. Many gang members view themselves as being part of a business, rather than a gang. Curry and Decker (2003) interviewed gang members in Chicago and found that many members "bristled at the characterization of their group as a gang, believing that such a term unfairly characterized them in negative terms" (10). However, other members did admit that they were involved in criminal activities and did consider themselves part of a gang.

Almighty Latin King and Queen Nation

One of the oldest and most organized gangs originating in Chicago is the Almighty Latin King and Queen Nation (ALKQN), also known as the Latin Kings, which is made up primarily of Hispanics. Started in the 1940s, the Latin Kings began as many other gangs did—to protect each other, to fight injustice, and to better themselves and their communities. However, over time, they became one of Chicago's most violent street gangs.

The ALKQN is governed by a constitution, which provides 10 commandments that govern the behavior of all members, a description of the royalty of the ALKQN, and directions for establishing new chapters of the gang. The top-level leaders are known as the Inca; the second-level leadership, or warlord level, is referred to as the Supreme Cacique; and the third level of command is the Royal Crown.

An estimated 25,000 members of the Latin Kings are active in Chicago. Sets within the Latin Kings are considered to be better organized than most other gangs in the Chicago area, each with a detailed constitution. They often have both male and female members and primarily focus on drug trafficking. Members are found both in the community and in prison. Gang members focus on the cultural aspects of their gang.

Symbols used by the Latin Kings include a lion, a sun, a diamond, a cross, a five-pointed crown, the number 5, and those symbols associated with the People Nation. The points of the five-pointed crown stand for respect, honesty, unity, knowledge, and love. Primary colors worn by the gang include black, gold, and red.

In 1995, Latin Kings gang members in New York City were investigated by the U.S. Attorney's Office, the FBI office in New York City, and the New York Police Department under the federal Racketeer Influenced and Corrupt Organizations (RICO) statutes. The investigation resulted in the arrest of several dozen gang members on charges ranging from arson to murder. All defendants, except for gang leader Luis Felipe, pleaded guilty. Following a jury trial, Felipe was found guilty and sentenced to life in prison without the possibility of parole.

Antonio "King Tone" Fernandez took over leadership of the New York chapter of ALKQN and attempted to improve the image of the gang by claiming that it was essentially a brotherhood of men and women who were trying to improve their lives and communities. However, in 1999, federal and state investigators examined the members and activities of the ALKQN and arrested more than 100 members, including Fernandez, charging them with narcotics possession, conspiracy to distribute narcotics, weapons possession, and murder. Fernandez pleaded guilty to charges of selling 700 grams of heroin and 3.5 kilos of cocaine and was sentenced to twelve-and-a-half years in prison.

Black Peace Stone Nation

The Black Peace Stone Nation gang, also known as Black P. Stones, started out as a political organization known as the Blackstone Rangers in the 1950s. Founded by Jeff Fort (see Chapter 5) and Eugene Hairston, the Blackstone Rangers developed into an association of more than 20 local gangs and political organizations in Chicago. Made up predominantly of African Americans, the gang split in 1968 following the investigation of Fort for embezzlement of government funds. Most of the gang members followed Fort, rather than Hairston, and the newly formed Fort gang became known as the Black Peace Stone Nation. Fort was convicted in 1972 of embezzlement and lying to government officials and served four years in prison, where he continued to direct the gang's activities.

Following Fort's release from prison in 1976, he joined the Moorish Temple of America in Milwaukee, became a Muslim, and changed the name of the gang alliance to El Rukn, from the Arabic for "foundation." In 1987, Fort and several other leaders of El Rukn were indicted for conspiring to transport explosives and commit violent acts on behalf of the government of Libya. He was convicted and sentenced to 80 years in prison and fined $225,000. With most of the gang's leadership in prison, the gang was dissolved in 1987 and reformed in 1988 under the name Black Peace Stone Nation (NDIC 2003b).

In 2003, the gang alliance was estimated to have a membership of between 6,000 and 8,000 members, including seven gangs in 20 states. The gang colors are black, red, and green; gang members also wear popular sports team jerseys, specifically the Chicago Bulls or the Phoenix Suns. Gang tattoos include a pyramid within a circle with a sun on top and the eye of Allah in the pyramid's left side, or a crescent moon, a five-pointed star, and the word "Allah" or the number 7 (for the seven prayers of the Koran).

The gang is associated with the People Nation alliance of gangs. Gang members illustrate this alliance by wearing a baseball cap with the brim to the left; folding up the left pants leg; or using red, green, or black shoelaces only in the left shoe (NDIC 2003b). Gang members are involved in a variety of criminal activities, including drug trafficking, assault, battery, murder, money laundering, extortion, and robbery.

18th Street

The 18th Street gang, sometimes referred to as Calle 18, was formed during the 1960s in Los Angeles. It is made up primarily of Hispanics, often illegal immigrants from Mexico and Central America, although some African Americans, Asians, whites, and Native Americans are members. The gang reportedly began as a result of racial prejudice. A Hispanic gang known as the Clanton Street gang was composed of Hispanics who were American citizens; other Hispanics in Los Angeles who were illegal immigrants or not 100 percent Hispanic wanted to join but were rejected. These youths created a new gang, the 18th Street gang, named after the street on which their organizer lived.

Tattoos include XVIII or 666 (which adds up to 18). Gang members primarily wear dark pants, usually brown or black, with a white T-shirt. The gang typically uses graffiti to mark their territory. They also travel to other cities and states to recruit new members; Valdez (2000a) believes they were the first Hispanic street gang to travel to other areas for this purpose. Criminal activities of gang members include drug trafficking, auto theft, carjacking, drive-by shootings, weapons trafficking, rape, and murder. The gang reportedly has connections with drug cartels in Mexico and Colombia and is heavily involved in drug trafficking (Valdez 2000a). Another frequent criminal activity is "tax collection": gang members collect a "tax" from all businesses within their territory, threatening to kill anyone who refuses to pay the tax.

Norteños

The Norteños ("northerner" in Spanish) gang was started in Folsom State Prison in 1968 by several Hispanic prisoners who wanted to protect themselves from the Mexican Mafia, a prison gang composed primarily of Southern Californians. The gang expanded into many communities as the gang members were released from prison and returned to their old neighborhoods. Gangs affiliated with the Norterños are generally found in northern California and in Colorado, Texas, New York, other western states, and some midwestern states.

Gang members associate themselves with the number 14 (N is the 14th letter of the alphabet) and the color red. They are often seen wearing San Francisco 49ers clothing and hats, University of Nebraska caps and clothing, or University of Nevada, Las Vegas (UNLV) clothing; they interpret the UNLV as "Us Norteños Love Violence." Some Norteños in California have been seen wearing the light blue University of North Carolina team clothing, interpreting the "NC" as "Northern California."

Sureños

Gangs affiliated with the Sureños ("southerner" in Spanish) are found in Southern California; throughout the western United States, with a major presence in Colorado, Arizona, New Mexico, and Utah; in the Midwest, primarily Illinois, Indiana, and Nebraska; and the South, in Georgia, North Carolina, and Florida. The Sureños started in the 1970s as the Mexican Mafia in the California prison system and grew throughout Southern California as gang members were released from prison. Gangs such as 18th Street and Mara Salvatrucha often identify themselves as Sureños.

Gang members associate themselves with the number 13 (M is the 13th letter of the alphabet), which stands for the Mexican Mafia and the color blue. Gang members illustrate their alliance with the gang by wearing a baseball cap with the brim to the right or folding up the right pants leg. Sureño gang members are primarily known for their involvement in drug trafficking, theft, and some human trafficking. Other symbols used include "Sur 13," "Los Sureños," "MM" (Mexican Mafia), or "E Eme" (The M).

Vice Lords

The Vice Lords gang was formed in Chicago in 1958 by several youths who met at the Illinois Training School for Boys in St. Charles, Illinois, and were looking for protection as well as ways to make money. It is the second-largest street gang in Chicago, with an estimated 20,000 members throughout Illinois. The Vice Lords have now expanded into other states, as well as other countries, including Central America and Spain. The gang is composed of many sets; each set has its own leaders and creates its own hierarchical structure. Members are primarily African American.

Gang members are involved in criminal activities, including drug trafficking, homicide, drive-by shootings, and weapons smuggling. Their symbols and tattoos include a five-pointed star, a top hat, a martini glass, a cane, crescent moons, and the Playboy bunny. The points of the five-pointed star represent love, justice, truth, freedom, and peace. The top hat indicates shelter or protection for the gang members. The martini glass symbolizes celebration and class. The cane indicates the strength of the gang, and, when seen intersecting a top hat, it shows that the gang controls that neighborhood. The crescent moons, when facing each other, represent the division of African Americans into two halves—the East and the West. The Playboy bunny symbolizes the quickness and alertness of gang members.

The gang's colors are gold, black, and red. The team jerseys they wear includes those of the Pittsburgh Steelers (football), University of Iowa, and Pittsburgh Penguins (hockey). They are also known to wear Louis Vuitton caps, which have the LV logo, and UNLV jackets—UNLV reversed is VLNU, or Vice Lords Nation United.

Mara Salvatrucha (MS-13)

The Mara Salvatrucha (*mara* meaning "posse," "salva" from El Salvador, and *trucha* meaning "street tough") gang, also known as MS-13, was founded in Los Angeles during the 1980s. Formed initially by Salvadorans in Los Angeles for protection from other local Hispanic gangs, MS-13 is a well-run organization operating throughout the United States, Canada, Mexico, El Salvador, and other Central American countries. It has been aligned with the Mexican Mafia and the Sureños. Symbols used by the gang in tattoos and graffiti include the number 13. According to Campos-Flores (2005), approximately 700,000 MS-13 gang members are active in the world; a large majority of them reside in Central America.

The gang is considered to be one of the most violent gangs in the world. Members are involved in a variety of criminal activities, including auto theft, home invasions, burglaries, extortion, murder, rape, weapons trafficking, carjacking, and witness intimidation. Drug trafficking activities include the sale and distribution of cocaine, marijuana, heroin, and methamphetamine. In some areas, gang members have also instituted a tax on certain business activities, taxing prostitutes and individuals involved in drug sales in their neighborhoods. The gang is also responsible for executing three federal agents and for numerous other assaults on law enforcement personnel (Valdez 2000b).

Law enforcement agencies have a difficult time monitoring the activities of MS-13, because the gang is spread throughout the United States and has a presence in many other countries, has a decentralized form of organization, and is involved in a wide variety of criminal activities. According to the FBI's Web site, MS-13 has between 6,000 and 10,000 members in 42 states and the District of Columbia (FBI 2008). The FBI operates the MS-13 National Gang Task Force, which coordinates the expertise and resources of several federal agencies and investigates the national and international activities of this gang.

State Statutes

Some type of legislation related to gangs has been enacted in more than 70 percent of all states. These statutes most often legislate gang activity, gang member recruitment, drive-by shootings, graffiti, enhanced penalties for participating in gang activities, and forfeiture of property used in or obtained through criminal gang activity. Some states have enacted legislation specific to street gangs, including street gang terrorism acts such as the Street Terrorism Enforcement and Prevention (STEP) Act first introduced in California. The STEP Act is well known because of its comprehensive attempt to control and prevent street gangs from committing criminal acts throughout the state.

Most law enforcement officials believe that state statutes are the most effective means of dealing with gang crime. A survey by the Institute for Law and Justice of local prosecutors found that respondents believe that general criminal statutes can deal with most crimes committed by gang members. Prosecutors in 36 states reported that they have filed charges against gang members using existing state criminal codes, while prosecutors in 14 states indicated that they have also used newly enacted state laws that target specialized gang offenses, such as drive-by shootings and carjackings (Johnson, Webster, and Connors 1995).

Federal Government Involvement in Prevention and Intervention Activities

The U.S. federal government has several programs to prevent youths from joining gangs and to intervene and stop gang activity. The FBI runs more than 160 task forces operating in its 56 field offices throughout the country; for example, 134 Safe Streets task forces focus on violent gangs and their activities. These task forces include federal, state, and local investigators, who share information, resources, staffing, and information on local gangs and gang activity.

The Bureau of Alcohol, Tobacco, Firearms and Explosives also has several ongoing efforts in its local offices to curb gang activity. For example, in 2006, the ATF in Minnesota established a task force with the St. Paul Police Department to investigate firearms-related crime; 75 percent of these crimes are gang related. Also in 2006, the ATF Violent Gang Task Force in Seattle arrested 47 gang members, charging them with federal and state firearms and drug charges. The ATF has become involved in international gang activities by cohosting a gang summit in Los Angeles in 2007 that focused on strengthening multilateral efforts toward transnational gangs; participants included chiefs of police from Belize, Honduras, El Salvador, and Guatemala.

Federal Legislation

Generally, most of the crimes committed by gang members are the responsibility of state and local law enforcement agencies;

states generally enact laws to prevent or suppress gang activity. However, the U.S. Congress has passed several laws that relate to gangs and gang behavior.

Anti-Drug Abuse Act of 1988 (P.L. 100-690)

This act established grant programs within the Office of Justice Programs and the Office of Juvenile Justice and Delinquency Prevention within the U.S. Department of Justice to address gang problems. Grants are provided to state, local, and tribal law enforcement agencies that can be used for a variety of activities, including antigang initiatives.

Violent Crime Control and Law Enforcement Act of 1994 (P.L. 103-322)

This act was the first to take a more comprehensive approach to dealing with gangs and contains several antigang initiatives. New or enhanced penalties for crimes that are associated with gangs were established, including the imposition of an additional term of imprisonment (up to 10 years) for gang-related crimes such as serious federal drug offenses or federal violent felonies affecting interstate or foreign commerce. The act also allows for the prosecution of juveniles who are 13 years old or older if the juvenile was in possession of a firearm during a violent crime. The act authorized funding for the Gang Resistance Education and Training Program, which provides grants to state and local law enforcement agencies and prevention programs that focus on schools. The Community Oriented Policing Services program was also authorized by this act; the program is designed to place more law enforcement officers on the streets to make local communities safer.

FY2005 Consolidated Appropriations Act (P.L. 108-447)

This act designated $10 million for the establishment of the National Gang Intelligence Center at the FBI, which serves as a clearinghouse for information from the FBI, ATF, and other federal law enforcement agencies. It also authorized funding to hire additional FBI agents and analysts to focus on the most violent gangs.

Racketeer Influenced and Corrupt Organizations (RICO) Act (18 U.S.C. 1961 *et seq.*)

Prosecutors in several states have used this legislation successfully, although it was not originally meant for gang activity. The RICO statute, enacted in 1970, has been fairly effective in combating organized criminal activity. Though it is used primarily against high-level criminal groups, some prosecutors have also used it to prosecute gang members engaged in criminal behavior. Most legal experts and many gang researchers believe that it can be used effectively against the large, well-organized gangs that are deeply involved in criminal activities but that state and local laws work best in combating most gang activity.

Bills before the 110th Congress (2007–2008 session)

Every year, bills are introduced in the U.S. Congress that are related to eliminating gang activity, encouraging youth to avoid gang involvement, or preventing or discouraging gang membership and activity. Most often, these bills never make it out of the respective House or Senate committees. As of the end of 2007, the following bills had been introduced in either the U.S. Senate or House of Representatives relating to gangs and gang activities.

H.R. 367—Gang Elimination Act of 2007

This act would require that the U.S. attorney general develop a national strategy to identify and eliminate the illegal operations of the top three international drug gangs that pose the greatest threat to law and order in the United States. It was introduced in the U.S. House of Representatives on January 10, 2007.

H.R. 1582—Gang Abatement and Prevention Act of 2007

This act would increase and enhance law enforcement resources committed to investigate and prosecute violent gangs, to deter and punish gang crime, to protect law-abiding citizens and communities from violent gangs, and to expand gang prevention programs. It was introduced in the House of Representatives on March 20, 2007, with a companion bill (S. 456—Gang Abatement and Prevention Act of 2007) in the U.S. Senate.

H.R. 1692—Fighting Gangs and Empowering Youth Act of 2007

This bill would help law enforcement agencies to fight violent criminal gangs. It was introduced in the House of Representatives on March 26, 2007. A companion bill (S. 990—Fighting Gangs and Empowering Youth Act of 2007) was introduced in the Senate.

H.R. 3150—Anti-Gang Enforcement Act of 2007

This act would provide increased commitment of law enforcement resources to investigate and prosecute violent gangs, to deter and punish gang crime, to aid in the prosecution of juvenile gang members who have committed violent crimes, and to improve gang prevention programs. It was introduced in the House of Representatives on July 24, 2007.

H.R. 3152—Anti-Gang Task Force Act of 2007

The act would provide funding for the creation and support of multijurisdictional antigang task forces. It was introduced in the House of Representatives on July 24, 2007.

H.R. 3547—Gang Prevention, Intervention, and Suppression Act

This act would provide similar provisions as the Gang Abatement and Prevention Act of 2007. It was introduced in the House of Representatives on September 17, 2007.

Gang-Related Definitions in Federal Statutes

The federal government has defined *criminal street gang* as follows (from Title 18, Part I, Chapter 26, § 521—Criminal Street Gangs):

> (a) Definitions—
> "conviction" includes a finding, under State or Federal law, that a person has committed an act of juvenile delinquency involving a violent or controlled substances felony.
> "criminal street gang" means an ongoing group, club, organization, or association of 5 or more persons–
> (A) that has as 1 of its primary purposes the commission of 1 or more of the criminal offenses described in subsection (c);

(B) the members of which engage, or have engaged within the past 5 years, in a continuing series of offenses described in subsection (c); and

(C) the activities of which affect interstate or foreign commerce.

"State" means a State of the United States, the District of Columbia, and any commonwealth, territory, or possession of the United States.

(b) Penalty—The sentence of a person convicted of an offense described in subsection (c) shall be increased by up to 10 years if the offense is committed under the circumstances described in subsection (d).

(c) Offenses—The offenses described in this section are

(1) a Federal felony involving a controlled substance (as defined in section 102 of the Controlled Substances Act (21 U.S.C. 802)) for which the maximum penalty is not less than 5 years;

(2) a Federal felony crime of violence that has as an element the use or attempted use of physical force against the person of another; and

(3) a conspiracy to commit an offense described in paragraph (1) or (2).

(d) Circumstances—The circumstances described in this section are that the offense described in subsection (c) was committed by a person who –

(1) participates in a criminal street gang with knowledge that its members engage in or have engaged in a continuing series of offenses described in subsection (c);

(2) intends to promote or further the felonious activities of the criminal street gang or maintain or increase his or her position in the gang; and

(3) has been convicted within the past 5 years for—

(A) an offense described in subsection (c);

(B) a State offense—

(i) involving a controlled substance (as defined in section 102 of the Controlled Substances Act (21 U.S.C. 802)) for which the maximum penalty is not less than 5 years' imprisonment; or

(ii) that is a felony crime of violence that has as an element the use or attempted use of physical force against the person of another;

(C) any Federal or State felony offense that by its nature involves a substantial risk that physical force against the person of another may be used in the course of committing the offense; or

(D) a conspiracy to commit an offense described in subparagraph (A), (B), or (C).

Gang-Related Definitions in State Statutes

Statutes in most states attempt to define gang membership. Table 6.1 provides excerpts from specific statutes related to definitions of gangs and gang activity.

TABLE 6.1

State statute definitions of *street gang, gang member,* and *gang activity*

State	Definition
Alabama § 13A-6-26	(a) For purposes of this section, the term "streetgang" means any combination, confederation, alliance, network, conspiracy, understanding, or other similar arrangement in law or in fact, of three or more persons that, through its membership or through the agency of any member, engages in a course or pattern of criminal activity.
Alaska § 11.81.900	(13) "criminal street gang" means a group of three or more persons (A) who have in common a name or identifying sign, symbol, tattoo or other physical marking, style of dress, or use of hand signs; and (B) who, individually, jointly, or in combination, have committed or attempted to commit, within the preceding three years, for the benefit of, at the direction of, or in association with the group, two or more offenses under any of, or any combination of, the following: . . .
Arizona § 13-105	"Criminal street gang" means an ongoing formal or informal association of persons whose members or associates individually or collectively engage in the commission, attempted commission, facilitation or solicitation of any felony act and who has at least one individual who is a criminal street gang member. 8. "Criminal street gang member" means an individual to whom two of the following seven criteria that indicate criminal street gang membership apply: (a) Self-proclamation. (b) Witness testimony or official statement. (c) Written or electronic correspondence. (d) Paraphernalia or photographs. (e) Tattoos. (f) Clothing or colors. (g) Any other indicia of street gang membership.

continues

TABLE 6.1   continued

State	Definition
Arkansas § 5-74-103	(3) "Criminal gang, organization, or enterprise" means any group of three (3) or more individuals who commit a continuing series of two (2) or more predicate criminal offenses that are undertaken in concert with each other; and (4) "Predicate criminal offense" means any violation of Arkansas law that is a crime of violence or a crime of pecuniary gain.
Arkansas § 5-74-202	a) "Criminal gang, organization, or enterprise" is defined as any group of three (3) or more individuals who commit a continuing series of two (2) or more predicate criminal offenses which are undertaken in concert with each other. b) "Predicate criminal offense" means any violation of Arkansas law which is a crime of violence or of pecuniary gain. c) "Crime of violence" means any violation of Arkansas law where a person purposely or knowingly causes, or threatens to cause, death or physical injury to another person or persons, specifically including rape, §5-14-103. d) "Crime of pecuniary gain" means any violation of Arkansas law that results or was intended to result, in the defendant's receiving income, benefit, property, money, or anything of value.
California § 186.22	(f) As used in this chapter, "criminal street gang" means any ongoing organization, association, or group of three or more persons, whether formal or informal, having as one of its primary activities the commission of one or more of the criminal acts enumerated in paragraphs (1) to (25), inclusive, of subdivision (e), having a common name or common identifying sign or symbol, and whose members individually or collectively engage in or have engaged in a pattern of criminal gang activity.
Colorado § 18-23-101	(1) "Criminal street gang" means any ongoing organization, association, or group of three or more persons, whether formal or informal: (a) Which has as one of its primary objectives or activities the commission of one or more predicate criminal acts; and (b) Whose members individually or collectively engage in or have engaged in a pattern of criminal gang activity.
Colorado § 19-1-103	(52) "Gang", as used in sections 19-2-205 and 19-2-508, means a group of three or more individuals with a common interest, bond, or activity, characterized by criminal or delinquent conduct, engaged in either collectively or individually.
Connecticut § 29-7n	(a) For the purposes of Sections 7-294l and 7-294x, Subsection (a) of Section 10-16b, Subsection (b) of this section and Sections 3 and 8 of public act 93-416, "gang" means a group of juveniles or youth who, acting in concert with each other, or with adults, engage in illegal activities.
Delaware § 616	(1) "Criminal street gang" means any ongoing organization, association, or group of 3 or more persons, whether formal or informal, having as one of its primary activities the commission of one or more of the criminal acts enumerated in Subdivision (a)(2) of this section, having a common name or common identifying sign or symbol, and whose members individually or collectively engage in or have engaged in a pattern of criminal gang activity.

continues

TABLE 6.1   continued

State	Definition
	(2) "Pattern of criminal gang activity" means the commission of, attempted commission of, conspiracy to commit, solicitation of, or conviction of 2 or more of the following criminal offenses, provided that at least one (1) of these offenses occurred after July 1, 2003, and that the last of those offenses occurred within 3 years after a prior offense, and provided that the offenses were committed on separate occasions, or by 2 or more persons . . . .
District of Columbia § 22-951	(1) "Criminal street gang" means an association or group of 6 or more persons that: (A) Has as a condition of membership or continued membership, the committing of or actively participating in committing a crime of violence, as defined by § 23-1331(4)); or (B) Has as one of its purposes or frequent activities, the violation of the criminal laws of the District, or the United States, except for acts of civil disobedience. (2) "Violent misdemeanor" shall mean (A) Destruction of property (§ 22-303); (B) Simple assault (§ 22-404(a)); (C) Stalking (§ 22-404(b)); (D) Threats to do bodily harm (§ 22-407); (E) Criminal abuse or criminal neglect of a vulnerable adult (§ 22-936(a)); (F) Cruelty to animals (§ 22-1001(a)); and (G) Possession of prohibited weapon (§ 22-4514).
Florida § 874.03	(1) "Criminal street gang" means a formal or informal ongoing organization, association, or group that has as one of its primary activities the commission of criminal or delinquent acts, and that consists of three or more persons who have a common name or common identifying signs, colors, or symbols and have two or more members who, individually or collectively, engage in or have engaged in a pattern of criminal street gang activity. (2) "Criminal street gang member" is a person who is a member of a criminal street gang as defined in subsection (1) and who meets two or more of the following criteria: (a) Admits to criminal street gang membership. (b) Is identified as a criminal street gang member by a parent or guardian. (c) Is identified as a criminal street gang member by a documented reliable informant. (d) Resides in or frequents a particular criminal street gang's area and adopts their style of dress, their use of hand signs, or their tattoos, and associates with known criminal street gang members. (e) Is identified as a criminal street gang member by an informant of previously untested reliability and such identification is corroborated by independent information. (f) Has been arrested more than once in the company of identified criminal street gang members for offenses which are consistent with usual criminal street gang activity. (g) Is identified as a criminal street gang member by physical evidence such as photographs or other documentation. (h) Has been stopped in the company of known criminal street gang members four or more times.

continues

TABLE 6.1 continued

State	Definition
Georgia § 16-15-3	(1) "Criminal street gang" means any organization, association, or group of three or more persons associated in fact, whether formal or informal, which engages in a pattern of criminal gang activity as defined in subsection (2) of this Code section. The existence of such organization, association, or group of individuals associated in fact may be established by evidence of a common name or common identifying signs, symbols, tattoos, graffiti, or attire or other distinguishing characteristics. (2) "Pattern of criminal gang activity" means the commission, attempted commission, conspiracy to commit, or solicitation, coercion, or intimidation of another person to commit at least two of the following offenses, provided that at least one of these offenses occurred after July 1, 1998, and the last of such offenses occurred within three years, excluding any periods of imprisonment, of prior criminal gang activity.
Idaho § 18-8502	(1) "Criminal gang" means an ongoing organization, association, or group of three (3) or more persons, whether formal or informal, that has a common name or common identifying sign or symbol, whose members individually or collectively engage in or have engaged in a pattern of criminal gang activity, having as one (1) of its primary activities the commission of one (1) or more of the criminal acts enumerated in Subsection (3) of this section. (2) "Criminal gang member" means any person who engages in a pattern of criminal gang activity and who meets two (2) or more of the following criteria: (a) Admits to gang membership; (b) Is identified as a gang member; (c) Resides in or frequents a particular gang's area and adopts its style of dress, its use of hand signs, or its tattoos and associates with known gang members; (d) Has been arrested more than once in the company of identified gang members for offenses that are consistent with usual gang activity; (e) Is identified as a gang member by physical evidence such as photographs or other documentation; or (f) Has been stopped in the company of known gang members four (4) or more times.
Illinois § 147/10	"Street gang" or "gang" or "organized gang" or "criminal street gang" means any combination, confederation, alliance, network, conspiracy, understanding, or other similar conjoining, in law or in fact, of 3 or more persons with an established hierarchy that, through its membership or through the agency of any member engages in a course or pattern of criminal activity. "Streetgang member" or "gang member" means any person who actually and in fact belongs to a gang, and any person who knowingly acts in the capacity of an agent for or accessory to, or is legally accountable for, or voluntarily associates himself with a course or pattern of gang-related criminal activity, whether in a preparatory, executory, or cover-up phase of any activity, or who knowingly performs, aids, or abets any such activity. "Streetgang related" or "gang-related" means any criminal activity, enterprise, pursuit, or undertaking directed by, ordered by, authorized by, consented to, agreed to, requested by, acquiesced in, or ratified by any gang leader, officer, or governing or policy-making person or authority, or by any agent, representative, or deputy of any such officer, person, or authority.

continues

204 Data and Documents

TABLE 6.1 continued

State	Definition
Indiana § 35-45-9-1	As used in this chapter, "criminal gang" means a group with at least five (5) members that specifically: (1) either: (A) promotes, sponsors, or assists in; or (B) participates in; or (2) requires as a condition of membership or continued membership; the commission of a felony or an act that would be a felony if committed by an adult or the offense of battery (IC 35-42-2-1).
Iowa § 723A.1	2. "Criminal street gang" means any ongoing organization, association, or group of three or more persons, whether formal or informal, having as one of its primary activities the commission of one or more criminal acts, which has an identifiable name or identifying sign or symbol, and whose members individually or collectively engage in or have engaged in a pattern of criminal gang activity. 3. "Pattern of criminal gang activity" means the commission, attempt to commit, conspiring to commit, or solicitation of two or more criminal acts, provided the criminal acts were committed on separate dates or by two or more persons who are members of, or belong to, the same criminal street gang.
Kansas § 21-4226	a) "Criminal street gang" means any organization, association or group, whether formal or informal: (1) Consisting of three or more persons; (2) having as one of its primary activities the commission of one or more person felonies, person misdemeanors, felony violations of the uniform controlled substances act, K.S.A. 65-4101 et seq., and amendments thereto, or the comparable juvenile offenses, which if committed by an adult would constitute the commission of such felonies or misdemeanors; (3) which has a common name or common identifying sign or symbol; and (4) whose members, individually or collectively, engage in or have engaged in the commission, attempted commission, conspiracy to commit or solicitation of two or more person felonies, person misdemeanors, felony violations of the uniform controlled substances act, K.S.A. 65-4101 et seq., and amendments thereto, the comparable juvenile offenses, which if committed by an adult would constitute the commission of such felonies or misdemeanors or any substantially similar offense from another jurisdiction. (b) "Criminal street gang member" is a person who: (1) Admits to criminal street gang membership; or (2) meets three or more of the following criteria: (A) Is identified as a criminal street gang member by a parent or guardian. (B) Is identified as a criminal street gang member by a state, county or city law enforcement officer or correctional officer or documented reliable informant. (C) Is identified as a criminal street gang member by an informant of previously untested reliability and such identification is corroborated by independent information. (D) Resides in or frequents a particular criminal street gang's area and adopts such gang's style of dress, color, use of hand signs or tattoos, and associates with known criminal street gang members.

continues

TABLE 6.1   continued

State	Definition
	(E) Has been arrested more than once in the company of identified criminal street gang members for offenses which are consistent with usual criminal street gang activity.
	(F) Is identified as a criminal street gang member by physical evidence including, but not limited to, photographs or other documentation.
	(G) Has been stopped in the company of known criminal street gang members two or more times.
	(H) Has participated in or undergone activities self-identified or identified by a reliable informant as a criminal street gang initiation ritual.
	(c) "Criminal street gang activity" means the commission or attempted commission of, or solicitation or conspiracy to commit, one or more person felonies, person misdemeanors, felony violations of the uniform controlled substances act, K.S.A. 65-4101, et seq., and amendments thereto, or the comparable juvenile offenses, which if committed by an adult would constitute the commission of such felonies or misdemeanors on separate occasions.
Louisiana § 15:1404	A. As used in this Chapter, "criminal street gang" means any ongoing organization association, or group of three or more persons, whether formal or informal, which has as one of its primary activities the commission of one or more of the criminal acts enumerated in Paragraphs (1) through (8) of Subsection B of this Section or which has a common name or common identifying sign or symbol, whose members individually or collectively engage in or have engaged in a pattern of criminal gang activity.
	B. As used in this Chapter, "pattern of criminal gang activity" means the commission or attempted commission of two or more of the following offenses, provided at least one of those offenses occurred after September 7, 1990 and the last of those offenses occurred within three years after a prior offense, and the offenses are committed on separate occasions or by two or more persons . . . .
Massachusetts § 265.44	Whoever commits an assault and battery on a child under the age of eighteen for the purpose of causing or coercing such child to join or participate in a criminal conspiracy in violation of section seven of chapter two hundred and seventy-four, including but not limited to a criminal street gang or other organization of three or more persons which has a common name, identifying sign or symbol and whose members individually or collectively engage in criminal activity . . . .
Minnesota § 609.229	As used in this section, "criminal gang" means any ongoing organization, association, or group of three or more persons, whether formal or informal, that:
	(1) has, as one of its primary activities, the commission of one or more of the offenses listed in section 609.11, subdivision 9;
	(2) has a common name or common identifying sign or symbol; and
	(3) includes members who individually or collectively engage in or have engaged in a pattern of criminal activity.
Mississippi § 97-44-3	"Street gang" or "gang" or "organized gang" or "criminal street gang" means any combination, confederation, alliance, network, conspiracy, understanding, or other similar conjoining, in law or in fact, of three (3) or more persons with an established hierarchy that, through its membership or through the agency of any member, engages in felonious criminal activity.

continues

TABLE 6.1 continued

State	Definition
	For purposes of this chapter, it shall not be necessary to show that a particular conspiracy, combination or conjoining of persons possesses, acknowledges or is known by any common name, insignia, flag, means of recognition, secret signal or code, creed, belief, structure, leadership or command structure, method of operation or criminal enterprise, concentration or specialty, membership, age or other qualifications, initiation rites, geographical or territorial situs or boundary or location, or other unifying mark, manner, protocol or method of expressing or indicating membership when the conspiracy's existence, in law or in fact, can be demonstrated by a preponderance of the competent evidence. However, any evidence reasonably tending to show or demonstrate, in law or in fact, the existence of or membership in any conspiracy, confederation or other association described herein, or probative of the existence of or membership in any such association, shall be admissible in any action or proceeding brought under this chapter. "Street gang member" or "gang member" means any person who actually and in fact belongs to a gang, and any person who knowingly acts in the capacity of an agent for or accessory to, or is legally accountable for, or voluntarily associates himself with a gang-related criminal activity, whether in a preparatory, executory or cover-up phase of any activity, or who knowingly performs, aids or abets any such activity. "Street gang related" or "gang-related" means any criminal activity, enterprise, pursuit or undertaking directed by, ordered by, authorized by, consented to, agreed to, requested by, acquiesced in, or ratified by any gang leader, officer or governing or policymaking person or authority, or by any agent, representative or deputy of any such officer, person or authority . . . .
Missouri § 578.421	(1) "Criminal street gang", any ongoing organization, association, or group of three or more persons, whether formal or informal, having as one of its primary activities the commission of one or more of the criminal acts enumerated in subdivision (2) of this section, which has a common name or common identifying sign or symbol, whose members individually or collectively engage in or have engaged in a pattern of criminal gang activity; (2) "Pattern of criminal street gang activity", the commission, attempted commission, or solicitation of two or more of the following offenses, provided at least one of those offenses occurred after August 28, 1993, and the last of those offenses occurred within three years after a prior offense, and the offenses are committed on separate occasions, or by two or more persons . . . .
Montana § 45-8-402	(1) "Criminal street gang" means any ongoing organization, association, or group of three or more persons, whether formal or informal, having as one of its primary activities the commission of one or more of the criminal acts enumerated in 45-8-405, having a common name or common identifying sign or symbol, and whose members individually or collectively engage in or have engaged in a pattern of criminal street gang activity. (2) "Pattern of criminal street gang activity" has the meaning provided in 45-8-405
Nevada § 193.168	6. As used in this section, "criminal gang" means any combination of persons, organized formally or informally, so constructed that the organization will continue its operation even if individual members enter or leave the organization, which: (a) Has a common name or identifying symbol; (b) Has particular conduct, status and customs indicative of it; and (c) Has as one of its common activities engaging in criminal activity punishable as a felony, other than the conduct which constitutes the primary offense.

continues

TABLE 6.1   continued

State	Definition
New Jersey § 2C.44-3	"Criminal street gang" means three or more persons associated in fact. Individuals are associated in fact if (1) they have in common a group name or identifying sign, symbol, tattoo or other physical marking, style of dress or use of hand signs or other indicia of association or common leadership, and (2) individually or in combination with other members of a criminal street gang, while engaging in gang related activity, have committed, conspired or attempted to commit, within the preceding three years, two or more offenses of robbery, carjacking, aggravated assault, assault, aggravated sexual assault, sexual assault, arson, burglary, kidnapping, extortion, or a violation of chapter 11, section 3, 4, 5, 6 or 7 of chapter 35 or chapter 39 of Title 2C of the New Jersey Statutes regardless of whether the prior offenses have resulted in convictions.
New York 9 NYCRR § 301.3	(d)(1) The term gang as used herein means any ongoing organization, association, or group of three or more persons, whether formal or informal, having as one of its primary activities the commission of one or more criminal acts, which has an identifiable name or with the identifying sign or symbol, and whose members individually or collectively engage in or have engaged in a pattern of gang activity. (2) The term gang member means any individual who is part of, associated with, or otherwise affiliated with a gang as defined in paragraph (1) of this subdivision. (3) Gang activity means the commission by a gang member, in a singular commission, attempt to commit, conspiring to commit, or the solicitation of a criminal act, on State property in the presence of two or more other gang members. (4) A pattern of gang activity means the commission, attempt to commit, conspiring to commit, or solicitation of two or more criminal acts, provided the criminal acts were committed on separate dates or by two or more persons who are members of, or belong to, the same gang.
North Carolina § 15A-1340.16	(d)(2a) . . . A "criminal street gang" means any ongoing organization, association, or group of three or more persons, whether formal or informal, having as one of its primary activities the commission of felony or violent misdemeanor offenses, or delinquent acts that would be felonies or violent misdemeanors if committed by an adult, and having a common name or common identifying sign, colors, or symbols.
North Dakota § 12.1-06.2-01	1. "Crime of pecuniary gain" means any violation of state law that directly results or was intended to result in the defendant alone, or in association with others, receiving income, benefit, property, money, or anything of value. 2. "Crime of violence" means any violation of state law where a person purposely or knowingly causes or threatens to cause death or physical bodily injury to another person or persons. 3. "Criminal street gang" means any ongoing organization or group of three or more persons, whether formal or informal, that acts in concert or agrees to act in concert with a purpose that any of those persons alone or in any combination commit or will commit two or more predicate gang crimes one of which occurs after August 1, 1995, and the last of which occurred within five years after the commission of a prior predicate gang crime. 4. "Participate in a criminal street gang" means to act in concert with a criminal street gang with intent to commit or with the intent that any other person associated with the criminal street gang will commit one or more predicate gang crimes.

continues

TABLE 6.1 continued

State	Definition
Ohio § 2923.41	As used in sections 2923.41 to 2923.47 of the Revised Code: (A) "Criminal gang" means an ongoing formal or informal organization, association, or group of three or more persons to which all of the following apply: (1) It has as one of its primary activities the commission of one or more of the offenses listed in division (B) of this section. (2) It has a common name or one or more common, identifying signs, symbols, or colors. (3) The persons in the organization, association, or group individually or collectively engage in or have engaged in a pattern of criminal gang activity. (B)(1) "Pattern of criminal gang activity" means, subject to division (B)(2) of this section, that persons in the criminal gang have committed, attempted to commit, conspired to commit, been complicitors in the commission of, or solicited, coerced, or intimidated another to commit, attempt to commit, conspire to commit, or be in complicity in the commission of two or more of any of the following offenses . . . .
Oklahoma § 21-856	F. "Criminal street gang" means any ongoing organization, association, or group of five or more persons that specifically either promotes, sponsors, or assists in, or participates in, and requires as a condition of membership or continued membership, the commission of one or more of the following criminal acts: . . .
South Dakota § 22-10A-1	(1) "Street gang," any formal or informal ongoing organization, association, or group of three or more persons who have a common name or common identifying signs, colors, or symbols and have members or associates who, individually or collectively, engage in or have engaged in a pattern of street gang activity; (2) "Street gang member," any person who engages in a pattern of street gang activity and who meets two or more of the following criteria: (a) Admits to gang membership; (b) Is identified as a gang member by a documented reliable informant; (c) Resides in or frequents a particular gang's area and adopts its style of dress, its use of hand signs, or its tattoos and associates with known gang members; (d) Is identified as a gang member by an informant of previously untested reliability if such identification is corroborated by independent information; (e) Has been arrested more than once in the company of identified gang members for offenses which are consistent with usual gang activity; (f) Is identified as a gang member by physical evidence, such as photographs or other documentation; or (g) Has been stopped in the company of known gang members four or more times; and (3) "Pattern of street gang activity," the commission, attempted commission, or solicitation by any member or members of a street gang of two or more felony or violent misdemeanor offenses on separate occasions within a three-year period for the purpose of furthering gang activity.
Tennessee § 40-35-121	(a) As used in this section, unless the context otherwise requires: (1) "Criminal gang" means a formal or informal ongoing organization, association, or group consisting of three (3) or more persons that has: (A) As one (1) of its activities the commission of criminal acts; and

continues

TABLE 6.1   **continued**

State	Definition
	(B) Two (2) or more members who, individually or collectively, engage in or have engaged in a pattern of criminal gang activity; (2) "Criminal gang member" is a person who is a member of a criminal gang, as defined in subdivision (a)(1), and who meets two (2) or more of the following criteria: (A) Admits to criminal gang involvement; (B) Is identified as a criminal gang member by a parent or guardian; (C) Is identified as a criminal gang member by a documented reliable informant; (D) Resides in or frequents a particular criminal gang's area, adopts their style or dress, their use of hand signs or their tattoos, and associates with known criminal gang members; (E) Is identified as a criminal gang member by an informant of previously untested reliability and such identification is corroborated by independent information; (F) Has been arrested more than once in the company of identified criminal gang members for offenses which are consistent with usual criminal gang activity; or (G) Is identified as a criminal gang member by physical evidence such as photographs or other documentation; . . .
Texas § 71.01	(d) "Criminal street gang" means three or more persons having a common identifying sign or symbol or an identifiable leadership who continuously or regularly associate in the commission of criminal activities.
Utah § 78-57-102	(2) "Gang activity" means any criminal activity that is conducted as part of an organized youth gang. It includes any criminal activity that is done in concert with other gang members, or done alone if it is to fulfill gang purposes. "Gang activity" does not include graffiti.
Virginia § 16.1-299.2	For purposes of this section "youth gang" means an ongoing organization, association or group (i) having common characteristics, including but not limited to initiation practices, hand signals, structured style of dress, specific geographic territorial claim or identifiable leadership and (ii) consisting of three or more individuals, at least one of whom is a juvenile, who identify themselves as a group by a name or symbol and are involved in a pattern of recurrent felonious criminal conduct.
Virginia § 18.2-46.1	"Criminal street gang" means any ongoing organization, association, or group of three or more persons, whether formal or informal, (i) which has as one of its primary objectives or activities the commission of one or more criminal activities; (ii) which has an identifiable name or identifying sign or symbol; and (iii) whose members individually or collectively have engaged in the commission of, attempt to commit, conspiracy to commit, or solicitation of two or more predicate criminal acts, at least one of which is an act of violence, provided such acts were not part of a common act or transaction.
Washington § 28A.600.455	(2) "Gang" means a group which (a) consists of three or more persons; (b) has identifiable leadership; and (c) on an ongoing basis, regularly conspires and acts in concert mainly for criminal purposes.

continues

TABLE 6.1   continued

State	Definition
Wisconsin § 939.22	I (9) "Criminal gang" means an ongoing organization, association, or group of three or more persons, whether formal or informal, that has as one of its primary activities the commission of one or more of the criminal acts, or acts that would be criminal if the actor were an adult, specified in Section 939.22 (21) (a) to (s); that has a common name or a common identifying sign or symbol; and whose members individually or collectively engage in or have engaged in a pattern of criminal gang activity. (9g) "Criminal gang member" means any person who participates in criminal gang activity, as defined in Section 941.38 (1) (b), with a criminal gang.
Wisconsin § 941.38	(b) "Criminal gang activity" means the commission of, attempt to commit or solicitation to commit one or more of the following crimes, or acts that would be crimes if the actor were an adult, committed for the benefit of, at the direction of, or in association with any criminal gang, with the specific intent to promote, further, or assist in any criminal conduct by criminal gang members: . . .

Source: Quoted statutes are taken from each state's criminal code. For more information, criminal codes may be accessed through each state's official state government Web site.

Summary of Significant Court Cases in U.S. Courts

In this section, summaries of several important cases are provided. They show the variety of cases that have been brought to the courts relating to gang members and their behavior as well as attempts by states and local jurisdictions to control gang activities.

Chalifoux v. New Caney Independent School District [976 F. Supp. 659 (S.D. Tex. 1997)]

David Chalifoux and Jerry Robertson were students at New Caney High School in Montgomery County, Texas. In 1997, they began wearing rosaries on the outside of their shirts in order to display their religious faith. They wore these rosaries for several weeks without any comment from school officials. They were not members of any gang and were never approached by any gang members. On March 6, 2007, two school district police officers approached the two students and advised them that they could not wear their rosaries outside their shirts, because the school had identified rosaries as gang-related apparel. Chalifoux and

Robertson challenged the school policy on the basis that it violated their First Amendment rights to free exercise of religion and free speech. The U.S. District Court ruled that the symbolic speech at issue in this case is a form of religious expression that is protected under the First Amendment and that the prohibition on wearing rosaries violated the plaintiffs' First Amendment rights as well. The court also voided the school district's regulation on gang-related apparel, claiming it failed to provide adequate notice regarding prohibited conduct.

City of Chicago v. Morales [527 U.S. 41 (1999)]

In 1992, the City Council of Chicago enacted the Gang Congregation Ordinance, which prohibited criminal street-gang members from loitering with each other in a public place. Jesus Morales and others were arrested for violating the ordinance in 1993. The Illinois chapter of the American Civil Liberties Union and the Cook County Public Defender challenged the law on behalf of Morales and the others who had been arrested. The trial court found that the law was unconstitutionally vague and dismissed the charges. The Illinois appellate court agreed that the ordinance violated the due process clause of the Fourteenth Amendment. The U.S. Supreme Court held that Chicago's anti-gang loitering ordinance was unconstitutionally vague.

Olesen v. Board of Education [676 F.Supp. 821 (N.D.Ill 1987)]

Darryl Olesen was a senior at Bremen High School in Midlothian, Illinois. The school's board of education established a rule prohibiting all gang activities at the school, including the wearing of gang symbols, jewelry, and emblems. The wearing of earrings by male students was included in that rule. Olesen wore an earring to school on several occasions, believing that it expressed his individuality and would be attractive to the female students. Each time he wore the earring, he was suspended. He challenged the constitutionality of the rule, arguing that it violated his First Amendment right of free speech and expression and his Fourteenth Amendment right to equal protection. The U.S. District Court dismissed Olesen's complaint, ruling that his message of individuality through the wearing of an earring was not within the protected scope of the First Amendment and that no discrimination had taken place, because the policy forbidding males to wear earrings while allowing females to wear earrings was based on the recognition that "the wearing of earrings by males generally connote gang membership. While girls may be gang members, they symbolize their affiliation in other ways."

Qutb v. Strauss [11 F.3d 488 (1993)]

The city of Dallas passed an ordinance in 1991 that established a curfew for youth under the age of 17 years old, prohibiting them from remaining in a public place from 11 p.m. until 6 a.m. on weeknights and from midnight until 6 a.m. on weekends. Exceptions were made if the youth was with his or her parents; on an errand for a parent; traveling to or from work; involved in work-related activities; or attending school, religious, or civic organization functions. Elizabeth Qutb and three other parents filed suit challenging the ordinance on the basis that it violated their children's First Amendment rights to associate. The U.S. Court of Appeals for the Fifth Circuit ruled that the ordinance did not violate the U.S. or Texas constitutions, suggesting that the curfew "furthers a compelling state interest, i.e., protecting juveniles from crime on the streets. We further conclude that the ordinance is narrowly tailored to achieve this compelling state interest."

Shuttlesworth v. City of Birmingham [382 U.S. 87 (1965)]

Pastor Fred Shuttlesworth was standing around with a group of his friends on a Birmingham, Alabama, sidewalk when a police officer asked them to clear the sidewalk so other pedestrians could get through. Following the officer's third request for them to move, everyone but Shuttlesworth began walking away. The officer arrested Shuttlesworth for violating the city ordinance that made it a crime to disobey a police officer's orders (Birmingham City Code §1231) and the ordinance that prohibited standing or loitering on the sidewalk and obstructing free passage of others (Birmingham City Code §1142). Shuttlesworth was convicted of violating both ordinances and appealed his conviction. Following appeals to the Alabama Court of Appeals and Alabama Supreme

Court, the U.S. Supreme Court overturned his conviction under §1231, suggesting that this section was specific to an officer directing vehicular, not pedestrian, traffic. The conviction under §1142 was set aside as well, in view of the possibility that it was based on an unconstitutional construction of the ordinance.

The People ex rel. Gallo v. Acuna [929 P.2d 596 (1997)]

In this case, a trial court issued a preliminary injunction against certain members of the Varrio Sureo Town or Varrio Sureo Treces gang, banning specific activities of the gang within a four-square-block neighborhood in San Jose, California. It barred them from activities such as "standing, sitting, walking, driving, gathering or appearing anywhere in public view with any other defendant . . . or with any other known [gang] member" as well as barring them from threatening or intimidating anyone in the neighborhood who complained about their activities. The Supreme Court of California held that the activities of the gang members qualified as a public nuisance and defendants' association was not entitled to protection under the First Amendment, because the gang was not formed for the purpose of engaging in protected speech or religious activities.

References

Bobrowski, Lawrence. 1988. *Collecting, Organizing, and Reporting Street Gang Crime.* Chicago: Special Functions Group, Chicago Police Department.

Campbell, Anne. 1984. *The Girls in the Gang: A Report from New York City.* Oxford: Basil Blackwell.

Campo-Flores, Arian. 2005. "The Most Dangerous Gang in America." *Newsweek*, March 28, 22.

Chin, Ko-Lin. 1990. *Chinese Subculture and Criminality: Non-traditional Crime Groups in America.* New York: Greenwood Press.

Collins, H. Craig. 1979. *Street Gangs: Profiles for Police.* New York: New York City Police Department.

Curry, G. David, and Scott H. Decker. 2003. *Confronting Gangs: Crime and Community,* 2d ed. Los Angeles: Roxbury.

Curry, G. David, Richard A. Ball, and Scott H. Decker. 1996. "Estimating the National Scope of Gang Crime from Law Enforcement Data." In *Gangs in America*, 2nd ed., edited by C. Ronald Huff, 21–36. Thousand Oaks, CA: Sage.

Curry, G. David, Scott H. Decker, and Arlen Egley, Jr. 2002. "Gang Involvement and Delinquency in a Middle School Population." *Justice Quarterly* 19 (2): 275–292.

Curry, G. David, Robert J. Fox, Richard A. Ball, and Darryl Stone. 1992. *National Assessment of Law Enforcement Anti-Gang Information Resources.* Washington, DC: Draft Report to the National Institute of Justice, U.S. Department of Justice.

Egley, Arlen, Jr., and Christina E. Ritz. 2006. *Highlights of the 2004 National Youth Gang Survey.* Washington, DC: Office of Juveniles Justice and Delinquency Prevention, U.S. Department of Justice.

Esbensen, Finn-Aage, and David Huizinga. 1993. "Gangs, Drugs, and Delinquency in a Survey of Urban Youth." *Criminology* 31 (4): 565–587.

Esbensen, Finn-Aage, and Frank M. Weerman. 2005. "Youth Gangs and Troublesome Youth Groups in the United States and the Netherlands: A Cross-National Comparison." *European Journal of Criminology* 2 (1): 5–37.

Fagan, Jeffrey. 1990. "Social Processes of Delinquency and Drug Use among Urban Gangs." In *Gangs in America*, edited by C. Ronald Huff. Newbury Park, CA: Sage.

Federal Bureau of Investigation (FBI). 2007. "The Gangs of L.A.: The City Fights Back." [Online information; retrieved 4/21/08.] http://www.fbi.gov/page2/jan07/lagangs012407.htm.

Federal Bureau of Investigation (FBI). 2008. "The MS-13 Threat: A National Assessment." [Online information; retrieved 4/21/08.] http://www.fbi.gov/page2/jan08/ms13_011408.html.

Harrell, Erika. 2005. *Violence by Gang Members, 1993–2003.* Washington, DC: Bureau of Justice Statistics, U.S. Department of Justice.

Institute for Law and Justice. 1994. *Gang Prosecution in the United States.* Washington, DC: Office of Justice Programs, National Institute of Justice, U.S. Department of Justice.

Johnson, Claire, Barbara Webster, and Edward Connors. 1995. *Prosecuting Gangs: A National Assessment.* Research in Brief. Washington, DC: Office of Justice Programs, National Institute of Justice, U.S. Department of Justice.

Knox, George. W. 2001. "The Gangster Disciples: A Gang Profile." [Online information; retrieved 4/21/08.] http://www.ngcrc.com/ngcrc/page13.htm.

Lee, Felicia R. 1991. "For Gold Earrings and Protection, More Girls Take Violence." *New York Times*, November 11, A1, 16.

Major, Aline K., and Arlen Egley, Jr. 2002. "2000 Survey of Youth Gangs in Indian Country." In *NYGC Fact Sheet*. Washington, DC: National Youth Gang Center.

Maxson, Cheryl L., Margaret A. Gordon, and Malcolm W. Klein. 1985. "Differences between Gang and Nongang Homicides." *Criminology* 23:209–222.

Miller, Walter B. 1975. *Violence by Youth Gangs and Youth Groups as a Crime Problem in Major American Cities*. Report for the National Institute for Juvenile Justice and Delinquency Prevention, Office of Juvenile Justice and Delinquency Prevention. Washington, DC: U.S. Government Printing Office.

Miller, Walter B. 1982. *Crime by Youth Gangs and Groups in the United States*. Washington, DC: Office of Juvenile Justice and Delinquency Prevention.

Moore, Joan. 1991. *Going Down to the Barrio*. Philadelphia: Temple University Press.

Moore, Joan, and John Hagedorn. 2001. "Female Gangs: A Focus on Research." In *Juvenile Justice Bulletin*. Washington, DC: Office of Juvenile Justice and Delinquency Prevention.

National Alliance of Gang Investigators' Associations (NAGIA). 2005. *2005 National Gang Threat Assessment*. Washington, DC: Bureau of Justice Assistance.

National Drug Intelligence Center (NDIC). 2003a. "Bloods." In *Drugs and Crime Gang Profile*. Washington, DC: NDIC, U.S. Department of Justice.

National Drug Intelligence Center (NDIC). 2003b. "Black Peace Stone Nation." In *Drugs and Crime Gang Profile*. Washington, DC: NDIC, U.S. Department of Justice.

National Youth Gang Center. 2007. *National Youth Gang Survey Analysis*. [Online report; retrieved 1/08.] http://www.iir.com/nygc/nygsa/.

Needle, Jerome A., and William Vaughn Stapleton. 1983. *Police Handling of Youth Gangs*. Washington, DC: Office of Juvenile Justice and Delinquency Prevention.

New Jersey State Police. 2007. *Gangs in New Jersey: Municipal Law Enforcement Response to the 2007 NJSP Gang Survey*. Trenton: New Jersey State Police.

New Mexico Department of Public Safety. 1994. *New Mexico Street Gangs: 1994 Update*. Albuquerque: New Mexico Department of Public Safety.

Office of Juvenile Justice and Delinquency Prevention (OJJDP). 2002. *National Youth Gang Survey Trends from 1996 to 2000.* Washington, DC: U.S. Department of Justice.

Office of Juvenile Justice and Delinquency Prevention (OJJDP). 2004. *Highlights of the 2002 National Youth Gang Survey.* Washington, DC: U.S. Department of Justice.

Regoli, Robert M., and John D. Hewitt. 2003. *Delinquency in Society,* 5th ed. Boston: McGraw-Hill.

Spergel, Irving A. 1983. *Violent Gangs in Chicago: Segmentation and Integration.* Chicago: School of Social Service Administration, University of Chicago.

Spergel, Irving A. 1986. "The Violent Gang in Chicago: A Local Community Approach." *Social Service Review* 60:94–131.

Spergel, Irving A., and G. David Curry. 1990. "Strategies and Perceived Agency Effectiveness in Dealing with the Youth Gang Problem." In *Gangs in America,* edited by C. Ronald Huff, 288–309. Thousand Oaks, CA: Sage.

Swecker, Chris. 2005. Congressional Testimony before the Subcommittee on the Western Hemisphere, House International Relations Committee, April 20.

Thornberry, Terrence P., Marvin D. Krohn, Alan J. Lizotte, and Deborah Chard-Wierschem. 1993. "The Role of Juvenile Gangs in Facilitating Delinquency Behavior." *Journal of Research in Crime and Delinquency* 30:55–87.

Thornberry, Terrence P., Marvin D. Krohn, Alan J. Lizotte, Carolyn A. Smith, and Kimberly Tobin. 2003. *Gangs and Delinquency in Developmental Perspective.* Cambridge, UK: Cambridge University Press.

Thrasher, Frederic M. 1927. *The Gang: A Study of 1,313 Gangs in Chicago.* Chicago: University of Chicago Press.

Valdez, Al. 2000a. "18th Street: California's Most Violent Export." [Online information; retrieved 4/21/08.] http://www.nagia.org/Gang%20 Articles/18th%20Street.htm.

Valdez, Al. 2000b. "Mara Salvatrucha: A South American Import" [Online information; retrieved 4/21/08.] http://www.nagia.org/Gang%20 Articles/Mara%20Salvatrucha.htm.

7

Directory of Organizations, Associations, and Agencies

This chapter describes organizations that work in a variety of ways with gangs and gang members as well as local community agencies that focus on stopping or preventing gang activity. They may be research oriented, prevention oriented, or service oriented. These organizations represent the types of services offered by programs throughout the country, but they are only a sampling of the many organizations now dealing with gangs and gang violence. Check with local agencies and police departments for area-specific programs, for information about specific police department gang units, and for other community-based education and recreation programs aimed at preventing youth from joining gangs.

Private, State, and Local Governmental Organizations

Adelphoi Village
1119 Village Way
Latrobe, PA 15650-1558
Telephone: 724-520-1111
Web site: http://www.adelphoivillage.org

Adelphoi Village is a private, nonprofit child care agency that offers specialized programs for young people who have taken alternative paths, including those involved in gangs. These programs include assessments, weekly group counseling, and family counseling and consultation. The program endeavors to educate youths on the major consequences of joining gangs; to provide an open, nonjudgmental forum for youths to discuss problems related to their gang activity; and to help them examine their lives and try to improve their situations. It also teaches them to accept responsibility for themselves and their actions and provides them with a support system to encourage positive behavior. Staff members help them to understand the cycles of drug, sexual, physical, and other criminal abuses connected with gang involvement and help them to face issues surrounding death, injury, and loss resulting from their gang activity. The program also helps young people develop good communication skills with their families as well as safeguards for a healthier lifestyle.

Al Wooten Jr. Heritage Center
9106 S. Western Ave.
Los Angeles, CA 90047
Telephone: 213-756-7203
Web site: http://www.wootencenter.org

This youth center offers after-school and weekend academic and recreational classes for young people in South Central Los Angeles who are between the ages of 8 and 18. Major goals are to offer alternatives to gang involvement, increase basic-skills test scores, reduce the high dropout rate, help youths reconnect with the community, assist in developing career and vocational skills and goals, and train youths to be leaders and positive role models in their communities. The outreach program aims to help young participants build positive self-images and develop maturity while improving academic performance. Staff members offer leadership development; recreational activities; community youth services; cultural activities; and academic training, including tutoring, literacy, and remedial courses. A mentoring program pairs successful business and community members with youths who need positive role models.

Boys & Girls Clubs of America
1275 Peachtree Street NE
Atlanta, GA 30309-3506
Telephone: 404-487-5700
Web site: http://www.bgca.org

Boys & Girls Clubs of America encourages and supports many individual Boys and Girls Clubs throughout the country. Its current approach to juvenile gang prevention emerged from its Targeted Outreach Delinquency Prevention effort. Between 1990 and 1992, the national Boys & Girls Club and 33 local clubs developed this prevention effort in order to reach youth at risk for gang involvement; they devised several strategies for reaching and providing services to youth living in areas with gang activity through the United States. The clubs focus on ways to provide services for these youths and to identify the strategies that have been most successful in treating at-risk youth.

California Wellness Foundation
Violence Prevention Initiative
6320 Canoga Ave., Suite 1700
Woodland Hills, CA 91367-7111
Telephone: 818-702-1900
Web site: http://www.tcwf.org

This foundation was created in 1992 as an independent, private organization to improve the health of California residents. It designs, develops, and evaluates health promotion and disease prevention programs and encourages individuals and communities to adopt healthy lifestyles. Through the Violence Prevention Initiative, the foundation hopes to develop and evaluate a comprehensive multidisciplinary approach to combating youth violence and gangs throughout California. This initiative has four components: a leadership program, a community action program, a policy program, and a research program. The leadership program promotes the importance of leadership in preventing acts of violence. The community action program provides resources and technical assistance to various communities to reduce youth violence through health promotion programs. The policy program advocates changes in public policy that might help reduce gang violence. The research program seeks to expand current knowledge about causes and prevention of youth violence; it will examine the relationships between violence and alcohol and other drugs, firearms and gang involvement, socioeconomic factors, and public health conditions.

The foundation also has established community action grants to provide resources and technical assistance to communities that want to reduce youth violence through pilot collaborative health promotion programs.

Center for the Study and Prevention of Violence
Institute of Behavioral Science
University of Colorado
1877 Broadway, Suite 601
Boulder, CO 80302
Telephone: 303-492-1032
Web site: http://www.colorado.edu/cspv

The primary purpose of the center, founded in 1992, is to provide information and assistance to groups and individuals studying the causes of violence and ways of preventing it, especially youth violence and gang activity. The center's information house gathers research literature relating to violence and offers bibliographic searches on requested topics via its online database, which contains abstracts and references to research papers, programs, curricula, videos, books and journal articles, and other sources of information about causes of violence and prevention strategies. Reviews of literature are conducted and currently include topics such as evaluating juvenile violence prevention; violence and the schools; the effects of the mass media on violence; the family and juvenile violence; gangs, guns, and violence; and alcohol and drugs and their influence on juvenile violence. These reviews combine an evaluation of the scientific literature and comments from current practitioners and policy makers. The center provides technical assistance to individuals and groups developing or evaluating programs that focus on violence prevention. The center also has a research component that analyzes data and develops and conducts studies to understand the causes of violence.

CHARGE Gang Task Force
City of Harrisonburg
101 N. Main St.
Harrisonburg, VA 22801
Telephone: 540-437-2643
Web site: http://www.ci.harrisonburg.va.us/index.php?id=660

The CHARGE (Combined Harrisonburg and Rockingham Gang Enforcement Unit) Gang Task Force is composed of two officers from the City of Harrisonburg Police Department and two deputies from the Rockingham County Sheriff's Office and was implemented in response to growing gang activity and violence in the city and county. Members of the task force track organized criminal activity, primarily focusing on gang activity; work to reduce overall gang activity through community awareness programs; encourage greater networking among local agencies; and encourage the rapid exchange of information among agencies to ensure public safety.

Dane County Narcotics and Gang Task Force
211 S. Carroll St.
Madison, WI 53710
Telephone: 608-266-4248
Web site: http://www.cityofmadison.com/police/taskforc.html

The Dane County Narcotics and Gang Task Force is a law enforcement group with members across jurisdictions, including federal, state, and local agencies. Its purpose is to identify and stop individuals involved in illegal gang activity, prostitution, and illegal gambling activities; develop and maintain an intelligence network for tracking drug and gang activities; disseminate information regarding drug and gang activities; provide training to law enforcement personnel; support community antidrug and antigang educational programs; solicit community support in the fight against drugs and gangs; and identify and arrest fugitives and violent offenders.

Fairfax Skindeep Tattoo Removal Program
Fairfax County Health Department
10777 Main St.
Fairfax, VA 22030
Telephone: 703-246-2411
Web site: http://www.fairfaxcounty.gov/hd/tattoo

The Fairfax Skindeep Tattoo Removal Program is a collaborative effort among the cities of Fairfax and Falls Church, Virginia; family members and/or caregivers; Fairfax County public human service agencies; and community organizations. The program encourages the removal of gang-related tattoos from area youth. The program works to provide positive alternatives to gang involvement through public- and private-sector collaboration, reduce violent crime threatening at-risk youth, support county human service planning, enhance educational opportunity, encourage participation in job and basic skills training, cooperate with other local organizations interested in tattoo removal, provide opportunities for community service, and create productive citizens. Youths who participate in this program are required to attend all classes offered and pass them with a grade of C or better, seek employment if they have met their educational objectives, maintain 100 percent drug and alcohol sobriety during program participation, comply with their participation agreement and/or signed rules of probation, improve self-esteem by removing socially stigmatizing and discrediting tattoos, and complete 40 hours of community service prior to tattoo removal.

Gang Alternatives Program
P.O. Box 408
San Pedro, CA 90733
Telephone: 310-519-7233
Web site: http://www.gangfree.org

The Gang Alternatives Program was started in 1986 to eliminate the base of gang membership by encouraging positive lifestyle changes that will discourage children from joining gangs. Services include gang prevention, community cleanup activities, resources on parenting, and referral services. Program components include provision of gang awareness and gang prevention education activities to elementary-school and middle-school-age children, a parent education component that supports children in resisting the temptation to join a gang, an outreach program for at-risk youth that includes counseling and referral services, and a graffiti removal and community cleanup service.

Gang Outreach
P.O. Box 655
Mundelein, IL 60062
Telephone: 847-249-0558
Web site: http://www.mundelein.org/police/
gang_outreach.htm

Gang Outreach is a nonprofit, faith-based organization focusing on gang prevention and intervention in Lake County, Illinois. Services are designed to provide at-risk youth with positive influences to help them reach their potential and avoid participation in gang activities. Weekly activities are conducted in schools, business areas, parks, jails, and neighborhoods where drugs and gangs are common. Its Transitions program is a support group for youths looking for a way to get out of gangs; meetings include group dialogue, Bible study, prayer, and one-on-one dialogues as needed. The Tattoo Removal Program removes gang tattoos from those who complete a six-month program; participants are required to demonstrate that they are no longer affiliated with a gang, they must actively participate in the Transitions program, and they must regularly participate in various community service programs. The Gang Color Trade-In Program helps youths who turn in their old gang-color clothing; they are taken shopping for new clothes that have no significance or relation to any gang. Gang Outreach's intervention and prevention program provides speakers for public schools, Neighborhood Watch meetings, community colleges, and conferences on gang violence; finds safe houses for youths attempting to leave their gangs; assists former gang members in finding employment; and works with law enforcement agencies in local communities.

Gang Resistance Is Paramount
16400 Colorado Ave.
Paramount, CA 90723
Telephone: 562-220-2120
Web site: http://www.paramountcity.com/ps.parksrecreation.cfm?ID=6 \Address}

Gang Resistance Is Paramount (GRIP) was started in 1982 as a collaborative effort with the city of Paramount, California. Formerly known as Alternatives to Gang Membership, GRIP works to curb gang membership and discourage participation in gangs by teaching children the harmful effects of gang participation and how to choose positive alternatives. The program's approach is based on the belief that interest in gangs begins at an early age and a successful antigang program must emphasize early identification of children at risk. The program has three components: an elementary school antigang curriculum, an intermediate school follow-up program, and neighborhood meetings. Counselors offer gang resistance lessons to elementary and ninth-grade students in the Paramount school system. Lessons in the elementary school curriculum focus on peer pressure, graffiti, the impact of gang activity on family members, drug use and abuse among gang members, and alternative activities. The intermediate school follow-up program reviews the information presented in the elementary school curriculum and also emphasizes self-esteem, the consequences of a criminal lifestyle, the importance of getting a higher education, and career opportunities. Neighborhood meetings, conducted by city staff members, educate parents about gang activity and provide parents with encouragement and assistance in preventing their children from joining gangs. Handouts, in English and Spanish, provide information on city programs, tattoo removal programs, and graffiti hotlines.

Great Lakes International Gang Investigators Coalition
P.O. Box 070167
Milwaukee, WI 53207
Web site: http://gligic.org

The Great Lakes International Gang Investigators Coalition was formed in 2000 as an independent nonprofit organization working to educate law enforcement agencies and the community concerning gang-related topics. It promotes the exchange of gang intelligence within the law enforcement community and conducts monthly intelligence networking meetings, biannual training seminars, and annual conferences. It publishes an electronic newsletter and maintains an electronic bulletin board for sharing information from each region.

Guardian Angels
717 Fifth Ave., Suite 401
New York, NY 10022
Telephone: 212-545-7676
Web site: http://www.guardianangels.org

In 1979, the Guardian Angels began as an anticrime patrol on the subways of New York City. As criminal acts have escalated over the years, the Guardian Angels' role has expanded as well. They are now asked to do more and more in communities trying to combat crime, such as organize patrols and assist residents in their fight against crime. The Guardian Angels are an international, multicultural, and multiethnic network of more than 90 chapters throughout the world. Patrolling in groups of four, they are well trained in what to do when they see a crime in progress, how to protect themselves and the victims, how to make a citizen's arrest, and how to work effectively with the police to put criminals in jail. Members are taught discipline, responsibility, respect, loyalty, and self-esteem. They escort senior citizens to appointments and to other activities, assist the handicapped, provide self-defense demonstrations and training courses, and distribute food to the hungry and homeless. Guardian Angels also speak at elementary, junior, and senior high schools and colleges about their program and how to prevent crime, as well as about the dangers of drugs, gangs, substance abuse, and peer pressure and the importance of staying in school. Members are trained extensively in self-defense, first aid and CPR, and ways to communicate effectively with people.

Hardcore Gang Division
Los Angeles County District Attorney's Office
210 W. Temple St., Room 17-1116
Los Angeles, CA 90012
Telephone: 213-974-3903
Web site: http://da.co.la.ca.us/gangs.htm

In response to the emergence of more than 1,400 street gangs in Los Angeles County, the Los Angeles County District Attorney's Office has created a comprehensive approach to fighting gang activity, including suppression, intervention, and prevention activities. The Hardcore Gang Division consists of more than 50 specially trained attorneys who prosecute the most serious gang-related murder cases in the county. Six Community Law Enforcement and Recovery program sites have been established to target members of specific gangs who pose the most dangerous threats to their communities; prosecutors, police, deputy sheriffs, probation officers, deputy city attorneys, and others work together to get them off the streets. In the Heightened Enforcement and Targeting program, prosecutors work most closely with police to monitor and prosecute the most dangerous gang members, often focusing on juvenile gang activity. Intervention programs include the Strategies Against Gang Violence program to fight and prevent crime. Prosecutors and community outreach personnel participate on the county's 13 interagency gang task forces to help develop effective gang prevention strategies.

Homies Unidos
1625 W. Olympic Blvd., Suite 706
Los Angeles, CA 90015
Telephone: 213-383-7484
Web site: http://www.homiesunidos.org

Founded in 1996 in San Salvador, El Salvador, Homies Unidos is a nonprofit organization focusing on the prevention of gang violence and intervention with projects located in San Salvador and Los Angeles, California. They focus on the development of creative alternatives to youth violence and drugs by providing access to alternative education, training in leadership development, self-esteem-building programs and activities, and health education programs. The program has evolved from providing support for transnational families affected by gang participation and gang violence to a comprehensive action-based program that has strategic alliances with a variety of national and international organizations.

Institute on Violence and Destructive Behavior
University of Oregon
Eugene, OR 97403-1215
Telephone: 541-346-3591
Web site: http://www.uoregon.edu/~ivdb/

The Institute on Violence and Destructive Behavior (IVDB) works with schools and social service agencies to help them address violence and destructive behavior in order to ensure safety and encourage the healthy social development and academic success of children and youth. The institute's goals are (1) to address systematically social problems that the public is concerned about in Oregon and nationally; (2) to provide faculty expertise on violence and destructive behavior; and (3) to integrate research, training, and service activities. Its three program components are research, instruction, and public service. Research activities focus on longitudinal and cross-sectional studies that examine the early family, school, and community factors that may lead to later violent behavior; identifying factors that can lead to as well as protect from violent behavior and gang affiliation; and studying effective intervention strategies. IVDB's instructional component focuses on providing training and technical assistance to families, schools, and the community to prevent violent behavior along with advocacy activities that encourage legislators, policy makers, and agency leaders to help implement successful prevention and intervention programs. As part of the public service component, the institute acts as a resource to local and state agencies.

Junior Players
4054 McKinney Ave., Suite 104
Dallas, TX 75204
Telephone: 214-526-4076
Web site: http://www.juniorplayers.org

This nonprofit organization focuses on the arts as a way to transform the lives of youth. Through participation in free summer and after-school workshops, Junior Players provides positive role models and increases self-esteem, literacy, and communication skills for thousands of Dallas youth. Discover Ourselves is a series of after-school workshops that provide a fun, structured learning environment and alternatives to gang involvement during the critical summer and after-school hours. Guided by professional artists from the Dallas community, participants learn basic skills in theater arts, with an emphasis on reading, writing, and oral communication skills. Peace Power is a violence prevention program that uses theater for at-risk students ages 11 to 15 in an after-school program in Dallas middle schools. Conflict resolution skills are taught to participants to help them in their daily lives. Students are also given the opportunity to voice their concerns regarding personal and social issues. At the end of the program, students write a short presentation on a topic of their choice.

Juvenile Diversion Program
Finney County Youth Services
907 Zerr Rd.
Garden City, KS 67846
Telephone: 316-272-3695
Web site: http://www.finneycounty.org/statusoffenders.asp

The Juvenile Diversion Program was designed to divert juvenile-status, first-time, or second-time offenders up to the age of 18 years from the formal judicial process and provide services that are designed to break the cycle of criminal behavior. The program has eight major services: Theft Prevention Class, Community Violence Awareness Class, Active Parenting of Teens, Youth Alternative Group, Adopt a Highway Project, Graffiti Removal Effort, Gang Training, and J.A.I.L. Program at Norton and Hutchinson state penitentiaries. The J.A.I.L. program takes male juveniles to one of the penitentiaries for a "scared straight" presentation on what life is like in the penitentiary. Juveniles who are charged with a violent crime may be placed in the Community Violence Awareness Class, which teaches them anger management, how to resolve conflicts through nonviolent means, gang resistance techniques, and the ways in which violence affects them as well as the community. The Graffiti Removal Effort paints over or otherwise cleans gang graffiti. The Gang Training program offers gang awareness training to parents and community groups.

Loudoun County Gang Response Intervention Team
18 E. Market St.
Leesburg, VA 20175
Telephone: 703-777-0303
Web site: http://www.loudoun.gov/Default.aspx?tabid=1110

The Loudoun County Gang Response Intervention Team is a multidisciplinary, multiagency team that coordinates the suppression, intervention, and prevention of street gang activity in Loudoun County. Relying on the expertise of its members, the team identifies youths at risk for becoming involved in gang activity, along with their families and their communities. Team members include the Commonwealth Attorney; Community Corrections Program; County Administrator's Office; Family Services; Juvenile and Domestic Relations Court Service Unit; Mental Health and Substance Abuse Services; Parks, Recreation, and Community Services; Sheriff's Office; and Loudoun Youth Initiative.

MAD DADS
555 Stockton St.
Jacksonville, FL 32204
Telephone: 904-388-8171
Web site: http://www.maddads.com

MAD (Men Against Destruction) DADS (Defending Against Drugs and Social Disorder) was founded in June 1989 in the basement of the Omaha Pilgrim Baptist Church by a group of men who were fed up with gang violence and the unimpeded flow of illegal drugs in their community. The group encourages all "strong, drug-free men" to act as positive parental role models and, by example, to address citywide issues concerning youths and their families. It conducts weekend street patrols in troubled areas, reporting crime, drug sales, and other destructive activities to the proper authorities. MAD DADS also offers positive community activities for youth, chaperones community events, and provides street counseling at any time. Its division of MOMS AND KIDS works with the MAD DADS. The organization now has more than 60 chapters in 15 states.

Mayor's Gang Prevention Task Force
City of San Jose
Department of Parks, Recreation and Neighborhood Services
200 E. Santa Clara St., 9th Floor
San Jose, CA 95113
Telephone: 408-535-3576
Web site: http://www.sanjoseca.gov/prns/mgptf.asp

The Mayor's Gang Prevention Task Force (MGPTF) was established in 1991 in response to the increasing levels of youth violence throughout the city. As an interagency, collaborative effort, the Task Force works to strengthen and formalize relationships among the city, the public schools, and other community-based organizations; to increase school attendance rates; to expand after-hours programs to provide youth with safe places after school; and to refer youth involved in gang activities to intervention programs. Chaired by the mayor of San Jose, the MGPTF consists of membership of more than 30 community-based organizations representing law enforcement, mental health, probation, substance abuse, health care, education, the justice system, recreation, and community service providers.

Memphis Shelby Crime Commission
119 S. Main St., Suite 450
Memphis, TN 38103
Telephone: 901-527-2600
Web site: http://www.memphiscrime.org

Established in 1997 by the Plough Foundation and Guardsmark, Inc. as an independent, nonprofit organization, the Memphis Shelby Crime Commission is a nongovernmental organization that works with all law enforcement agencies and community-based groups to help implement model crime reduction programs. The program works to coordinate and engage in selected strategic community partnerships that enhance the local criminal justice system, and then disengage itself from them; works with the community and criminal justice system as required; responds to time-sensitive community requirements for expertise and advocacy; and researches, builds, and measures the best practices in criminal justice as required for community safety. The Best Practices Committee addresses all aspects of crime and public safety, including crime prevention, courts, law enforcement, juvenile justice, gangs, technology, victim assistance, domestic violence, drugs, corrections, and legislation. The committee makes recommendations based on the crime commission's key organizational goals and objectives.

Metro Denver Partners
701 S. Logan St., Suite 109
Denver, CO 80209
Telephone: 303-777-7000
Web site: http://www.metrodenverpartners.org

Founded in 1968 in response to growing rates of juvenile delinquency, Metro Denver Partners matches at-risk youths with adult volunteers who are trained to act as a caring, positive role models and advocates for the youths. Youths are referred to the program by community agencies, including courts, schools, mental health agencies, and other social services agencies. A variety of services are provided through five specific programs. The Denver Diversion Program, the original partners program, works with boys and girls ages 8 to 17 who have had some type of involvement with the juvenile justice system. The Adams County Program serves 8- to 12-year-old boys and girls from homes where substance abuse is or has been present. It assists both youths and families in overcoming substance abuse problems and the resulting dysfunctional behaviors. The Adolescent Females Program offers weekly meetings to girls between the ages of 9 and 14 years to discuss youth leadership, life skills building, family involvement and support, school success, and career options. The Douglas County Mentoring Program works with boys and girls ages 8 to 14 in Douglas County who have been referred to the program by schools, the District Attorney's juvenile diversion programs, and other social services agencies. The program provides them with mentors who meet weekly with them for tutoring and other support services. In the Northeast Denver Tutoring Program, adult volunteers meet with 9- to 14-year-old boys and girls to help with basic academic skills. The Youth Mentoring Collaborative Program helps fifth and sixth graders who are homeless or eligible for the Temporary Assistance for Needy Families program's help. The Gang Rescue and Support Project (www.graspyouth.org) meets weekly to support youths trying to stay out of the gang lifestyle. Directed by former gang members who have committed themselves to helping others avoid gang involvement, mentors work with participants on education; job skills; and responsibilities to themselves, their families, and their communities.

Mothers Against Gang Wars
42 N. Sutter St., Suite 215
Stockton, CA 95202
Telephone: 209-464-6607
Web site: http://home.inreach.com/gangbang

Mothers Against Gang Wars (MAGW) was founded in 1991 by Sandra Davis, a former gang member, to stop gang violence. The program staff works with schools, local governments, and other social service agencies by coordinating efforts to stop gang violence in San Joaquin County. Former gang members work with MAGW to help them understand the ways to get out of the gang life and become successful contributors to society. The goal is to work with gang members to help them make positive changes in their lives.

National Association of Police Athletic Leagues
658 W. Indiantown Rd., #201
Jupiter, FL 33458
Telephone: 561-745-5535
Web site: http://www.nationalpal.org

One of the largest juvenile-crime prevention programs with more than 3 million members, the National Association of Police Athletic Leagues provides a forum for sharing information, promotes national training seminars, develops fund-raising programs, initiates public-awareness projects, develops regional and national tournaments, and publishes a national newspaper. It promotes competition for the advancement of sportsmanship and citizenship. Local chapters throughout the United States offer a variety of activities, including sports programs, arts and crafts, dance, music, drama, social services, vocational guidance, remedial reading, gardening, field trips, and other popular youth activities. The organization works with neighborhood youths who are bored, apathetic, lonely, and dealing with the countless problems of living in the city; the long-term goal is to reach these youths before they become delinquent or involved in gang activities.

National Concerned Officers Organization on Gang Activities, Inc.
831 Ocean Park Ave.
Cobblestone Village, #161
Ocean Township, NJ 07712
Telephone: 732-460-0804
Web site: http://hometown.aol.com/CO3GA/index.html

The National Concerned Officers Organization on Gang Activities is made up of educators, clergy, law enforcement officers, former gang members, concerned citizens, and children who encourage communities to work together to resolve the problems they face, including gangs, school violence, and bullying. They offer seminars, in-service training, keynote speakers, conflict resolution, community awareness, community policing, youth motivation, and other intervention and prevention activities to increase understanding of the reasons why youths join gangs, how to prevent them from gang participation, how to recognize gang activity, and how to help them get out of a gang. Some of their activities include participation in positive programs that address the needs of youth; assistance to law enforcement and other outside agencies in their efforts to stop juvenile delinquency; provision of guidance and programs for identified gang members and those members seeking to leave the gang lifestyle; working to motivate youths to be respectful and productive citizens of the community; and raising community awareness of youth gangs.

National Council on Crime and Delinquency
1970 Broadway, Suite 500
Oakland, CA 94612
Telephone: 510-208-0500
Web site: http://www.nccd-crc.org

A nonprofit organization, the National Council on Crime and Delinquency (NCCD) focuses its attention on developing and promoting criminal justice and juvenile justice strategies that are fair, humane, effective, and built on a solid economic foundation. It researches critical criminal justice issues, formulates innovative approaches to controlling crime, and implements unique programs. The NCCD has developed standards and guidelines for probation and parole professions as well as strategies to help criminal justice professionals effectively manage corrections systems. It provides studies and policy recommendations for juvenile and criminal justice reform. The goal of the NCCD is to help federal and state officials, criminal justice professionals, and community organizations develop and implement programs that will improve the criminal justice system.

National Council of Juvenile and Family Court Judges
P.O. Box 8970
Reno, NV 89507
Telephone: 775-784-6012
Web site: http://www.ncjfcj.org

The National Council of Juvenile and Family Court Judges (NCJFCJ) provides counsel on juvenile and family law to America's juvenile and family jurists. Training, technical assistance, and continuing education are offered to judges, referees, probation officers, social workers, law enforcement personnel, and other juvenile justice professionals. The NCJFCJ stays abreast of changes in laws concerning child abuse and neglect, crack babies, foster care, custody issues, school violence, gangs, and serious juvenile crime and offers programs to address current topics in these areas. Its research division, the National Center for Juvenile Justice, has been the primary source of information on the nature of juvenile crime for more than 30 years.

National Crime Prevention Council
1700 K St. NW, Second Floor
Washington, DC 20006-3817
Telephone: 202-466-6272
Web site: http://www.ncpc.org

The National Crime Prevention Council is a private, nonprofit organization with a major focus on enabling people to help prevent crime and build safer, more caring communities. It manages a public service advertising campaign, provides information and referral services and technical assistance, conducts training in crime prevention skills and techniques, and conducts demonstration programs and research to discover the most effective ways to prevent crime in local communities. Its Youth as Resources project started as a demonstration project in three Indiana cities in 1987. This locally based program provides small grants to youths to help them design and carry out projects to meet their community's needs. Youth as Resources is based on the premise that young people, given the opportunity, have the desire and ability to organize and act effectively to help solve some of society's most pressing problems.

Publications: *Giving Youth a Voice* is a packet of information designed to help teens deal with the many difficult issues they face, including gangs, abuse, Internet safety, vandalism, and crime prevention. *She's a Gang Leader* describes how after-school programs and activities can keep young people from getting involved with gangs and other high-risk activities.

National Gang Crime Research Center
P.O. Box 990
Peotone, IL 60468
Telephone: 708-258-9111
Web site: http://www.ngcrc.com

The National Gang Crime Research Center (NGCRC) is a nonprofit independent organization focusing on gangs and gang violence. The NGCRC carries out large-scale research on gangs and gang members; disseminates up-to-date information about gangs and gang problems through its official publication, the *Journal of Gang Research;* and provides training and consulting services to federal, state, and local government agencies.

Publications: *Findings from the K–12 Survey Project* reports on the results of the 2006 School Survey of Gang-Related Issues, which examined gang and other related problems faced by schools. *The Problem of Gangs and Security Threat Groups (STG's) in American Prisons Today: Recent Findings from the 2004 Prison Gang Survey* examines gangs and related groups that threaten security within the U.S. prison system. NGCRC also publishes the *Journal of Gang Research,* a peer-reviewed quarterly journal focusing on gangs and gang problems.

National Resource Center for Youth Services
University of Oklahoma
Schusterman Center
4502 E. 41st St., Bldg. 4W
Tulsa, OK 74135-2512
Telephone: 918-660-3700
Web site: http://www.nrcys.ou.edu

The National Resource Center for Youth Services provides training, technical assistance, publications, conference planning, and information and referral services on a variety of adolescent issues. Its programs focus on a number of serious issues concerning youth, including runaways and homelessness, AIDS/HIV, independent living, substance abuse, residential care, sexual abuse, and cultural diversity. The center provides training materials and services to professionals and agencies that work with at-risk youth. The Managing Aggressive Behavior program provides trainer certification in skills needed to manage the aggressive behavior of children with whom the participants work and offers consultation on how to plan training sessions. Direct training is also provided for recognizing a developing crisis and intervening appropriately.

National School Safety Center
141 Duesenberg Dr., Suite 11
Westlake Village, CA 91362
Telephone: 805-373-9977
Web site: http://www.schoolsafety.us

In 1984, a presidential directive created the National School Safety Center to meet the growing demand by school professionals for additional training and education in the areas of school crime and violence prevention. The center is a partnership of the U.S. Department of Justice, the U.S. Department of Education, and Pepperdine University. Its purpose is to promote safe schools as well as to ensure quality education for all children. Its mandate is to focus national attention on cooperative solutions to problems that disrupt the education of children, with a special emphasis on ways to eliminate crime, violence, and drugs from schools, as well as programs that focus on improving student discipline, attendance, achievement, and school climate. It provides technical assistance, legal and legislative aid, and publications and films, and it conducts training programs and provides technical assistance for education and law enforcement practitioners, legislators, and other governmental policy makers. Staff members work with governors, attorneys general, school officials, and communities in every state to develop customized and safe school training and planning programs. The center also serves as a clearinghouse for current information on school safety issues and maintains a resource center with more than 50,000 articles, publications, and films.

New Mexico Youth at Risk Foundation, Inc.
1208 San Pedro NE, #206
Albuquerque, NM 87110
Telephone: 505-888-1801
Web site: http://www.infoimagination.org/nmyar

This nonprofit, all-volunteer organization deals with troubled youth throughout New Mexico. Its program goes beyond traditional prevention and intervention models to address issues of human and adolescent development. One component, the Community Partners for Youth program, works to alter the attitudes and core beliefs that youths have about themselves, others, their circumstances, and life itself. Young people identified by the agency attend a presentation about the program; if they choose to participate, they undergo a comprehensive enrollment process. Staffers of the year-long program work to increase the youths' self-esteem; help them learn to take responsibility for their choices, actions, and past mistakes; help them get along better with family and friends; teach them to communicate more effectively; help them seek higher education; teach them that fighting and violence are not the answer to solving problems; encourage them to stop selling drugs; help them refuse to join gangs; and assist them in developing long-range goals. The program includes a five-day nonresidential intensive course and a 14-month follow-through after-care program.

Night Basketball and Books
P.O. Box 32
Pasadena, CA 91102
Web site: http://www.nbab.org

Night Basketball and Books (NBAB) was founded in 1994 to provide a refuge of safety, hope, and change from a life of drugs and gang violence that affected many children in the Pasadena area. Young people met with adult mentors, played basketball, and shared meals. The program has expanded to include five major components: effective study skills, parental/guardian involvement, mentoring, academic achievement and tutoring, and sports. New participants entering the program are evaluated to determine their specific needs. Then staff work with the youths' parents or guardians, teachers, and counselors to design a plan to succeed. NBAB's mission is to assist at-risk children, youths, and young adults by providing a safe, caring place to go after school and evenings, and an environment in which they can acquire the skills to achieve self-sufficiency.

Omega Boys Club/Street Soldiers
P.O. Box 884463
San Francisco, CA 94188
Telephone: 415-826-8664
Web site: http://www.street-soldiers.org

Founded in 1987, the Omega Boys Club is for youths and young African American males between the ages of 12 and 25. The club believes in the extended family and the idea that unrelated adults and youths can come together and have an impact on the issues of drugs, gangs, and violence. The club's academic program prepares and assists members who are interested in pursuing a college degree. It provides non-college-bound members with verbal, academic, keyboard, and computer literacy skills to successfully enter the job market and encourages and facilitates the development of entrepreneurial capabilities. Omega's violence prevention effort also reaches out to the community at large. Major components include a weekly radio call-in talk show; an annual youth conference, in which participants seek solutions to the violence in their communities; and Street Soldier training, in which members learn to conduct violence prevention work in other communities.

Open Door Youth Gang Alternatives
1615 California St., Suite 712
Denver, CO 80202
Telephone: 303-893-4264; 1-800-275-4264 (ASK-GANG)
Web site: http://www.therev.org

Open Door Youth Gang Alternatives is a community-based, nonprofit organization founded in 1988 and designed to discourage participation in gangs and reduce gang-related violence in the Denver metropolitan area. Professional staff and volunteers focus on preventing elementary-school-age children from joining gangs through programs tailored for schools, corporations, other nonprofit agencies, and civic groups. The After School Education, Bonding and Character Program works with children from 5 to 12 years old, providing them with after-school homework help, mentoring, and sports activities. The Summer Day Camp and Teen Program provides day activities, a residential camp, and job training and employment for teenagers. The Daily Program provides day care, supervision, and educational opportunities for elementary-school-age children. Community education activities are provided through speaking engagements to churches, civic organizations, schools, and businesses to increase awareness of gang activity. Former gang members participate in public awareness prevention activities.

Project SOAR Mentoring Initiative
College of Education
Northern Arizona University
P.O. Box 5774
Flagstaff, AZ 86011
Telephone: 520-327-3425
Web site: http://coe.nau.edu/mentor_kids

Project SOAR (Student Opportunity for Academic Renewal) is a school-university mentoring program for students who have multiple risk factors in their lives. Some of the factors include gang involvement, chronic truancy, trouble with academics, and teenage pregnancy. Supported by the Arizona Supreme Court and Northern Arizona University Center for Excellence in Education, Academic Outreach, and Special Projects, Project SOAR has developed programs to help children resist pressure to join gangs and engage in other potentially life-altering behavior. It has created a model that provides a basic program structure upon which organizations can create their own individualized plans and includes academic support, skill-building and leadership-enhancing opportunities, parental involvement, and social and personal interaction. Mentoring is provided by college-level students, frequently from the field of education, serving as one-to-one mentors for students ranging from 5th to 12th grade. Each mentor spends an average of 5 to 10 hours per week tutoring, sharing social activities, becoming acquainted with the student's family, and attending Project SOAR meetings, which are focused on the problems frequently encountered by school-age children and their parents. Mentors receive a wage for the first five hours of mentoring per week, but frequently spend additional volunteer time with their mentees.

Salinas Barrios Unidos
1817 Soquel Ave.
Santa Cruz, CA 95062
Telephone: 831-457-8208
Web site: http://www.barriosunidos.net

Salinas Barrios Unidos is a grassroots, nonprofit organization dedicated to working closely with youths who are at risk of gang violence. It works to prevent violence, gang affiliation, and drug abuse among Hispanic youths by providing them with the tools necessary to make positive changes in their lives. Salinas Barrios Unidos believes that community workers who have experienced and overcome the challenges facing young people today are more effective in persuading youth to choose life-affirming behavior. The program focuses on building positive self-esteem and cultural pride through meaningful activities, education, job training, leadership development, and community services. Programs offered focus on three areas: leadership development, educational outreach, and community outreach. Each of these components provides positive activities for youths that will prevent them from becoming involved with gangs. The community outreach programs are based on the belief that gang violence is a community concern.

Salt Lake City Gang Project
Salt Lake County Sheriff's Department
3365 South 900 West
Salt Lake City, UT 84119
Telephone: 801-743-5864
Web site: http://www.slsheriff.org/html/org/metrogang/slagpage.html

This gang task force works to prevent and suppress gang activity by coordinating services at the local, county, and state levels. Members include police officers, prosecutors, community activists, business leaders, city department directors, and county and state government personnel, who meet monthly to discuss problems and develop strategies to resolve gang-related problems. The gang unit helps to provide at-risk youth with alternatives to the gang life by working with local business, government, and community leaders to provide work opportunities, including a job corps and apprenticeships. Youths are referred to drug rehabilitation and education programs if necessary. Police officers patrol known gang areas, conduct sting operations, and maintain a database that contains names of gang members, gang crimes committed, and the location at which these crimes were committed. The unit's community coordinator educates neighborhood groups on how to spot, deter, and report gang activity.

Seattle Team for Youth
City of Seattle Human Services Department
Youth Development and Achievement Division
Seattle Municipal Tower
700 5th Ave., Suite 5800
P.O. Box 34215
Seattle, WA 98124
Telephone: 206-386-1001
Web site: http://www.seattle.gov/humanservices/youth/
academic/teamforyouth.htm

The Seattle Team for Youth program offers case management and support services for youths who have dropped out of school or are at risk for dropping out, including those who are involved in gangs or at risk of gang involvement. Students eligible to receive services are those between the ages of 11 and 21 years from low-income families who have been suspended or expelled from school or have disciplinary issues, school attendance issues, or failing grades, are truant, or have already dropped out of school. Youths are provided access to case managers who assess each youth's needs and then develop a case management plan specifically tailored to the individual. Participants receive assistance in navigating the school and court systems and getting help in tutoring, housing, health, mental health, employment, and other treatment services.

Society for Prevention of Violence
3439 W. Brainard, Room 206
Woodmere, OH 44122
Telephone: 216-591-1876
Web site: http://spvmail.home.att.net

The Society for Prevention of Violence focuses on the reduction of violent acts and asocial behaviors in children and adults through education programs and activities. It teaches children and adults skills intended to build their character, help them acquire a strong value system, motivate them to develop their communication skills, and promote positive interpersonal relationships. The society works to help participants integrate social and academic skills in order to develop positive alternatives and reach their full potential. It encourages people to contribute to society by making decisions and solving problems through effective and appropriate means. A variety of workshops, such as "Gangs, Guns, Drugs, and Violence," are aimed at school personnel.

Strategy Against Gang Involvement
Los Angeles County District Attorney's Office
Bureau of Crime Prevention and Youth Services
320 W. Temple St., Suite 1162
Los Angeles, CA 90012
Telephone: 213-974-7401
Web site: http://da.co.la.ca.us/cpys/cpm.htm

Strategy Against Gang Involvement (SAGE) is aimed at taking back Los Angeles's streets from gangs and the accompanying problems of drugs and violence. SAGE places experienced deputy district attorneys in cities or areas to work with established agencies to develop new programs to combat gangs. Key to SAGE's success are civil injunctions (court orders) designed to reduce drug dealing, violence, graffiti, and loitering. Injunctions may prohibit gang members from carrying cellular phones, beepers, and walkie-talkies; from drinking on the street; from being on the street after midnight; and from harassing residents. SAGE deputies are active members of the communities in which they work, teaching residents how to recognize early signs of gang involvement in their children, how to divert their children from gangs, how to improve their neighborhoods, and how to effectively use the services provided by law enforcement. The program is tailored to each community in which it is activated.

Street SMART/Targeted Outreach Strategic Approaches
Boys & Girls Clubs of America
Health and Life Skills Initiatives
1230 W. Peachtree St., NW
Atlanta, GA 30309
Telephone: 404-487-5700
Web site: http://www.bgca.org/programs/healthlife.asp

The Boys & Girls Clubs of America created Street SMART, a national gang and violence prevention program that employs a team approach to help young people between the ages of 11 and 13 years to understand the destructive lifestyle of gangs and how to resist pressure to join gangs, resolve conflicts, and recognize and value individual differences. It is made up of four program areas—gang awareness and prevention, conflict resolution, peer leadership training, and valuing differences. It also allows them the opportunity to hold annual events that celebrate antigang, antiviolence themes. Street SMART serves as the National Project for Torch Clubs annually and is available for all Boys and Girls Clubs to use.

Teens Against Gang Violence
1486 Dorchester Ave.
Dorchester, MA 02124
Telephone: 617-825-8248
Web site: http://www.tagv.org

Founded in 1990 by Dr. Ulric Johnson in response to Boston's growing gang violence problem, Teens Against Gang Violence (TAGV) is a community-based gang and substance abuse prevention program. Its mission is to empower youth leaders so that they will be able to educate others about nonviolence. The program offers violence prevention education and intervention services to youths, families, and youth service providers through training, consultation, presentations, and workshops. Beginning in 1994, TAGV also provides programs for family members of TAGV participants. Children Against Gang Violence (CAGV) is composed of the siblings of the TAGV, and Parents Against Gang Violence (PAGV) includes the parents of the TAGV and CAGV.

United Community Action Network
44231 N. Division St.
Lancaster, CA 93534
Telephone: 661-948-3000
Web site: http://www.ucanav.com

The United Community Action Network (UCAN) works with at-risk youth to prevent them from joining gangs and using drugs. It operates a 24-hour tip and help line (805-266-HELP) that receives information concerning gang and drug activity in the community. The First Time Offender Juvenile Diversion Program works with first-time juvenile offenders to prevent them from offending again. Police officers bring truant youths to the Truancy Receiving/Holding Center, which provides a safe place for them to stay until their parents can pick them up; their parents receive information on and help in keeping their child from getting into more trouble. A summer job program provides jobs for youths, in the hope of keeping them off the streets and out of trouble.

Violence-Free Zone Initiative
Center for Neighborhood Enterprise
1625 K Street, NW, Suite 1200
Washington, DC 20006
Telephone: 202-518-6500
Web site: http://www.cneonline.org/pages/
Violence-Free_Zone

The Center for Neighborhood Enterprise (CNE) was founded in 1981 to assist the residents of low-income neighborhoods in addressing the problems of their communities, with a primary emphasis on youth violence. One of the major initiatives of the center is the Violence-Free Zone Initiative, which grew out of the House of Umoja program in Philadelphia during the 1980s. The center supported a local group in bringing together the leaders of two warring gangs following the shooting death of a 12-year-old boy in a Washington, D.C., public housing neighborhood. A truce was negotiated, and the youths involved in both gangs were provided with life skills and jobs. The center provides technical assistance to local grassroots organizations that focus on stopping violence in their communities. Local leaders who are trusted in their communities are identified and given guidance, technical assistance, and sources of support to create strong community-based organizations that will implement Violence-Free Zones. The local leaders identify youth advisors who are trained and act as hall monitors, mentors, and counselors in schools and after-school programs to encourage young people to avoid gang participation. Violence-Free Zone projects have been created in Atlanta; Baltimore; Dallas; Milwaukee; Washington, D.C.; and Prince George's County, Maryland.

VisionQuest
600 N. Swan Rd.
P.O. Box 12906
Tucson, AZ 85732
Telephone: 520-881-3950
Web site: http://www.vq.com

VisionQuest was founded in 1973 by two men who borrowed the name from the Native American practice of sending a boy entering manhood away for solitary fasting, meditation, and dreaming to pursue a vision from the Great Spirit. The founders worked in the corrections field and decided to leave after seeing too many young people incarcerated needlessly at a high cost to themselves and society. The program offers a broad network of responsive program alternatives for youths, many of whom have been referred from the juvenile justice or mental health systems. These juveniles range in age from 13 to 21, tend to have trouble developing and maintaining healthy relationships with family members and friends, and may also have trouble adapting to the school environment. Programs offered include impact camps, wagon trains, sailing, biking, backpacking trips, group homes, at-home treatment, alternative schools, and diagnostic and shelter care. As a national organization, it contracts with several government agencies in order to provide specialized services. The goal of the program is to help these youths return to their homes and communities with new self-respect and social survival skills. Staff members develop a program tailored to an individual's behavioral, health, and educational needs. Services provided include educational assessment, behavioral and psychological assessment, evaluation and diagnosis, health assessment and medical referrals, program planning and quarterly review, individualized educational programming, psychological and/or psychiatric counseling, individual and group counseling, parent counseling, family intervention and support, crisis intervention, and recreational activities. The programs focus on breaking down gang affiliations and replacing them with new, positive connections.

Youth Against Gang Activity
Family Service Association of San Antonio, Inc.
702 San Pedro Ave.
San Antonio, TX 78212
Telephone: 210-299-4494
Web site: http://www.family-service.org/yaga.htm

Led by teenagers, the Youth Against Gang Activity provides support, acceptance, and public service activities to keep youths from using drugs and alcohol and from joining gangs by working primarily in middle and high schools and in public housing units. Its goals are to increase youth self-esteem; improve school performance; increase knowledge of the dangers of alcohol, tobacco, and other drugs; emphasize the positive impact of community service projects; provide positive alternatives to violence, drugs, and gang activities; provide positive mentoring and role models; and provide tutoring for youth experiencing difficulty in school.

Federal Government Programs

California Gang Investigators Association
P.O. Box 861143
Los Angeles, CA 90086
Telephone: 888-229-CGIA (2442)
Web site: http://www.cgiaonline.org

Founded in 1977 to encourage better relationships and networking among all agencies working with street gangs and gang prevention in California, the California Gang Investigators Association is composed of law enforcement officers, including corrections personnel, prosecutors, parole personnel, and probation officers. They work with other gang investigators' associations around the United States to promote a coordinated approach to gang investigations, training, and information exchange.

East Coast Gang Investigators Association
P.O. Box 478
Mullica Hill, NJ 08602
Telephone: 631-523-6555
Web site: http://www.ecgia.org

The East Coast Gang Investigators Association (ECGIA) was founded in 1998 as a result of the need for information concerning street gangs on the East Coast. A small group of dedicated law enforcement professionals began sharing information with each other on a regular basis; as the gang problem grew, so did the number of law enforcement and other professionals interested in the intervention and prevention of gang activity. As of 2007, the ECGIA has more than 2,200 members from 16 states and Canada. It provides training to law enforcement personnel as well as public awareness programs concerning street gang awareness and identification to parents, teachers, professionals, and young people.

Florida Gang Investigators Association
Web site: http://www.fgia.com

The Florida Gang Investigators Association was founded in 1993 to promote and facilitate the exchange of information concerning criminal street gangs. The primary goal of the association is to work to eliminate gang violence and its effects on individual gang members and the community. It holds an annual training conference to promote gang awareness and to advocate for the development of effective techniques to help criminal justice professionals in identifying, documenting, and prosecuting criminal street gangs and their members.

Gang-Free Schools and Communities Program
Office of Juvenile Justice and Delinquency Prevention
810 Seventh St., NW
Washington, DC 20531
Telephone: 202-307-5914
Web site: http://ojjdp.ncjrs.org/programs/ProgSummary
.asp?pi=6&ti=&si=&kw=&PreviousPage=ProgResults

The Gang-Free Schools and Communities Program was started in 2000 to reduce youth gang activity in schools and communities throughout the United States. Four sites were selected: East Cleveland, Ohio; Houston; Miami/Dade County, Florida; and Pittsburgh. The program consists of two phases. In the first phase, each site created a steering committee and assessment team and assessed the local gang problem by tapping multiple sources of information, including law enforcement records, school records, community leaders, parents, students, teachers, and gang members. Each site then developed a strategic plan for implementing the Office of Juvenile Justice and Delinquency Prevention's Comprehensive Gang Model. In the second phase, each site implemented its strategic plan, including community mobilization, social intervention, educational and vocational opportunities, suppression, and organizational change. COSMOS Corporation is conducting the evaluation of the program.

Gang Reduction Program
Office of Juvenile Justice and Delinquency Prevention
810 Seventh St., NW
Washington, DC 20531
Telephone: 202-307-5914
Web site: http://ojjdp.ncjrs.org/programs/ProgSummary
.asp?pi=38&ti=&si=&kw=&PreviousPage=ProgResults

The Gang Reduction Program was developed to reduce gang activity in certain targeted neighborhoods using a wide range of interventions developed as a result of research on intervention and prevention. The program utilizes federal, state, and local resources and incorporates relevant prevention, intervention, and suppression strategies to curb gang activity. The program is funding pilot sites in four communities that have a significant amount of gang activity, existing program investment, and strong citizen involvement. The sites are East Los Angeles; Milwaukee; North Miami Beach; and Richmond, Virginia. The Urban Institute is conducting a three-year evaluation of these programs.

Georgia Gang Investigators Association
Web site: http://www.ggia.net

The Georgia Gang Investigators Association is composed of law enforcement and criminal justice professionals throughout the state. Members work to increase communication and information sharing among all members and to help educate each other on the problems and issues facing gang investigators.

Juvenile Justice Clearinghouse
Office of Juvenile Justice and Delinquency Prevention
National Institute of Justice
U.S. Department of Justice
P.O. Box 6000
Rockville, MD 20849-6000
Telephone: 800-638-8736
Web site: http://www.ncjrs.gov

The Office of Juvenile Justice and Delinquency Prevention (OJJDP) established the Juvenile Justice Clearinghouse as a component of the National Criminal Justice Reference Service (NCJRS) in 1979. The clearinghouse is a comprehensive resource on a variety of juvenile justice topics, including gangs and gang-related information. Juvenile justice professionals and anyone else seeking information can speak with an information specialist about specific areas of inquiry The clearinghouse coordinates the distribution of OJJDP publications and disseminates information about research sponsored by OJJDP, training projects, and program initiatives. It also provides access to the NCJRS library, which is one of the world's most comprehensive sources of criminal justice and juvenile justice literature. The NCJRS also has an electronic bulletin board on the Internet that provides timely information on a variety of topics of interest to juvenile justice professionals.

Publications: *Gang Suppression and Intervention: Community Models* provides a framework for creating promising approaches to reducing the problems created by juvenile gangs. *Early Precursors of Gang Membership: A Study of Seattle Youth* describes the results of the Seattle Social Development Project concerning youths who join gangs. *Youth Gang Programs and Strategies* describes programs that have been developed to discourage the appeal of gangs and reduce gang participation and violence.

Mid-Atlantic Regional Gang Investigators Network
Washington Baltimore High Intensity Dug Trafficking Area
Program
9001 Edmonston Rd., Suite 300
Greenbelt, MD 20770
Telephone: 301-489-1700
Web site: http://www.gomargin.us

Started in 1992 as an informal group of gang investigators representing seven law enforcement agencies from throughout the Washington, D.C., metropolitan area, the Mid-Atlantic Regional Gang Investigators Network (MARGIN) now includes federal, state, and local law enforcement/criminal justice officers representing more than 75 separate agencies throughout Maryland, Virginia, and Washington, D.C. MARGIN's primary goal is to enhance officer and overall public safety by providing relevant gang information to law enforcement officers.

Midwest Gang Investigator's Association
P.O. Box 510455
Milwaukee, WI 53203
Telephone: 414-278-5136
Web site: http://www.mgia.org

The Midwest Gang Investigator's Association is a professional, nonprofit organization that is made up of law enforcement officers and other members of the criminal justice community in Illinois, Indiana, Iowa, Michigan, Minnesota, Missouri, Nebraska, Ohio, Wisconsin, and Kentucky.

National Alliance of Gang Investigators' Associations
Web site: http://nagia.org

The National Alliance of Gang Investigators' Association (NAGIA) was formed in 1998. It is a cooperative organization currently composed of representatives from 17 regional gang investigators' associations representing more than 15,000 gang investigators across the country, as well as federal agencies and other organizations involved in gang-related matters. The NAGIA is a unique alliance of criminal justice professionals dedicated to the promotion and coordination of national antigang strategies. The NAGIA also advocates the standardization of antigang training, establishment of uniform gang definitions, assistance for communities with emerging gang problems, and input to policy makers and program administrators. The NAGIA is not meant to replace or duplicate the services provided by any other entity. Rather, it facilitates and supports regional gang investigators' associations, the Regional Information Sharing Systems (see below), and federal, state, and local antigang initiatives. NAGIA maintains an online library of articles on a variety of gang-related topics, provides a list of links to all regional investigators' associations and other regional information, and maintains links to gang conferences.

National Major Gang Task Force
338 S. Arlington Ave., Suite 112
Indianapolis, IN 46219
Telephone: 317-322-0537
Web site: http://www.nmgtf.org

Strategic goals and objectives of the National Major Gang Task Force include networking, training, and establishing information-sharing standards regarding gangs and security threat groups management in correctional settings. The task force has been recognized nationally in the criminal justice system for creative gang intervention and management strategies.

Publications: "A Study of Gangs and Security Threat Groups in America's Adult Prisons and Jails" and "Understanding Gangs and Gang Processes."

National Youth Gang Center
Institute for Intergovernmental Research
P.O. Box 12729
Tallahassee, FL 32317
Telephone: 850-385-0600
Web site: http://www.iir.com/nygc/

The National Youth Gang Center was created to gather and enhance the critical knowledge about youth gangs and provide information on the most effective responses to them. The center helps state and local jurisdictions collect, analyze, and exchange information on gang-related demographics, legislation, research, and promising program strategies. It also coordinates activities of the Office of Juvenile Justice and Delinquency Prevention Youth Gang Consortium, which is composed of federal agencies, representatives from gang programs, and service providers.

North Carolina Gang Investigators Association
Web site: http://www.ncgangcops.org

The North Carolina Gang Investigators Association (NCGIA) includes criminal justice professionals from across the state. NCGIA focuses on preventing and controlling gang activity throughout the state by exchanging information among all jurisdictions; offering training and other educational programs for members and the general public; and working with state legislators to enact laws to effectively control gangs. The association also encourages the use of a definition of *gang membership* that is consistent across jurisdictions.

Northern California Gang Investigators Association
Web site: http://www.ncgia.com

Formed in 1984 by law enforcement professionals concerned about the growing gang problem in northern California, the Northern California Gang Investigators Association focuses on intervention and prevention of gang activities. Members work to promote closer working relationships among all law enforcement personnel, encourage and support legislation designed to decrease gang activity, encourage public support through education and crime prevention activities, encourage the development of new techniques in gang member identification and apprehension, and cooperate with other agencies to discourage gang violence.

Northwest Gang Investigators Association
Web site: http://www.nwgia.com/

Established in 1994, the Northwest Gang Investigators Association (NWGIA) consists of law enforcement and other criminal justice personnel in Washington, Oregon, Idaho, and Montana. The mission of the NWGIA is to encourage the gathering of gang enforcement, associated drug trafficking, and intelligence information; develop new and effective techniques of managing gangs; encourage fraternalism among criminal justice professionals; and promote mutual cooperation in all areas of gang enforcement, including the open exchange of information.

Oklahoma Gang Investigators Association
Web site: http://www.ogia.net

The Oklahoma Gang Investigators Association is a nonprofit organization composed of law enforcement and associated professionals set up to share information concerning gangs with law enforcement agencies throughout the state and to educate the public.

Ontario Gang Investigators Association
Don Mills Station
P.O. Box 464
Don Mills, ON M3C 2T2
CANADA
Web site: http://www.ongia.org

The Ontario Gang Investigators Association (ONGIA) is made up of members of the law enforcement and criminal justice communities throughout Ontario, Canada, and North America. Membership is open to all sworn members of law enforcement agencies, including police, probation, corrections, immigration, and customs officers. ONGIA encourages networking between its members and the community to increase knowledge concerning gang-related issues.

Regional Information Sharing Systems Program
State and Local Assistance Division
Bureau of Justice Assistance
810 Seventh St., NW
Washington, DC 20531
Telephone: 202-616-7829
Web site: http://www.iir.com/riss
http://rissinfo.com

The Regional Information Sharing Systems (RISS) Program was created to link law enforcement agencies throughout the country to combat criminal networks that operate across jurisdictional lines. It assists local, state, federal, and tribal law enforcement agencies in protecting the public by providing secure, nation-wide information and intelligence-sharing capabilities and other investigative support services. The program operates six regional centers that share intelligence and coordinate efforts. They focus on increased violent activity by terrorists, drug traffickers, street gangs, cybercriminals, and other organized criminals. Each of the centers selects its own target crimes and the range of services it provides to member agencies. The RISS Program is a federally funded program administered by the U.S. Department of Justice, Bureau of Justice Assistance.

RISS utilizes a specialized database, the RISS National Gang Database, or RISSGang, to collect and disseminate information on gangs and gang members. The database provides law enforcement agencies with access to a variety of topics regarding gangs, including suspects, organizations, weapons, locations, and vehicles, along with images of gang members, gang symbols, and gang graffiti. Prior to 2005, access to the database was limited to RISS member agencies; however, in 2005, access was expanded to include nonmember criminal justice agencies.

The six RISS centers are:

1. The Middle Atlantic–Great Lakes Organized Crime Law Enforcement Network (MAGLOCLEN)
   140 Terry Dr., Suite 100
   Newtown, PA 18940
   Telephone: 1-800-345-1322

   The MAGLOCLEN geographical region includes Delaware, Indiana, Maryland, Michigan, New Jersey, New York, Ohio, Pennsylvania, and the District of Columbia, as well as Australia, Canada, and the United Kingdom.

2. The Mid-States Organized Crime Information Center (MOCIC)
   1610 E. Sunshine St., Suite 100
   Springfield, MO 65804
   Telephone: 417-883-4384.

   The MOCIC geographical region includes Illinois, Iowa, Kansas, Minnesota, Missouri, Nebraska, North Dakota, South Dakota, Wisconsin, and Canada.

3. The New England State Police Information Network (NESPIN)
   124 Grove St., Suite 105
   Franklin, MA 02038
   Telephone: 1-800-343-5682

   The NESPIN geographical region includes Connecticut, Maine, Massachusetts, New Hampshire, Rhode Island, and Vermont, as well as Canada.

4. The Rocky Mountain Information Network (RMIN)
   2828 N. Central Ave., Suite 1000
   Phoenix, AZ 85004
   Telephone: 1-800-821-0640

   The RMIN geographical region includes Arizona, Colorado, Idaho, Montana, Nevada, New Mexico, Utah, and Wyoming, as well as member agencies in Canada.

5. The Regional Organized Crime Information Center (ROCIC)
   545 Marriott Dr., Suite 850
   Nashville, TN 37214
   Telephone: 1-800-238-7985

   The ROCIC geographical region includes Alabama, Arkansas, Florida, Georgia, Kentucky, Louisiana, Mississippi, North Carolina, Oklahoma, South Carolina, Tennessee, Texas, Virginia, and West Virginia, as well as Puerto Rico and the U.S. Virgin Islands.

6. The Western States Information Network (WSIN)
   P.O. Box 903198
   Sacramento, CA 94203
   Telephone: 1-800-952-5258

   The WSIN geographical region includes Alaska, California, Hawaii, Oregon, and Washington, as well as Canada and Guam.

Southeastern Connecticut Gang Activities Group
P.O. Box 634
Waterford, CT 06385
Telephone: 860-437-0552
Web site: http://www.segag.org

The Southeastern Connecticut Gang Activities Group (SE-GAG), a nonprofit law enforcement association, was founded by the law enforcement and criminal justice agencies of southeastern Connecticut to combat the rise in violent youth and gang activities in the region. SE-GAG gathers and disseminates information to law enforcement and related criminal justice agencies to educate school administrators, teachers, parents, students, businesses, communities, and police in gang awareness and to encourage community involvement in making the communities safe.

Tennessee Gang Investigators Association
Web site: http://www.tn-gia.org

The Tennessee Gang Investigators Association (TNGIA) coordinates the efforts of gang investigators in order to quickly disseminate and exchange information concerning gang-related incidents, suspects, and investigations. The TNGIA also examines and encourages new methods and techniques to identify and apprehend gang members suspected of crimes.

Virginia Gang Investigators Association
Web site: http://www.vgia.org

The Virginia Gang Investigators Association is a nonprofit organization of law enforcement and related professionals organized for the purpose of sharing information concerning gangs and gang crime. It offers an annual conference to its members to facilitate sharing of the latest information and research concerning gangs.

8

Selected Print and Nonprint Resources

This chapter contains descriptions of recently published books, manuals, journal articles, and training guides on issues relating to gangs and gang behavior. Because many such books and journal articles have been published recently, this chapter lists the best known and more readily available materials on a variety of topics within this field; by no means is it a comprehensive listing of the current literature. Also described are selected videos and DVDs on gangs as well as Web sites that provide valuable information concerning gangs.

Books

Alexander, Claire. 2000. *The Asian Gang: Ethnicity, Identity, Masculinity*. London: Berg Publishers. 192 pages. Bibliography, index. ISBN 1-85973-319-0.

Alexander spent three years conducting fieldwork with young Bangladeshi men who lived in London's inner city. Based on society's view of groups of young Asian men as gangs and as a new and growing social problem, the book explores the myths and reality surrounding common societal stereotypes of contemporary Asian youth. This in-depth analysis of ethnicity and masculinity on a very personal level challenges our society's traditional views and provides valuable insights regarding Asian culture and youth delinquency.

Barrios, Luis, and David C. Brotherton. 2004. *Street Politics and the Transformation of a New York City Gang.* New York: Columbia University Press. 397 pages. Bibliography, index. ISBN 0-231-11418-4.

Barrios and Brotherton provide a fascinating look at the transformation of the Latin Kings and Queens, from a violent gang to the Almighty Latin King and Queen Nation (ALKQN), an organization that advocated for the poor and disenfranchised in society. Members encouraged peaceful means to achieve their goals and required that their members stay in school. Part 1 describes the basic parameters and methodology of the study as well as theories of street gang formation and organization. Part 2 presents their findings, including history of the gangs; the emergence of King Tone, the reformed ALKQN's charismatic leader; and the influence of other nongang groups, such as the Black Panthers and Young Lords, on the ALKQN. Part 3 discusses the group's level of organization, characteristics of members who joined the ALKQN during its transformation, the importance of ethnic and cultural identity, the goals of the organization, and the individuals and groups who are perceived as ALKQN's enemies.

Chin, Ko-Lin. 2000. *Chinatown Gangs: Extortion, Enterprise, and Ethnicity.* New York: Oxford University Press. 256 pages. Bibliography, index. ISBN 0-19-513627-6.

In this examination of gangs in New York City's Chinatown, Chin gathered first-hand information from gang members, victims of gang violence, community leaders, and law enforcement personnel. The gangs in Chinatown have been seen as a closed society, with no outsider allowed in. Chin demonstrates the widespread nature of the gangs; their influence, longevity, and existence as a local institution; and the fear that they engender in the Chinese community. He examines their role in the economic viability of the community, lawlessness, and their links to political economy and social history. Individual chapters focus on his research strategies and methods, the severity of gang victimization, patterns of gang extortion, victim reactions to gang extortion, gang characteristics, gang violence, the gang as an enterprise, and controlling Chinese gangs.

Choo, Kyung-Seok. 2007. *Gangs and Immigrant Youth.* New York: LFB Scholarly Pub. 200 pages. Bibliography, index. ISBN 1-59332-148-1.

Choo examines youth gangs in the Asian community, focusing on one Korean-affiliated Chinese youth gang in New York City and a Korean group of delinquent youths in New Jersey who are not considered to be a gang. He provides an analysis of the socio-economic and cultural characteristics of Korean immigrants, their demographics, and their unique lifestyle and relates these characteristics to the delinquent behavior of Korean young people. Individual chapters provide a discussion of current research, Choo's research design, the quality of Korean community life, assimilation, and descriptions of the delinquent group and the youth gang.

Christensen, Loren W. 1999. *Gangbangers: Understanding the Deadly Minds of America's Street Gangs.* Boulder, CO: Paladin Press. 200 pages. ISBN 1-58160-047-X.

As a former military policeman and gang enforcement officer in the police department in Portland, Oregon, Christensen talked with current and former gang members, police who work in gang units, prison corrections officers, parole and probation officers, teachers, social workers, and other professionals in an attempt to understand how gang members think and what makes them do what they do. In their own words, current and former gang members talk about killing people and about getting killed themselves, they describe who their targets are and how they determine who becomes a target, and they offer suggestions on ways to reduce the growing presence of gangs in the United States.

Covey, Herbert C. 2003. *Street Gangs throughout the World.* Springfield, IL: Charles C. Thomas. 267 pages. References, index. ISBN 0-398-07428-3.

The author provides a summary of knowledge of street gangs around the world. In Chapter 1, Covey explains why the study of street gangs is important and how demographic changes throughout the world lead to the development of street gangs, presents methodological issues, explores gang structures, compares street gangs with other groups (skinheads, mobs, casuals, taggers, hooligans, and organized crime), and describes the community's and mass media's role in encouraging or discouraging gang behavior. Chapter 2 briefly summarizes research on street gangs in the United States. Ensuing chapters examine street gangs in Europe, Canada, Central and South America, Russia, Asia, Africa, the Middle East, Australia, and the Pacific Islands. The final chapter compares findings from individual countries and examines worldwide trends.

Curry, G. David, and Scott H. Decker. 2003. *Confronting Gangs: Crime and Community.* **2nd ed. Los Angeles: Roxbury Park. 211 pages. Bibliography, index. ISBN 1-891487-52-3.**

The authors have designed this book for use in college-level courses on criminology, gangs, delinquency, violence, social problems, juvenile justice, and criminal justice. Focusing on community and neighborhood, the authors examine the nature and variety of gangs, the connection between gangs and delinquency, the role of drugs in contemporary gangs, female gang involvement, and the relationship between gangs and social institutions. The authors discuss the connection between the current literature on gangs and traditional approaches to gangs. The book also examines recent research and policy findings on gangs.

Decker, Scott, ed. 2003. *Policing Gangs and Youth Violence.* **Belmont, CA: Wadsworth. 320 pages. Bibliography, index. ISBN 0-534-59841-2.**

Part of the Wadsworth Professionalism in Policing series, this book describes current practices used by police and juvenile justice professionals based on a community-policing model. A variety of experts in their fields describe various problem-solving and suppression-based approaches and programs throughout the United States. Part 1 offers an introduction to gangs, community policing, and problem solving. Part 2 examines problem-solving approaches to gangs and youth violence, describing specific programs in Boston; Los Angeles; Indianapolis; Chicago; and Mountlake Terrace, Washington. Suppression-based approaches are examined in Part 3, which also includes descriptions of programs in St. Louis, Detroit, Southern California, and Dallas. The final part provides an analysis of the current status of gangs, youth violence, and policing efforts and offers suggestions for the future.

Decker, Scott H., and Frank M. Weerman, eds. 2005. *European Street Gangs and Troublesome Youth Groups*. New York: AltaMira Press. 338 pages. Index. ISBN 0-7591-0793-9.

Because youth gangs are common in the United States, many people believe that they are primarily an American phenomenon. However, street gangs and other violent youth groups exist in other countries. In this book, Decker and Weerman have gathered well-known contributors who provide the reader with information on European youth gangs and with comparisons with American youth gangs. Topics discussed include the impact of immigration on the growth and development of youth gangs, the contribution of rapid urbanization in many countries to the growth of gangs, and prevention and intervention strategies.

Delaney, Tim. 2006. *American Street Gangs*. Upper Saddle River, NJ: Prentice-Hall. 352 pages. References, index. ISBN 1-13-171079-6.

Written for college courses on gangs, criminology, social problems, and other courses in sociology and criminal justice departments, Delaney's book offers a review of the major issues related to gang life and gang violence. He discusses the major theories and socioeconomic reasons to explain the existence of gangs and describes the various types of gangs, including small, regional, and super-sized (nations) gangs. He examines the techniques used by law enforcement agencies to combat the serious problems created by gangs, along with efforts currently being made by law enforcement and private organizations to keep young people out of gangs. Individual chapters examine definitions of gangs, the history of gangs, theoretical and socioeconomic explanations for the existence of gangs, gang structure and processes, female gangs, criminal activities, prevention and suppression of gangs, treatment, and implications for the future.

Donahue, Sean, and Clint Willis, eds. 2002. *Gangs: Stories of Life and Death from the Streets*. New York: Thunder's Mouth. 364 pages. Bibliography. ISBN 1-56025-425-4.

A collection of fiction, nonfiction, and journalistic accounts of gangs, both past and present, this book provides 14 stories of attempts to survive in tough neighborhoods, written by individuals with experience on the streets. For example, Kody Scott, a former member of the Crips, describes the commitment he made as a gang member to murder those interfering with his gang. Piri Thomas (author of *Down These Mean Streets*) describes joining a gang as a means of survival in Spanish Harlem during the 1940s. The triads in Chinatown, crack cocaine and gangs, New York gangs, and Vietnamese gangs are also examined.

Duffy, Maureen P., and Scott Edward Gillig, eds. 2004. *Teen Gangs: A Global View*. Westport, CT: Greenwood. 248 pages. Index. ISBN 0-313-32150-7.

Duffy and Gillig have provided the reader with a collection of essays that provide a description of the nature and extent of gang culture in 14 countries, including Australia, the Bahamas, Honduras, Ireland, Israel, Italy, Jamaica, Malaysia, Papua New Guinea, Puerto Rico, Taiwan, Trinidad and Tobago, the United Kingdom, and the United States. Gangs are examined within the larger context of socioeconomic conditions within each country. The reader will notice that definitions vary from country to country. The conditions that cause gangs to form, including poverty, marginalization, and self-identity issues, are examined within each country, and society's responses to dealing with gangs are discussed. Also available as an e-book.

Egley, Arlen, Cheryl L. Maxson, Jody Miller, and Malcolm W. Klein, eds. 2007. *The Modern Gang Reader*. 3rd ed. Oxford University Press. 408 pages. Bibliography, index. ISBN 0-19533-066-8.

The editors have gathered articles from leading scholars and researchers to provide a comprehensive introduction to the study of gangs. Drawing on the knowledge of the leading gang scholars, the book provides diverse, wide-ranging views of the major contemporary issues in gang research. Section 1 provides current definitions of a gang, a history of gang research, a framework for understanding gangs, antecedents of gang membership, and getting into and leaving gangs. Section 2 discusses the distribution and structures of gangs, including patterns of gang problems, the evolution of street gangs, a cross-national perspective, and prison gangs. Section 3 discusses race, ethnicity, and gender in gangs, including Chinese gangs; a Frankfurt, Germany, street gang; female gangs; and the impact of sex composition on gangs. Section 4 looks at gangs, violence, and drugs. The final section examines programs and policies that have proven successful in preventing youths from joining gangs and those helping youths end their participation in gangs.

Esbensen, Finn-Aage, Stephen G. Tibbetts, and Larry Gaines, eds. 2004. *American Youth Gangs at the Millennium.* Long Grove, IL: Waveland. 389 pages. Bibliography. ISBN 1-57766-324-1.

The editors have gathered articles from leading scholars and researchers to provide a comprehensive review of the current status of American youth gangs. Divided into four sections, the book explores definitions and current trends in gang research and behavior, the wide variety of gangs, gang activities, and various responses to gangs. Section 1 focuses on issues surrounding official definitions of gangs, criminal behavior of youth gangs, and patterns of gang problems. Section 2 examines the variety of gangs, including Chicano and Chicana gangs, middle-school gangs, gender dynamics, and hybrid gangs. Section 3 looks at gang initiation activities, alcohol and violence, financial activities of gang members, organized crime, and gang homicide. The final section looks at the various responses to gang problems, including community and police intervention, prevention options, and civil gang injunctions.

Grennan, Sean, Marjie T. Britz, Jeffrey Rush, and Thomas Barker. 2000. *Gangs: An International Approach.* Upper Saddle River, NJ: Prentice-Hall. 479 pages. Index. ISBN 0-13-324856-9.

The authors provide an in-depth perspective on gangs throughout the world in this book, written primarily for college students. They examine the formation of gangs, history of criminal activities, and future of gangs. Gangs throughout the world are examined in terms of their historical background; the ethnic, racial, or religious makeup of the gang; initiation rites; length of membership; availability of upward mobility; and gangs' illegal activities. Groups examined include Italian organized crime; outlaw motorcycle gangs; supremacists and militias; street gangs; Jamaican and Nigerian gangs; Chinese gangs; Japanese, Vietnamese, and Korean gangs; Hispanic gangs; Russian and Israeli gangs; and other worldwide organized crime groups.

Hagedorn, John M., ed. 2007. *Gangs in the Global City: Alternatives to Traditional Criminology.* Urbana: University of Illinois Press. Bibliography, index. ISBN 0-252-03096-3.

Gangs are no longer simply an American phenomenon, but are found throughout the world. Researchers have not yet examined the transformation of gangs into worldwide enterprises, especially as this transformation is related to other changes that have occurred as a result of globalization. Hagedorn has gathered sociologists, gang experts, and other researchers to explore the relationships among the worldwide expansion of gangs, criminology, and globalization. Part 1 discusses theoretical perspectives, including gangs, institutions, race, space, globalization, and social exclusion. Part 2 examines spaces of globalization, such as the global city; New Zealand gangs; and the effects of rapid urbanization, migrant indigenous youth, and gangs. Part 3 focuses on identities of resistance, looking at female gangs, extremist youth groupings in Germany, and gangs and spirituality. Part 4 discusses responses to neoliberalism, examining gangs as a social movement, and Americanization and the racial aspect of youth crime and disorder.

Huff, C. Ronald, ed. 2002. *Gangs in America III*. Thousand Oaks: CA: Sage. Bibliography, index. ISBN 0-7619-2423-X.

In this third edition, Huff has pulled together fellow experts on gang research, including Cheryl Maxson, John Hagedorn, Malcolm Klein, and James Diego Vigil, to examine contemporary gangs and how communities respond to them. Part 1 examines the changing boundaries of youth gangs, joining gangs, and getting out of gangs. Part 2 focuses on areas in which gangs can be found, looking at neighborhoods and schools, as well as issues in developing and maintaining a regional gang incident tracking system. The increasing diversity of gangs is looked at in Part 3, and Part 4 examines research on gangs, antiloitering and public nuisance laws, new approaches to preventing gang violence, and gangs and public policy.

Jackson, Robert, and Wesley D. McBride. 2000. *Understanding Street Gangs*. Belmont, CA: Wadsworth. 160 pages. ISBN 0-942-72817-3.

As leading authorities on gang activities, Jackson and McBride describe the escalating dangers of street and prison gangs. They offer a unique approach to dealing with the problem, on a local as well as national level. Topics discussed include definitions of gangs, gang structure and organization, the causative factors involved in the creation of gangs, family structures and profiles, socioeconomic pressures to join gangs, the influence and role of drugs in various gang activities, and measurements of gang violence. The authors also suggest possible solutions to the problems related to street gangs.

Johnson, Claudia Durst. 2004. *Youth Gangs in Literature*. Westport, CT: Greenwood Press. 264 pages. ISBN 0-313-32749-1.

Johnson offers a unique perspective in an examination of how gangs have been portrayed in literature. Chapters are organized chronologically and by topic; each chapter offers a description of one or more works of fiction on that topic and then an analysis of different kinds of gangs and their characteristics. Topics include outlaw gangs, the Irish immigrant, a heritage of guns, the 1920s in Chicago, Jewish gangs, the 1940s in Harlem, Nazis and gangs, a girl gang in the 1950s, Vietnam and civil rights, prep schools, Watergate, family disintegration in the 1980s, the 1960s in Los Angeles, barrio gangs of the 1960s and 1970s, Filipino Americans, Vietnamese gangs and skinheads, and Chinese gangs.

Katz, Charles M., and Vincent J. Webb. 2006. *Policing Gangs in America*. New York: Cambridge University Press. 310 pages. References. ISBN 0-52185-110-6.

This book is focused on gang unit officers and their working environment, details how police gang units respond to gang problems in their communities, and discusses the issues and problems that characterize the police response to gangs. Individual chapters focus on studying the police response to gangs, a historical analysis of gangs and ways used to control gangs, the nature of the current gang problem, characteristics of the typical police gang unit and the participating officers, and community policing. A final chapter draws conclusions and discusses implications of the role that police gang units play in controlling gang activity.

Klein, Malcolm W. 2004. *Gang Cop: The Words and Ways of Officer Paco Domingo*. Walnut Creek, CA: AltaMira Press. 194 pages. ISBN 0-7591-0546-4.

Klein's purpose in writing this book is to provide a unique approach to understanding gangs. The lead character, Paco

Domingo, is a composite, constructed from real people the author has met over the years. The book helps the reader understand the personality and focus of law enforcement officials who work with gangs, as well as the nature of street gangs. In a different approach from that of the typical textbook, Klein uses Paco and his perspectives to describe current knowledge about gangs.

Klein, Malcolm W. 2005. *The American Street Gang: Its Nature, Prevalence, and Control.* **New York: Oxford University Press. 288 pages. Notes, index. ISBN 0-19-511573-2.**

Klein believes that we need to understand the American street gang "for intellectual purposes, to seek to control its excesses and prevent its continuing regeneration, and also to understand our society better" (3). With gangs currently found in more than 800 U.S. cities and towns, Klein believes that we need to understand them because society creates them and we must understand our relationship to them before the number of gangs will decline. In this book, he provides the reader with a discussion of the basic issues, including gang proliferation, the connections between gangs and drugs, and the role of group processes and dynamics in gang control. He offers a historical background and a discussion of the contemporary street gang situation, dealing with the problem, gang suppression, and prospects for the future. His final chapter attempts to answer the question of whether American street gangs are unique to this country or whether other countries are experiencing similar issues with youth gangs.

Klein, Malcolm W., and Cheryl L. Maxson. 2006. *Street Gang Patterns and Policies.* **New York: Oxford University Press. 310 pages. Bibliography, index. ISBN 0-19-516-344-3.**

Klein and Maxson explore the patterns of behavior and general characteristics of street gangs in contemporary America. They examine the relevant and promising approaches to developing effective gang policies and compare and contrast these policies and their similarities. Part 1 explores gang prevalence, proliferation, migration, crime patterns, and six major gang-control programs. Based on this information, the authors suggest that law enforcement agencies and policy makers reexamine current programs and policies focusing on controlling gang behavior. Part 2 examines risk factors for joining gangs, gang structures, and group processes and community contexts, which provide the foundation for reconsidering programs and policies. Part 3 looks at multiple goals for gang-control programs and policies and offers a model for policy choices.

Kontos, Louis, David Brotherton, and Luis Barrios, eds. 2003. *Gangs and Society: Alternative Perspectives.* **New York: Columbia University Press. 352 pages. Index. ISBN 0-231-12141-5.**

The editors have gathered a wide variety of experts in the field to examine the nature and complexity of gangs. They demonstrate that the "gang problem" is a complex one, mirroring the complexities of society as a whole. In Part 1, individual contributors discuss the limits of conventional theories concerning gangs, including American street gangs, Mexican American youth gangs, gangs and drug distribution in New York City during the 1990s, and homeless youth in Australia. Part 2 examines gangs and politics, including gang goals and street activism. The ways in which gangs use rituals and spiritualism and their search for individual and collective empowerment are discussed in Part 3. Contributors to Part 4 look at the role of females in gangs. The relationships between gangs and social control are examined in Part 5, which looks at gangs and the law as well as gangs in Massachusetts prisons. Finally, Part 6 examines the functions and politics of different approaches to gang photography and includes a photo essay.

McCorkle, Richard C., and Terance D. Miethe. 2002. *Panic: The Social Construction of the Street Gang Problem.* **Upper Saddle River, NJ: Prentice-Hall. 340 pages. Bibliography, index. ISBN 0-13-094458-0.**

McCorkle and Miethe, both criminologists, examine the focus that was placed on street gangs during the 1980s and early 1990s and the ensuing panic throughout the country concerning the growth and spread of street gangs. The authors argue that gangs were seen as a social problem as a result of the overblown claims of law enforcement officials, the media, and researchers who became interested in the gang phenomenon. As a result, the United States saw an increase in crime, widespread expansion of ineffective antigang policies, and the waste of millions of dollars in an attempt to fix the problem.

Miller, Jodie. 2001. *One of the Guys: Girls, Gangs, and Gender.* New York: Oxford University Press. 288 pages. References, index. ISBN 0-19-513078-2.

Are girls who participate in gangs just followers of their boyfriends, in essence victims of the gang mentality, or are they full participants in all the violence and aggression that is part of gang life? Miller examines the reasons why girls join gangs, the nature of their participation, and how gang membership leads to violence and victimization for females. The book includes interviews with female gang members in St. Louis, Missouri, and Columbus, Ohio, who provide vivid first-person accounts of gang life. The ways in which gender affects gang experience and the implications for gender and crime are explored.

Miranda, Marie. 2003. *Homegirls in the Public Sphere.* Austin: University of Texas Press. 231 pages. Bibliography, index. ISBN 978-0-292-70192-2.

For more than two years, Miranda conducted field research in Fruitvale, California, working with Chicana gang members, who disagree with many popular representations of Chicana youth. They also describe their own lives and involvement in gangs through a video, *It's a Homie Thang!* Miranda describes the community of Fruitdale, the debates about an urban underclass, the development of a working relationship between her and the girls in the study, the production of the video project, and how the girls view themselves, as they speak at public meetings and community agencies. She looks at the communication process and, in an appendix, provides answers to frequently asked questions about gangs and the girls who participated in her study.

Petersen, Rebecca D., ed. 2004. *Understanding Contemporary Gangs in America: An Interdisciplinary Approach.* Upper Saddle River, NJ: Prentice-Hall. 400 pages. Index. ISBN 0-130-39474-2.

Written for undergraduate and graduate courses in juvenile delinquency, juvenile justice, deviance, and other courses in criminology departments, this book provides a comprehensive examination of gangs in the United States. Petersen has pulled together experts in the field to provide diverse viewpoints on gangs, gang behavior, and gang violence. Part 1 of the book provides an overall introduction to and current definitions of a gang.

Part 2 examines gender issues, including girls in the gang, differences between gang girls and gang boys, and the meaning of family and kinship among homegirls. The third part covers race and ethnicity in gangs, including Chicano, Navajo, and Chinese gangs. Gangs in prisons and schools are the focus of Part 4. Violence, drugs, and gangs are examined in Part 5. Part 6 looks at gang victimization, and the final part discusses promising prevention and intervention strategies. Questions designed to encourage critical thinking of the materials presented are provided at the end of each chapter.

Sheldon, Randall G., Sharon K. Tracy, and William B. Brown. 2004. *Youth Gangs in American Society.* **3d ed. Belmont, CA: Wadsworth. 336 pages. References, index. ISBN 0-534-61569-4.**

In this third edition, the authors review recent research and current impressions and understanding of gangs in American society. The first chapter provides a history of gangs in society and explores current definitions and understanding of what constitutes a gang. Chapter 2 attempts to describe what gangs and gang members look like. The gang subculture is explored in Chapter 3, criminal activities in which gangs are involved are examined in Chapter 4, and membership and participation of girls in gangs is discussed in Chapter 5. Chapter 6 examines the various theories proposed on why gangs exist. The existence of gangs as a result of inequalities in American society is discussed in Chapter 7. Chapters 8 and 9 explore community-based and national intervention strategies and legal intervention strategies.

Short, James F., Jr., and Lorine A. Hughes, eds. 2006. *Studying Youth Gangs.* **Lanham, MD: AltaMira Press. 288 pages. Bibliography, index. ISBN 0-7591-0938-9.**

Short and Hughes have gathered a broad and respected group of gang researchers and social scientists to examine the dynamics of youth gangs. Short begins by discussing the reasons why studying gangs is important. From there, contributors examine the issues surrounding the effect of studying gangs, the neighborhood effects on street gang behavior, social dynamics, social network analysis, whether hate groups should be considered street gangs, gangs in Australia, the global impact of gangs, and a community-wide gang program model. The editors conclude the volume by examining the ways to move gang research forward.

Tita, George, K. Jack Riley, Greg Ridgeway, Clifford Grammich, Allan F. Abrahamse, and Peter W. Greenwood. 2003. *Reducing Gun Violence: Results from an Intervention in East Los Angeles.* **Santa Monica, CA: RAND Corporation. 76 pages. Bibliography. ISBN 0-8330-3475-8.**

The Boston Gun Project, also known as Operation Ceasefire, was established to reduce youth violence by working to reduce gang and gun violence through the use of sanctions, incentives for prevention, or a combination of sanctions and services developed for specific situations. The program was successful, and the RAND Corporation set out to determine if a similar program would work in other urban areas. This report describes the application of this program to a gang-infested area in East Los Angeles. Through the use of increased police presence and stricter enforcement of housing codes and gun laws, along with other intervention activities, crime rates were reduced. More important, crime rates in nearby areas did not increase, reinforcing the finding that crime rates were indeed reduced, rather than the belief that criminals simply moved out of one neighborhood and into another.

Totten, Mark D. 2000. *Guys, Gangs and Girlfriend Abuse.* **Orchard Park, CA: Broadview Press. 239 pages. References. ISBN 1-55222-341-4.**

This book reports the results of a study that Totten conducted on marginal male gang members; the reasons why they abuse their girlfriends, including physical, sexual, and emotional abuse; and how they rationalize this behavior. He extends this analysis to examine how the abuse of young women, gays, and racial minorities is related to views of family and gender. He reviews the study of male violence, learning and developing familial and gender ideologies, and summarizes the findings in his study. Appendices provide the screening interview questions and the in-depth interview questions in the study.

Tovares, Raul Damacio. 2002. *Manufacturing the Gang: Mexican American Youth Gangs on Local Television News.* **Westport, CT: Greenwood. 192 pages. Bibliography, index. ISBN 0-313-31827-1.**

Tovares examines the ways in which Mexican American youth gangs have been portrayed on local television news in Austin, Texas. In addition to portrayals in local news media, the reactions of the police and community leaders are also examined, specifically the ways in which myths about gangs have been created. Society is led to believe, using media clichés, that a rising tide of violence is occurring, drug use and addiction have grown, and minority youth are alienated from the larger society. Tovares argues that these beliefs are gross exaggerations of reality and have led to reinforcing stereotypes concerning Mexican American youth. Continuing distortions and selective reporting by the press and television only encourage these stereotypes of young Mexican American males as prone to violence and a danger to society.

Umemoto, Karen. 2006. *The Truce: Lessons from an L.A. Gang War.* Ithaca, NY: Cornell University Press. 232 pages. Bibliography, index. ISBN 0-8014-4372-5.

For 10 months in 1993, a Los Angeles neighborhood was the center of gang violence that began with a fight among individuals, some of whom were affiliated with local gangs. In the end, 17 people were murdered and more than 50 were injured. Umemoto lived near this neighborhood and spent two years conducting ethnographic research during the violence and the truce that followed. She conducted interviews with gang members, local residents, business leaders, law enforcement officers, and gang intervention program officials. She provides an in-depth analysis of contemporary urban conflict in the United States and the lack of agreement in interpretations for the cause of the problems.

Vigil, James Diego. 2002. *A Rainbow of Gangs: Street Cultures in the Mega-City.* Austin: University of Texas Press. 231 pages. References, index. ISBN 978-0-292-78749-0.

Recent research into the process of adapting to American culture does not frequently include an examination of those who struggle or are unable to adapt. Vigil attempts to fill that research void by offering an in-depth multicultural analysis of Chicano, African American, Vietnamese, and Salvadoran gangs in Los Angeles. He describes the gang experience as being shaped by the history and culture of each ethnic group and individual family and their interaction with the larger society.

Vigil, James Diego. 2007. *The Projects: Gang and Non-Gang Families in East Los Angeles.* Austin: University of Texas Press. 256 pages. References, index. ISBN 0-292-71730-5.

Vigil examines the dynamics of living in the Pico Gardens housing development in East Los Angeles in an attempt to determine the variables that may make some families more likely to become involved in gangs and how some families were able to avoid the pressures to join a gang. The wide variety of income and social status among residents, who are primarily Mexican American, is explored, and family histories are provided to illustrate many of the issues facing the residents.

Weisel, Deborah Lamm. 2002. *Contemporary Gangs: An Organizational Analysis.* **New York: LFB Scholarly Publishing. 226 pages. Bibliography, index. ISBN 1-931202-30-3.**

Weisel conducted field research to gather information on the organizational characteristics of gangs; she focused on four criminal gangs in Chicago and San Diego. She conducted semi-structured face-to-face interviews with gang members to examine each gang's purpose, growth, and evolution over time in order to develop an understanding of the gang within an organizational framework. Specific areas examined include gang size and changes in size over time, age distribution, residence, recruitment practices, gang history, gang goals, objectives of individual gang members, the environment in which the gang operated, and the gang's response to that environment. Individual chapters focus on a literature review of relevant research on gangs, a description of the research methodology, interview findings and analysis of data gathered, and a discussion of significant findings and suggested directions for further research. Findings indicate that community conditions and norms contribute to the formation of gangs—that individual youths do "drift into gang membership, influenced predominantly by the collective experience of growing up in the neighborhood in which family and friends belong to the gang" (193).

Wiener, Valerie. 1999. *Winning the War against Youth Gangs: A Guide for Teens, Families, and Communities.* **Westport, CT: Greenwood. 224 pages. Bibliography, index. ISBN 0-31330-819-5.**

Describing young people as the "shadow generation" because of their search for answers to the question "who am I?" and the influence that this search has on everything they do, Wiener analyzes the attraction of belonging to a gang. Part 1 discusses the resolution of young people's need for self-acceptance, self-esteem, and self-respect, including the impact of peer groups and friends. Part 2 offers a history of gangs in the United States, the different types of gangs, and various gang structures. Part 3 suggests a variety of solutions to the gang problem, encouraging collaboration among law enforcement agencies, schools, the media, and families. The final part examines the modern family and offers practical suggestions to adults and youths for avoiding gangs or getting out of them. Quotes from interviews Weiner conducted with young people are provided throughout the book.

Yablonsky, Lewis. 1998. *Gangsters: Fifty Years of Madness, Drugs, and Death on the Streets of America.* **New York: New York University Press. 280 pages. Notes, index. ISBN 0-814-79688-5.**

Yablonsky, a sociologist and criminologist, explores the reasons that young people find gang life so attractive and why they join gangs. He provides a brief history of gangs and discusses black and Chicano gangs and why gangs kill, including the observation that black gangs primarily attack other black gangs, Chicano gangs attack other Chicano gangs, and white gangs attack other white gangs. Also discussed are the major characteristics of gangs and various treatment approaches used to intervene in or suppress gang involvement and violence. Recommended approaches to prevent gang violence are examined.

Journal Articles

Bjerregaard, Beth. 2002. "Self-Definitions of Gang Membership and Involvement in Delinquent Activities." *Youth and Society* **34:31–54.**

According to Bjerregaard, significant differences exist among researchers regarding conceptual and operational definitions of gang membership. One of the major stumbling blocks is allowing respondents to identify themselves as gang members; as a result, this study examined the relationship between the differing methods of operationalizing gang membership and involvement in delinquent activities. Results indicate that those individuals who reported that they were gang members were more likely to report that their gangs had the characteristics that are usually associated with street gangs. These individuals were also more likely to participate in all types of delinquent behavior.

Cadwallader, Tom W., and Robert B. Cairns. 2002. "Developmental Influences and Gang Awareness among African-American Inner City Youth." *Social Development* 11:245–265.

In a study of almost 500 African American youth in the first, fourth, and seventh grades in inner-city schools, Cadwallader and Cairns examined the students' knowledge of gangs in their local community and their social networks. The researchers found that as the girls and boys grew older, their knowledge of local gangs increased, depending on their social peer groups. Local neighborhoods were shown to have a strong effect on youths' social development.

Craig, Wendy M., Frank Vitaro, Claude Gagnon, and Richard E. Tremblay. 2002. "The Road to Gang Membership: Characteristics of Male Gang and Nongang Members from Ages 10 to 14." *Social Development* 11:53–68.

In this study, the authors examined the effect of gang membership on early adolescents, their behavior profiles, their family characteristics, and friendships of gang and nongang members. The study sample consisted of 142 boys, ages 11 through 14 years, who met certain criteria. An analysis of the data indicated that while gang membership was stable for the boys between the ages of 13 and 14, it was not stable at younger ages. The boys with stable gang memberships were more likely than nongang members to be rated by their teachers as displaying fighting behavior characteristics, hyperactivity, and oppositional behavior and to self-report delinquent behaviors. Peers also claimed gang members were more aggressive than nongang members.

Gottfredson, Denise C., and Gary D. Gottfredson. 2002. "Quality of School-Based Prevention Programs: Results from a National Survey." *Journal of Research in Crime and Delinquency* 39:3–35.

Using the data from a national survey of 3,691 school-based prevention activities during the spring of 1998, the authors analyzed the quality of school-based prevention programs. They found that the quality of these prevention programs is low, specifically as they are implemented in schools. A review of the data suggests that the quality of prevention could be improved with better implementation of the programs, including their implementation into the regular school activities.

Henderson, Eric, Stephen J. Kunitz, and Jerrold E. Levy. 1999. "The Origins of Navajo Youth Gangs." *American Indian Culture and Research Journal* 23:243–264.

Representatives of the Navajo Nation estimated that approximately 60 youth gangs were active in Navajo Country in 1997. The authors interviewed approximately 50 Navajo males between 21 and 45 years of age who were asked about their knowledge of or experience with gangs when they were younger. If they responded that they knew of gangs or had been members of gangs, they were questioned at length about their involvement. The authors describe cultural changes over the years in Navajo Country and present a historical perspective on Navajo male youth groups, the origin and distribution of youth gangs, and characteristics of core gang members.

Hunt, Geoffrey P., and Karen Joe Laidler. 2001. "Alcohol and Violence in the Lives of Gang Members." *Alcohol Research and Health* 25:66–71.

For participants in a gang, life includes two endemic features— alcohol and violence. While other researchers have largely focused on the relationship of violence to drugs, Hunt and Laidler examine alcohol as an integral part of gang life. Alcohol is a social lubricant, used to encourage social behavior and reinforce masculinity and male togetherness. Drinking is also done in two important rites in gang life—initiation and funerals. The authors argue that if the links between drinking and violence can be understood, law enforcement officials and researchers will be more likely to be able to determine the social processes that encourage violent acts after drinking.

Katz, Charles M. 2003. "Issues in the Production and Dissemination of Gang Statistics: An Ethnographic Study of a Large Midwestern Police Gang Unit." *Crime and Delinquency* 49:485–516.

While researchers, law enforcement officials, and other professionals have debated various aspects of the collection of gang data, little research has been conducted to investigate the processes used by individuals and organizations to collect and disseminate these data. Katz employs a multimethodological approach to examine the issues concerning the ways that one midwestern gang unit produces and disseminates gang statistics. Unlike previous research that has examined gang data, Katz's findings did not reveal that the gang unit of the police department influenced the reporting of gang data for the benefit of the department. Instead, findings revealed that the development of gang statistics was influenced by serious problems in the ways the department processed the information. Gang statistics were not developed by using official, or informal, definitions of a gang or gang member, but were the result of problematic communication within the gang unit and between the gang unit and the environment in which it operated.

Lane, Jodi. 2002. "Fear of Gang Crime: A Qualitative Examination of the Four Perspectives." *Journal of Research in Crime and Delinquency* **39:437–471.**

Even though crime rates have gone down, according to Lane, the public's fear of becoming victims of crime has remained high. This high level of fear indicates that the increased focus by many law enforcement agencies and the federal government is not enough to calm the public's fears of crime. Fear-of-crime researchers examining these levels of fear have developed four theoretical perspectives based on social disorganization theory to explain fear on the basis of a variety of environmental factors other than crime. Lane gathered qualitative data from focus groups in 1997 in Santa Ana, California, which she uses to describe what individuals think about gang crime and the reasons they give for being afraid.

Lopez, D. A., and Patricia O'Donnell Brummett. 2003. "Gang Membership and Acculturation: ARSMA-II and Choloization." *Crime and Delinquency* **49:627–642.**

Many researchers studying Latino gangs employ the concept of choloization, which asserts that gang members are less acculturated than nongang members. Lopez and Brummett attempt to quantify data on this concept, using a sample of Latino youths from Los Angeles County who are incarcerated ($N = 370$). The researchers hypothesized that Latino gang members have more of a Mexican orientation than Latinos that are not gang members. The results supported this hypothesis, providing empirical evidence for choloization. Lopez and Brummett suggest that the findings can help professionals working in delinquency intervention activities, but they caution that the results may also have the effect of further disenfranchising Latino gang members.

Sheehan, Karen, Joseph A. DiCara, Susan LeBailly, and Katherine Kaufer Christofel. 1999. "Adapting the Gang Model: Peer Mentoring for Violence Prevention." *Pediatrics* 104:50–54.

The authors examine the effectiveness of peer mentoring programs in the inner city in modifying attitudes toward violence as well as violent behavior among participating youth. The study compared 50 children who were enrolled in a peer mentoring program with 75 control children. There were no differences between the scores of the two groups prior to participation in the mentoring program. Following the completion of the program, the data suggest that peer mentoring programs for young children may be effective in reducing youth violence. The authors suggest additional research is needed.

Taylor, Carl S., Richard M. Lerner, Alexander von Eye, Deborah L. Bobek, Aida Bilalbegovic Balsano, Elizabeth M. Dowling, and Pamela M. Anderson. 2004. "Internal and External Developmental Assets among African American Male Gang Members." *Journal of Adolescent Research* 19:303–322.

Forty-five African American members of inner-city Detroit gangs and 50 African American adolescent males living in the same communities but not participating in gang activities were compared to determine similarities and differences in their development characteristics. Findings indicate that youths involved in community programs that promote healthy, positive development were more likely than the gang members to have characteristics that indicate positive youth development.

Tsunokai, Glenn T., and Augustine J. Kposowa. 2002. "Asian Gangs in the United States: The Current State of the Research Literature." *Crime, Law and Social Change* 37:37–50.

According to Tsunokai and Kposowa, criminologists have been interested in and fascinated by Asian gangs since the late 1980s. Although a large increase was seen in books and articles concerning Asian gangs during the 1990s, they believe that no consensus has been reached on the nature and characteristics of Asian gangs. In this paper, the authors describe current research on Asian gangs and examine various criminological theories that might help explain the cause of this growth. Similarities and differences between African American gangs and Asian gangs are analyzed. The authors offer a variety of research and policy recommendations.

Yoder, Kevin A., Les B. Whitbeck, and Dan R. Hoyt. 2003. "Gang Involvement and Membership among Homeless and Runaway Youth." *Youth and Society* **34:441–467.**

The authors use a sample of 602 homeless and runaway youth from four midwestern states to analyze and describe the extent of gang involvement and gang membership among these youth. They also compare several characteristics of gang members with youth who are peripherally involved in gangs but not members, as well as those of nongang youth, including socioeconomic and demographic characteristics, family background, school experiences, street experiences, emotional problems, alcohol and drug use, and other delinquent and deviant behaviors. The researchers found that a statistically significant number of these young people were gang members (15.4 percent of the sample) or involved in gangs (32.2 percent of the sample). More family legal problems were reported by gang members and gang-involved youth; they were also more likely to have been suspended from school, ran away at a younger age, displayed more frequent use of alcohol and drugs, were more likely to come into contact with other delinquent youth, and were more likely to have attempted suicide than nongang youth in the study. Not surprisingly, youth gang members were more likely to have lower amounts of parental monitoring and to have experienced more severe abuse and more street victimization than either gang-involved or noninvolved youth.

Manuals and Training Materials

Arbreton, Amy J. A., Jessica Sheldon, and Carla Herrera. 2005. *Beyond Safe Havens: A Synthesis of 20 Years of Research on the Boys & Girls Clubs.* **Philadelphia: Public/Private Ventures.**

Philadelphia Public/Private Ventures undertook an evaluation of findings from studies of Boys & Girls Clubs that were conducted over the past 20 years. It reviewed the research conducted on individual programs as well as the results of participant evaluations to determine specific areas in which participants had positive experiences. The organization also describes the general strategies of the programs and factors leading to the success or failure of the programs. Finally, it identified various aspects of the evaluations that indicate that participation in these clubs provides positive experiences to the participants.

Howell, James C. 2000. *Youth Gang Programs and Strategies.* **Washington, DC: Office of Juvenile Justice and Delinquency Prevention.**

The author, relying on more than 50 years of gang program evaluations, provides a summary of what has been learned about prevention, intervention, and suppression programs; effective strategies that employ multiple techniques; multiagency initiatives; comprehensive approaches to gang problems; and legislation. Prevention programs discussed include community organization, early childhood programs, school-based programs, and after-school activities. Intervention programs include programs focusing on detached workers, crisis intervention, violence-free zones, gang summits and truces, and emergency room intervention, as well as Boys & Girls Clubs. Suppression programs include prosecution programs, police response, and geomapping and tracking systems.

Manwaring, Max G. 2005. *Street Gangs: The New Urban Insurgency.* **Carlisle, PA: Strategic Studies Institute.**

The primary purpose of this monograph is to identify and describe the most relevant characteristics of criminal street gangs and explore their links to insurgent activities. Manwaring believes that gang-related crime, along with the instability it causes governments, is a serious national security and sovereignty problem in many parts of the world. He identifies important issues that need to be understood individually and together in order to develop effective strategies to deal with the criminal and political nature of these gangs.

Mellor, Brian, Leslie MacRae, Monica Pauls, and Joseph P. Hornick. 2005. *Youth Gangs in Canada: A Preliminary Review of Programs and Services.* **Calgary: Canadian Research Institute for Law and the Family.**

The Department of Public Safety and Emergency Preparedness Canada awarded the Canadian Research Institute for Law and the Family a grant to collect and analyze data on youth gangs and to identify programs providing services to youth involved with gangs throughout the country. The researchers were specifically tasked with developing a multidimensional framework to understand the reasons why youths become involved in gangs, identifying programs and services that focus on youth in gangs and categorizing program goals based on their level of prevention. The authors identified 24 primary prevention programs, 27 secondary prevention programs (focusing mostly on intervention activities), and 8 tertiary prevention programs (focusing essentially on rehabilitation and/or getting youth out of gangs). Twelve programs are a combination of primary and secondary prevention programs, and six programs offer a combination of secondary and tertiary prevention activities.

Miller, Walter B. 2001. *The Growth of Youth Gang Programs in the United States: 1970–1998*. Washington, DC: Office of Juvenile Justice and Delinquency Prevention.

Miller presents information concerning the statistical trends in the development of youth gang problems from 1970 to 1998. The report offers a description of youth gang problems in the United States, a summary of gang localities, a list of cities and counties experiencing gang problems, a description of regional trends in gang cities and counties, and a summary of the findings. He concludes that in the United States during the study period, communities experienced more problems with gangs in more locations than ever before.

National Alliance of Gang Investigators Association (NAGIA). 2005. *2005 National Gang Threat Assessment*. Washington, DC: Bureau of Justice Assistance.

This report examines recent trends in gang activity and gang migration from one area to another. A collaborative effort among the members of the NAGIA, the report provides a regional and national picture of the threat posed by gangs so that policy makers at all levels of government will understand the extent of the gang problem. Some of the trends are as follows: gangs are the primary distributors of drugs throughout the country, they have connections with organized crime, they are sophisticated users of computers, the number of Hispanic gangs and gang members is growing, Native American participation in gangs is growing, and the role of women in gangs is evolving.

Reed, Winifred L., and Scott H. Decker, eds. 2002. *Responding to Gangs: Evaluation and Research.* **Washington, DC: Office of Justice Programs, U.S. Department of Justice.**

A major focus of the National Institute of Justice is to encourage and support research that helps establish effective policies that will assist law enforcement and other local agencies and organizations in developing effective programs in deterring youth participation in gangs. Topics include a summary of research during the past decade; the evolution of street gangs; female participation in gangs; gang homicides; evaluation of the Gang Resistance Education and Training Program, the Nevada antigang legislation and gang prosecution units, and a task force approach to gangs; gang prevention programs for female adolescents; gang reduction in Boston; and development of a regional gang incident tracking system.

Spergel, Irving A., Kwai Ming Wa, Sungeun Ellie Choi, Susan Grossman, Ayad Jacob, Annot Spergel, and Elisa M. Barrios. 2004. *Evaluation of the Gang Violence Reduction Project in Little Village.* **Chicago: Illinois Criminal Justice Information Authority.**

The Gang Violence Reduction Project was the first in a series of demonstration programs designed to address serious youth gang problems. Funded by the Illinois Criminal Justice Information Authority and sponsored by the Chicago Police Department, the project focused on grassroots organization, using former gang leaders and members as outreach youth workers, and involved a number of community organizations. Findings of the evaluation are reported, including the finding that the program appeared to be most successful during its first three years of operation, and community residents believed that the program was successful in reducing violent gang behavior. (The report is available at http://www.icjia.state.il.us/public/pdf/ResearchReports/GVRP_Eval.pdf.)

Starbuck, David, James C. Howell, and Donna J. Lindquist. 2001. *Hybrid and Other Modern Gangs.* **Washington, DC: Office of Juvenile Justice and Delinquency Prevention, Juvenile Justice Bulletin.**

Describing the nature of modern youth gangs, the authors focus on hybrid gang culture, which is "characterized by mixed racial and ethnic participation within a single gang, participation in multiple gangs by a single individual, vague rules and codes of conduct for gang members, use of symbols and colors from multiple—even rival—gangs, collaboration by rival gangs in criminal activities, and the merger of smaller gangs into larger ones" (1). The authors provide a short history of hybrid gangs, along with their characteristics, emerging information on these gangs, and policy and program implications.

Troutman, David R., M. Elaine Nugent Borakove, and Steven Jansen. 2007. *Prosecutor's Comprehensive Gang Response Model*. Alexandria, VA: National District Attorneys Association, American Prosecutors Research Institute.

As part of the National District Attorneys Association Special Topics Series, this monograph is a result of a three-day symposium in which prosecutors, police, juvenile justice experts, state and local government officials, school professionals, representatives from community-based organizations and faith-based groups, and researchers met to create a comprehensive response to the gang problems they face in their communities. The comprehensive gang response model helps local prosecutors and allied professionals design individually tailored gang initiatives. This publication provides an overview of the model, ways to assess the local community's need for a coordinated response to local gangs, a plan of action, suggestions for ways to gather community support and develop a plan of implementation, and evaluation methods.

Videos and DVDs

Canceled Lives: Letters from the Inside

Type:	VHS
Length:	20 minutes each (three-video series)
Date:	1997
Cost:	$199.00
Source:	Available from the National Resource Center for Youth Services,
Telephone:	1-800-274-2687

This video series provides a powerful portrait of the criminal justice system as seen through the eyes of young boys and girls who are serving time in juvenile facilities as well as men and women who are serving hard time in prison. Heart-breaking, emotion-filled visions of life in prison are provided to at-risk, predelinquent youth and juvenile offenders. The first two videos in the series focus on youths and adults incarcerated as a result of their involvement with substance abuse, violence, and gangs. The third video provides a painful portrait of the reality of prison life.

Catching Them Early

Type:	VHS, DVD
Length:	58 minutes
Date:	1998
Cost:	$99.95 (VHS); $89.95 (DVD)
Source:	Films Media Group
	P.O. Box 2053
	Princeton, NJ 08543-2053
Telephone:	800-257-5126
Fax:	609-671-0266
Web site:	http://www.filmsmediagroup.com

At-risk youth in Richmond, California, constantly face gang violence, drug abuse, and teenage pregnancy. This video reports on the activities of a coalition of community agencies working to intervene and help youth avoid these issues. Personnel from Lincoln Elementary School and the city's Lions Club, Familias Unidas, Child Haven, and Head Start are shown working together to provide wholesome, safe activities that will encourage young people to develop traits that will help keep them out of trouble, including self-confidence, cultural identity, and life skills training.

Changing Lives, Saving Lives: Criminals and Gang Members Anonymous

Type:	VHS, DVD
Length:	23 minutes
Date:	2004
Cost:	$99.95 (VHS); $89.95 (DVD)
Source:	Films Media Group
	P.O. Box 2053
	Princeton, NJ 08543-2053
Telephone:	800-257-5126

Fax: 609-671-0266
Web site: http://www.filmsmediagroup.com

A hard-core gang member, Richard Mejico, is in prison for murder. So is his son, Steven, who happens to be his cellmate. Mejico formed Criminals and Gang Members Anonymous (CGA), a 12-step program to help individuals who are addicted to crime and violence break the cycle. The video describes his journey and includes interviews with other convicts who have joined CGA, as well as an emotional interview with his wife, Martha.

18 with a Bullet: El Salvador's American-Style Gangs
Type: VHS, DVD
Length: 57 minutes
Date: 2006
Cost: $139.95 (VHS); $129.95 (DVD)
Source: Films Media Group
              P.O. Box 2053
              Princeton, NJ 08543-2053
Telephone: 800-257-5126
Fax: 609-671-0266
Web site: http://www.filmsmediagroup.com

During the 1990s, the United States deported thousands of Salvadoran nationals who were living illegally in the United States. Some of these individuals belonged to gangs while in the United States, and when they left, they took Los Angeles gang culture with them. This video follows the transnational gang known as 18, which is a Salvadoran variation of the name of the 18th Street gang in Los Angeles. The viewer sees teenage gang members patrol their turf in the streets of San Salvador; make prospective members go through initiation rituals such as violent beatings; encourage gang activity within prisons; battle their enemies; and help El Salvador rank as one of the most violent countries in the world.

Gang Terror
Type: VHS, DVD
Length: 45 minutes
Date: 1997
Cost: $99.95 (VHS); $89.95 (DVD)
Source: Films Media Group
              P.O. Box 2053
              Princeton, NJ 08543-2053

Telephone: 800-257-5126
Fax: 609-671-0266
Web site: http://www.filmsmediagroup.com

Produced by CBS News, this video offers a view into life in a gang. Shown are the deadly struggles between the Crips and the Bloods, who are fighting for control of the drug trade; the effects of living in a neighborhood in Chicago that is controlled by gangs; the rough experiences of female gang members who are out to prove that they are tough; and the struggles between the police and gang members for influence over at-risk youth in Hartford, Connecticut.

Gangs: The American Evolution
Type: DVD
Length: 120 minutes
Date: 2005
Cost: $13.00
Source: Available from the Idaho RADAR Network
               Center, Boise State University, 1910 University
               Drive, Boise, ID 83725
Telephone: 208-426-2946

Sergeant Harold M. Rochon is a 20-year veteran of the Detroit Police Department and author of *Terrorists and Designer Jeans*. He believes that the growth and spread of gangs throughout the United States has reached an epidemic. This DVD was developed for use to train law enforcement and other professionals in the field. Rochon examines the history of gangs, explains the various ways to identify and classify gang members, explores gang ideology and recruiting techniques, and discusses the drug use by gang members.

Gangs: It's Your Life
Type: VHS (three tapes)
Length: 20 minutes each (60 minutes)
Date: 2001
Cost: $195.00
Source: Chariot
Web site: www.chariotdist.com/violence/its_your_life.htm

A three-part series on gangs, this program examines the reasons why young people join gangs, the serious consequences of gang life, and the ways that youth can make a choice to stay out of gangs by taking advantage of viable alternatives.

The Limits of Justice
Type: VHS, DVD
Length: 58 minutes
Date: 1998
Cost: $99.95 (VHS); $89.95 (DVD)
Source: Films Media Group
             P.O. Box 2053
             Princeton, NJ 08543-2053
Telephone: 800-257-5126
Fax: 609-671-0266
Web site: http://www.filmsmediagroup.com

In Boston, during the funeral of a gang member, members of a rival gang stormed the church where the service was being held. As a result, local community leaders met with law enforcement officials and decided to work together to reduce violent crime in Boston. Police and parole officers team up to patrol the streets, enforcing probation and deterring violence; mentors experienced with life on the streets are paired with at-risk youth; and other community organizations provide education, day care, job training, and food. This video documents the development and experiences of this program.

Nuestra Familia, Our Family
Type: DVD
Length: 54 minutes
Date: 2006
Cost: $149.95
Source: Films Media Group
             P.O. Box 2053
             Princeton, NJ 08543-2053
Telephone: 800-257-5126
Fax: 609-671-0266
Web site: http://www.filmsmediagroup.com

Two Latino gangs, Nuestra Familia and the Mexican Mafia, are at war in Salinas, California. This video, using interviews with gang members from Nuestra Familia and law enforcement officials, describes the formation and development of the gang, its militarylike structure, and its power throughout the local community and the country. A joint task force between the Salinas Police Department and the Federal Bureau of Investigation, known as Operation Black Widow, was developed to suppress and destroy this gang. The video describes the involvement of one family in Nuestra Familia across multiple generations.

Street Gangs in Los Angeles

Type:	VHS, DVD
Length:	23 minutes
Date:	2000
Cost:	$159.95 (VHS); $149.95 (DVD)
Source:	Films Media Group
	P.O. Box 2053
	Princeton, NJ 08543-2053
Telephone:	800-257-5126
Fax:	609-671-0266
Web site:	http://www.filmsmediagroup.com

This video provides the audience with a frightening view of gang life in Los Angeles. Gangs that control large areas of the city and the ease with which they murder others are shown as evidence that life in Los Angeles can be frightening. Gang members' attraction to the thrills and dangers of life is examined, along with the efforts of communities to keep their neighborhoods safe.

Street Life: Inside America's Gangs

Type:	VHS, DVD
Length:	43 minutes
Date:	1999
Cost:	$99.95 (VHS); $89.95 (DVD)
Source:	Films Media Group
	P.O. Box 2053
	Princeton, NJ 08543-2053
Telephone:	800-257-5126
Fax:	609-671-0266
Web site:	http://www.filmsmediagroup.com

ABC news correspondent Cynthia McFadden takes a look inside an American gang, interviewing female members of two Los Angeles gangs, the Drifters and Tepa 13. Correspondent John Quinones interviews King Tone, the leader of New York City's

Latin Kings gang. The video also contains clips from videos shot by the gang members themselves.

Street Life: One Man's Struggle
Type: VHS, DVD
Length: 23 minutes
Date: 2000
Cost: $79.95 (VHS); $69.95 (DVD)
Source: Films Media Group
             P.O. Box 2053
             Princeton, NJ 08543-2053
Telephone: 800-257-5126
Fax: 609-671-0266
Web site: http://www.filmsmediagroup.com

Former gang member Johnny Montalvo used to be a ruthless criminal, selling drugs and killing without any guilty feelings. This video portrays his journey, as he is now confined to a wheelchair as a result of his criminal activities and is working hard at being a single parent. ABC news correspondent Chris Bury offers an in-depth examination of Montalvo's life as he continues to struggle with the lure of the gang and the desire to change his life.

World's Most Dangerous Gangs
Type: DVD
Length: 52 minutes
Date: 2006
Cost: $19.95
Source: National Geographic
             Washington, DC
Telephone: 1-800-437-5521

In this compelling DVD, Lisa Ling from National Geographic Explorer gives the viewer a first-hand view of the MS-13 gang, an extremely violent gang that is experiencing rapid growth in large and small communities throughout the United States, known for recruiting the most desperate members of society, including children. The gang's culture and rituals are described in interviews with current gang members, with members who are trying to escape the gang, and with investigators attempting to stop the growth and activities of the gang.

Internet Resources

Community Oriented Policing Services (COPS)
U.S. Department of Justice
Web site: http://www.cops.usdoj.gov

The COPS office originated in 1994 as part of the Violent Crime Control and Law Enforcement Act of 1994. Its purpose is to promote community policing as an effective means to improve public safety in responding to criminal, including gang, activity. The office provides grants to state, local, and tribal law enforcement agencies to hire and train community policing personnel, use cutting-edge crime-fighting technologies, and examine innovative strategies for policing local communities. It focuses on crime and social disorder using traditional police services as well as other innovative strategies.

The Coroner's Report
P.O. Box 1932
North Little Rock, AR 72115
Telephone: 301-940-GANG
Web site: http://www.gangwar.com

Set up and run by a former coroner and a nationally recognized gang researcher, Steve Nawojczyk, this Web site provides an overview of American gangs, information on gang graffiti, articles and links on youth gangs, a gang war blog, book recommendations, and a featured link.

Graffiti Related Links on the World Wide Web
Web site: http://www.dougweb.com/grlinks.html

This Web site provides a variety of links to information concerning graffiti and antigraffiti programs. Information is divided into several subjects, including city, law, and police pages related to graffiti; educational materials regarding graffiti; gangs; graffiti magazines and Web pages of graffiti advocates; neighborhood graffiti organizations and abatement projects; and other miscellaneous links.

Into the Abyss: A Personal Journey into the World of Street Gangs
http://www.faculty.missouristate.edu/M/MichaelCarlie/

Maintained by sociologist Mike Carlie, this Web site features the entire contents of his book *Into the Abyss* along with additional articles, updates, and links to other Web sites providing information on street gangs.

Juvenile Justice Clearinghouse
U.S. Department of Justice
Web site: http://www.ncjrs.gov

The clearinghouse is a comprehensive resource for information on a variety of juvenile justice topics, including gangs. Juvenile justice professionals and anyone else seeking information on juvenile justice topics can speak with an information specialist concerning specific requests for information. Access is provided to the National Criminal Justice Reference Service library, which is one of the world's most comprehensive sources of criminal justice and juvenile justice literature. An electronic bulletin board can be found on the Internet, which provides timely information on a variety of topics of interest to juvenile justice professionals.

Michigan State University Libraries
Criminal Justice Resources: Gangs
Web site: http://www.lib.msu.edu/harris23/crimjust/gangs.htm

This Web site provides links to a wide variety of resources, including other Web sites, documents, and other resources that focus on youth gangs.

National Alliance of Gang Investigators Associations (NAGIA)
http://www.nagia.org

NAGIA is an association composed of criminal justice professionals and organizations that focus on promoting and coordinating national antigang strategies (see Chapter 7). The Web site includes an online library of articles and links to the local and regional gang investigation associations.

National Gang Crime Research Center
Web site: http://www.ngcrc.com/

The National Gang Crime Research Center was founded in 1990 and conducts research on gangs and gang members, offers training and consulting services, and disseminates information. The site contains sections on resources, reports and publications, training conference information, and profiles of major gangs.

National Youth Gang Center (NYGC)
Web site: http://www.iir.com/nygc/

The NYGC is operated and funded by the Office of Juvenile Justice and Delinquency Prevention in the U.S. Department of Justice and provides statistical data collection and analysis focusing on gangs, an analysis of gang legislation, gang literature review, identification of promising gang program strategies, and consortium coordination activities. Its Web site offers detailed information about the NYGC and its activities and resources for further information, including gang-related news, legislation, publications, conference and training links, funding links, and a listserv mailing list to discuss all aspects of youth gang crime.

Streetgangs.com
http://www.streetgangs.com

This Web site was created and is maintained by gang researcher Alejandro A. Alonso, a doctoral student of geography at the University of Southern California in Los Angeles. It offers a wide variety of information concerning gangs, including a history of gangs in Los Angeles, recent news concerning gangs, media information, legal information concerning laws and injunctions, a book club, a magazine, a speakers bureau, and movie reviews. It is intended to help parents, educators, and youths understand how and why gangs have become so pervasive in American society.

Violent Gangs
Federal Bureau of Investigation (FBI)
Web site: http://www.fbi.gov/hq/cid/ngic/violent_gangs.htm

The FBI's Web site on violent gangs contains recent news, facts and photos, and other resources on violent gangs, including links to the MS-13 National Gang Task Force and the National Gang Intelligence Center.

Glossary

alliance The grouping together of two or more gangs for a variety of purposes, including control of certain areas, sale and distribution of drugs, or safety.

banger An individual gang member or the person who shoots during a drive-by shooting.

cartel A criminal syndicate that is organized to control the distribution and reduce competition, such as a drug cartel.

colors A means to identify individual members from a specific gang. The gang color may be displayed by clothing, shoelaces, bandannas, or other items worn by the gang member.

defendant A person or entity (such as an organization) charged with a civil or criminal action.

home invasion Breaking into a home in order to commit a criminal act while the residents are at home.

homey Fellow gang member.

hood Slang term for neighborhood.

injunction An order issued by a court to an individual or group of individuals requiring them to refrain from some behavior, such as loitering.

migration Movement of gang members from one location to another.

O.G. Original gangster or old gangster.

parole The release from prison of a convicted criminal prior to the official completion of his or her original sentence. While on parole, the individual must meet certain conditions, such as staying away from criminal activities and drugs, and must report to a parole officer at certain predetermined intervals.

plaintiff The person or entity who institutes a legal claim or action.

recidivism   The tendency to relapse into a previous pattern of behavior. In the field of gang research, the term usually refers to a former gang member rejoining a gang.

set   A smaller subset of a larger gang, usually named after local streets or neighborhoods.

status offense   Behavior or action that is considered to be an offense only if it is carried out by a minor; includes curfew violations, truancy, running away from home.

Index

About the Author

Karen L. Kinnear holds an MA in sociology and is a paralegal, as well as a professional researcher, editor, and writer with more than 25 years of experience in sociological, economic, statistical, and financial analysis. Among her previous publications are *Violent Children: A Reference Handbook; Childhood Sexual Abuse: A Reference Handbook; Women in the Third World: A Reference Handbook;* and *Single Parents: A Reference Handbook,* all part of ABC-CLIO's Contemporary World Issues series.